SCHELLING
AND THE END OF IDEALISM

SUNY Series in Hegelian Studies
William Desmond, Editor

SCHELLING
AND THE END OF IDEALISM

DALE E. SNOW

STATE UNIVERSITY OF NEW YORK PRESS

Published by
State University of New York Press, Albany

© 1996 State University of New York

All rights reserved

Printed in the United States of America

No part of this book may be used or reproduced in any manner whatsoever without written permission. No part of this book may be stored in a retrieval system or transmitted in any form or by any means including electronic, electrostatic, magnetic tape, mechanical, photocopying, recording, or otherwise without the prior permission in writing of the publisher.

For information, address State University of New York Press
State University Plaza, Albany, N.Y. 12246

Production by M. R. Mulholland
Marketing by Nancy Farrell

Library of Congress Cataloging-in-Publication Data

Snow, Dale E., 1955–
    Schelling and the end of idealism / Dale E. Snow.
      p. cm.—(SUNY series in Hegelian studies)
    Includes bibliographical references and index.
    ISBN 0-7914-2745-5 (alk. paper).—ISBN 0-7914-2746-3 (pbk. : alk. paper)
    1. Schelling, Friedrich Wilhelm Joseph von, 1775–1854. I. Title II. Series.
B2898.S66   1996
193—dc20   95-4245
                                                                       CIP

10 9 8 7 6 5 4 3 2 1

CONTENTS

Acknowledgments   vii

Introduction   1

1. The Enlightenment under Attack
   I. Kant's Early Reception   11
   II. Jacobi and the Pantheism Controversy   14
   III. Faith or Reason?   24

2. The Knowledge of Reality
   I. The Problem of the Thing in Itself   33
   II. Fichte: The Self as First Principle   36
   III. The Early Schelling's Concept of the Self   45
   IV. How Is Knowledge of Reality Possible?   55
   V. Genius: The "Sunday's Children" Problem   62

3. The Philosophy of Nature
   I. The Essential Role of the Philosophy of Nature   67
   II. Arguments against the Mechanistic Model of Nature   70
   III. The Development of the Concept of Matter   74
   IV. Necessity and Scientific Objectivity   77
   V. *On the World Soul*   82
   VI. Dynamism, Polarity, and the Philosophy of Organism   86

4. Metaphors for Nature
   I. From the Philosophy of Nature to the System   93
   II. Metaphors of Dominance and Control   98
   III. Kant   99
   IV. Fichte   102
   V. Hegel   106
   VI. Schelling   110

5. The Emergence of the Unconscious
   I. The Purpose of the *System*   119
   II. A Clash of Paradigms   123
   III. Paradoxes in the *System*   130
   IV. Aesthetic Idealism   135

6. Of Human Freedom
   I. The Idealism of Freedom   141
   II. Difficulties   146
   III. The Introduction: A Redefinition of Freedom   151
   IV. The "Real and Vital Conception of Freedom"   158
   V. "Man's Being Is Essentially His Own Deed"   165
   VI. An End of Idealism?   174

7. Beyond Idealism? *The Ages of the World*
   I. Schelling's Later Philosophy   181
   II. The Doctrine of the Fall   185
   III. The Historical Character of Reality: The Philosophy of Time   192
   IV. Gottsein and Dasein: The Ontology of What is Not   197
   V. The Controversy of 1811—12 and Beyond   205
   VI. Conclusion   213

Notes   217

Selected Bibliography   241

Index   261

ACKNOWLEDGMENTS

I would like to take this opportunity to acknowledge the financial support of the DAAD (Deutscher Akademischer Austauschdienst) during the early years of work on this project and of the Humanities Center of Loyola College in Maryland for the Junior Faculty Sabbatical which made possible a semester's leave during the fall of 1990. I remain indebted to Joseph Lawrence, Jitendra Mohanty, Michael Vater, and Merold Westphal, who were kind enough to offer their assessments of my project to the Humanities Center Steering Committee.

It is often difficult to pinpoint the moment of birth of an idea, but the basic conception of this book took its present form during the summer of 1989 while I was attending the NEH Summer Seminar "What is Enlightenment?" directed by James Schmidt at Boston University. I had already been exploring some of the parallels between Jacobi and Schelling in my article "F. H. Jacobi and the Development of German Idealism," which appears here in revised form as chapter 1, but I came to see Schelling as a critic not just of the Enlightenment concept of reason but the rationalist tradition as well.

I am grateful to Rudolf Makkreel, who first introduced me to Schelling, and whose continued interest in my work has been a source of inspiration. I also profited from the editorial advice of Joseph Lawrence on what appears here as chapter 5, originally published in slightly different form as "The Role of the Unconscious in the *System of Transcendental Idealism*." William Desmond and an anonymous reader for the State University of New York Press offered many valuable suggestions which helped me to improve and extend my argument.

My most heartfelt appreciation is for my husband, Jim Snow, whose ability to produce domestic tranquility is only exceeded by his philosophical acumen. My work would not be possible without him, but the errors that remain are mine alone.

INTRODUCTION

> Far from it being true that man and his activity makes the world comprehensible, he is himself the most incomprehensible of all, and drives me relentlessly to the view of the accursedness of all being, a view manifested in so many painful signs in ancient and modern times. It is precisely man who drives me to the final despairing question: Why is there something? Why not nothing? (13:7)[1]

Schelling is finally beginning to emerge from the long dark shadow cast by the eminence and popularity of Hegel's philosophy. The preeminence of Hegel's philosophy during his own lifetime relegated Schelling to virtual oblivion. Although Hegel's star dimmed considerably following his death in 1831, the renewed interest in Hegel's philosophy in the latter half of the twentieth century again served to eclipse Schelling's philosophy. Schelling is, however, beginning to emerge from the shadows of Hegelianism and claim his rightful place in the history of philosophy. As Hermann Braun has recently written, there is an emergent "need for Schelling"[2] at the present historical moment. In one respect, then, the present study is contiguous in purpose with a newly emerging body of literature that seeks to awaken the philosophical community to the value of Schelling's philosophy.[3]

One means of accomplishing this is to document Schelling's considerable influence on thinkers as diverse as Feuerbach, Marx, and Kierkegaard in the nineteenth century, and Heidegger, Cassirer, Jaspers, Tillich, Bloch, Habermas, and Derrida in the present century. While I gladly acknowledge the value of this approach and recognize that Schelling's influence has been tremendous, this is not how I approach Schelling's philosophy in this study.

Another possibility is to show not only that Schelling exerted a great influence on the aforementioned philosophers but that in Schelling's philosophy itself, there is an anticipation of philosophical concerns dominating the contemporary philosophical conversation. This kind of approach is not surprising given the fact that contemporary philosophy is concerned again to question the possibility of metaphysics, and even philosophy itself. Schelling himself raises precisely these questions, albeit in idioms peculiar to the nineteenth century. If one sees through Schelling's idioms, he can be seen as exploring a problematic akin to that of Richard Rorty, Donald Davidson, and others. Andrew Bowie's recent study is an admirably lucid attempt to situate Schelling's philosophy in this conversation.

In the present study, I have opted for yet another approach to Schelling's philosophy, one that attempts to encounter Schelling on his own terms. Those sympathetic to Hegel, and often correspondingly unsympathetic to Schelling, are quick to point out that Schelling never developed a mature philosophical system; in fact, Schelling is often read as something of a philosophical chameleon, defending a position only to quickly abandon it for another, and then another. In other words, he is read as offering a succession of unsatisfactory attempts to provide a system comparable in scope to the systems of Hegel or Schopenhauer. If we look at a thinker such as Schopenhauer, who devotes an entire philosophical life to the unfolding of a single thought, to the construction of a grand system that is a metaphysics of the will, Schelling, by contrast, will indeed seem chameleon-like.

In this study I show that Schelling, like Fichte and other post-Kantians of the early nineteenth century, initially sees his vocation as not only the completion of Kant's philosophy but as constructing a philosophical system. And like Fichte, Schelling at the same time explores the concept of system itself. Yet it is not a defeat

Introduction 3

that Schelling never finally arrives at such a system. Rather, he eventually brings into serious question the possibility of systematic philosophy itself. As Joseph Esposito has expressed it: "It was Schelling who drew up the table of contents of German idealism, defined the problems philosophers would concern themselves with for decades, and indeed, probably took idealism as far as it could go in the process."[4]

There is, I argue, a fundamental tension that pervades all of Schelling's writings, that serves as the impetus for bringing into question the possibility of metaphysics. When Schelling was called to Berlin in 1841 to expunge the *Drachensaat des Hegelschen Pantheismus*, it was widely understood as a direct challenge to the Hegelians.[5] In the celebrated Berlin Lectures (lectures attended by Feuerbach, Ruge, Kierkegaard, and others), Schelling did not in any way temper his criticisms of Hegel's philosophy. According to Schelling, Hegel's system amounts to concepts without meaning, a closed dance of abstractions. "Is philosophy then only concerned with the *essences* of things? And has it nothing to do with their existence?"[6] Hegel, according to Schelling, ignores existence. Hegel fails to offer, as Schelling promises to do (a promise never finally realized), a philosophy that answers to life, a philosophy useful to human beings. Against Hegel, Schelling declares that we need a philosophy that can measure itself by life; a philosophy that would take its force from reality itself and would then also produce something actual and lasting. Whether or to what extent these criticisms of Hegel are warranted is another matter; perhaps they are not.[7] What is revealed, however, in the criticisms Schelling directed against his former friend and roommate at Tübingen is the very tension operative throughout Schelling's entire philosophical career: the tension between system and life.

The tension between system and life, reason and unreason, conscious and unconcious, God and evil, is the key hermeneutical principle for understanding Schelling's philosophy. If we see this tension emerging as the central problematic for Schelling, we can begin to see that Schelling's thought is indeed evolutionary rather than chameleon-like. Whether or not there can be a philosophy that answers to life remains a question worth pondering; Schelling does remind us that the question matters terribly, and attempting to answer this question has largely defined the vocation of philosophers since Schelling, whether they acknowledge Schelling or not.

One of the most prominent of the multiple ironies inherent in reducing Schelling to one of Hegel's forerunners is that it renders Schelling's critique of the Western metaphysical tradition all but invisible. This critique culminates, as A. O. Lovejoy and Paul Tillich, among others, have argued, in the middle and later works in an evolutionary theology. Their claim that Schelling is therefore the first philosopher in the Western tradition to make a break with the static "devolutionist" metaphysics originating with Plato and Plotinus is now fairly well known.[8] Still, this is by no means the only or even the most important ramification of Schelling's critique of the Enlightenment and its metaphysical assumptions.

I present the evolution of Schelling's thought as the story of a metaphysical quest, one which takes man supremely seriously. It is man who presents us with the riddle of the world. It thus behooves us to remember that the young Schelling came of age intellectually during an extraordinarily complex time. Although from a twentieth-century vantage point we regard Kant's achievement as secure, almost monumental, recent scholarship strongly suggests that even Kant owes his influence and reputation largely to his role in the pantheism controversy of 1785–89.[9] One of the purposes of this book is to provide a reminder of the precarious and unsettled intellectual atmosphere in which Kant and his successors were writing. A part of that atmosphere was writers and men of letters who questioned, passionately, what they perceived to be the malign hegemony of reason: the most influential of these figures, for both Schelling and Hegel, was F. H. Jacobi.

Introduction

A titanic struggle was being waged between the defenders of the Enlightenment (among them, Kant) and their numerous opponents, who claimed that an overemphasis on reason had resulted in a devaluing of faith, feeling, and immediate intuitive connection to God. This very real tension between the claims of faith and the claims of reason was both exploited and crystallized by Jacobi in his polemical assertion that there are only two possible types of philosophical system, dogmatism and criticism. Still more provocative was Jacobi's insistence that we cannot choose between systems on an intellectual basis; they can be distinguished only by the values they embody, the kind of life they make possible.

Schelling took this challenge seriously, as can be seen from his correspondence and the "Philosophical Letters on Dogmatism and Criticism" of 1796, and he saw his philosophical task as facing the implications of it. The stakes are very high: if, in the final analysis, the choice of philosophical system rests on something preconceptual and fundamental in each of us, this has two vitally important consequences. First, reason has been dethroned, in the sense that rational argument has been exposed as insufficient to compel agreement; second, we realize that we have been rudely awakened from the dream that progressively increasing rationality will ultimately reveal universal truth, which was the central myth of the Enlightenment.

Always concerned with origins, Schelling began at the beginning as he understood it: with the concept of the self. His earliest philosophical efforts took the form of a search for a more satisfactory concept of the self than either Kant or Fichte had provided. Chapter 1 provides the historical background necessary to understand what this quest for the self meant in the last decade of the eighteenth century. The battle lines were drawn with respect to the Enlightenment view of reason: reason was defended by Kant and Moses Mendelssohn; it was attacked by that self-appointed defender of the faith, Jacobi.

Chapter 2 examines Fichte's and Schelling's early concepts of the self as they emerged from Kant's Copernican revolution. Kant states his defining concerns in the famous questions: "What can I know? What must I do? What may I hope?" Schelling does not disdain these Kantian questions but rather thinks that they would be illuminated by an understanding of their origin, the self itself, as he sometimes calls it. He is wrestling with a more fundamental, indeed a more metaphysical question. As a young man, he identifies "the original conflict in the human spirit" with the question of "*emergence out of the absolute*; for we would all agree concerning the absolute if we never left its sphere, and if we did not emerge from it, we would have no other realm concerning which we could be in conflict" (1:294). In other words, for Schelling, any genuine concept of the self must be capable of shedding light on that first question of all: "Why is there something rather than nothing?" (1:310) Thus the self remains characterized by the search for truth; the Enlightenment tradition of faith in the eventual triumph of universal truth is not so much rejected by Schelling as it is *historicized*. That is, Schelling remained sufficiently a child of his age to hold fast to the value of the search for truth. Yet both the shape of the quest and the nature of the truth sought altered dramatically in the course of his philosophical career.

Chapters 3 and 4 describe Schelling's reconsideration and rejection of the mechanistic assumptions of Enlightenment science for an evolutionary and developmental understanding of nature. Some of the implications of what he sometimes called the philosophy of organism are revealed in his special interest in medicine and a philosophy of medicine which is based upon the very contemporary-sounding insight that body and spirit are aspects of one subjectivity. I also argue that a close consideration of the language and imagery of Schelling's philosophy of nature indicates a deep and essential break from the other German idealists with respect to the understanding of man's place in nature in a way that anticipates contemporary controversies, particularly in feminist scholarship.

The *System of Transcendental Idealism* (1800) was intended to demonstrate the complete parallelism between natural history and the history of spirit. However, when the structure of the dynamic forces (later potencies) in nature, always composed of the tension and equilibrium of opposing tendencies, is predicated of spirit as well, the need for a force opposing consciousness produces a theory of the unconscious. In chapter 5 the dynamic structure of forces in opposition is revealed as the basis of the natural world, and shown to have laid the groundwork for the move away from the static faculty psychology of Kant to a theory of the primacy of the will and the role of unconscious forces which anticipates Freud.

Chapter 6 provides an assessment of that equivocal masterpiece, *The Essence of Human Freedom* (1809), in which Schelling struggles with the most difficult challenge to any thinker who wants to make sense of the experience of being human: the problem of evil. Schelling undergoes a metamorphosis in this work. Prior to 1809 his writing style had been detailed to the point of verbosity, burdened by an abstract and formalistic style, and concerned, independently of topic, with systematic completeness. *Freedom* is tantalizingly brief, composed in a richly metaphorical, almost poetic, style, and abandons the rigors of system for the attempt to do justice to life. Schelling's enduring passion for origins leads him to rephrase his question in this context as, "has creation a final purpose at all, and if so, why is it not attained immediately, why does perfection not exist from the very beginning?" (7:403). This challenge leads him to introduce the concepts of God's life and personality.

In *Freedom*, Schelling shattered the assumptions that had provide the framework for his earlier thought. Chapter 7 examines the ways in which the later Schelling moved beyond idealistic metaphysics and challenged the very limits of philosophy. In the *Stuttgart*

Lectures (1810) and *The Ages of the World* (1811–15), he addresses the problem of the relation between the finite and the infinite by introducing a doctrine of the fall. The historicizing of reality makes a fundamental rethinking of the concept of time necessary, and the enterprise of philosophical inquiry itself is reconceived as evolutionary by showing how the life of God can be adequately grasped only in this way.

This last effort led Schelling into the public controversy of 1811–12 with Jacobi, whom he perhaps erroneously perceived as unfairly critical of his new concept of God; in that conflict can be seen how far the mature Schelling has traveled. It was Jacobi who had provided him with the original impetus to reconsider what it means to claim truth for a particular philosophical viewpoint, Jacobi, who had described the philosopher's mission as "to reveal existence" [*Daseyn zu enthüllen*] (1:156) and pleaded for a connection between philosophy and life. Thus there is both melancholy and irony in the fact that the last work Schelling published (although he would lecture and write for another forty-two years) was the polemic of 1811–12 against Jacobi.

The details of the controversy were complex, but the impetus behind it simple: although Jacobi had once served in the invaluable role of the outside agitator, noisily shouting inconvenient truths when he maintained that philosophies that did not have a demonstrable connection with reality were insubstantial webs of abstractions, he also insisted that this connection be immediate and intuitive. For Schelling, as indeed for Kant before him, such *Schwärmerei* was nonsense, and dangerous nonsense at that: the very meaning of philosophy is to find a home for man in being, and any 'intuitive' shortcut inevitably divides humanity into true believers and everyone else. Worse yet, Jacobi had over the years fallen into an increasingly pronounced tendency to denigrate reason in order to glorify faith, culminating in what Schelling described as "the promulgation of a general hatred of reason" (8:47).

Introduction

Schelling's philosophical development had led him to a radically transformed understanding of reason, but not its abandonment. He does turn away from his earlier focus on the relationship of nature and spirit to the effort to understand their common ground. Although this leads him in the direction of the awareness that the "true basic substance of all life and being is just what is terrible" (8:339), he never gives up striving to reach this ground. The realization that this ground cannot be adequately explicated by a 'negative philosophy' of concepts and abstractions leads the later Schelling to defend the possibility of grasping existence with a 'positive philosophy', one which undertakes to complete the task of reconceiving the truths of revelation as truths of reason.

Schelling's metaphysical quest may have ended, in a sense, with the discovery of the *Angst* which is the human reaction to awareness of "the accursedness of all being" (13:7), but he was quick to point out that this was at most a rediscovery. Many ancient myths attempt to symbolically grasp the ineffable mystery of creation and provide an answer to that first of all questions: Why is there something rather than nothing? The philosophy of mythology, and later the philosophy of revelation, illustrates the many common elements in these accounts. Most importantly, the late philosophy, like all of Schelling's writings, demonstrates the unending tension between the passion of the mind to know and the despair born of the realization that it is impossible to know the mystery at the heart of being.

1

The Enlightenment under Attack

I. Kant's Early Reception

Hegel's *Lectures on the History of Philosophy* is seldom more dramatic than in his description of the deleterious effects of the philosophies of both Kant and Jacobi on the stature of philosophy in the minds of the learned public. Schelling grew up in the atmosphere Hegel describes; what lessons did he take from the attack on some of the most cherished beliefs of the Enlightenment, represented by Kant's attempt to limit reason and Jacobi's bid to discredit it entirely? Answering this question will require some familiarity with the intellectual battles being waged in the last two decades of the eighteenth century. Hegel makes his opinion exquisitely clear:

> . . . until the Kantian philosophy was reached the interest in philosophy was general, it was accessible, and men were curious to know about it, it pertained to the ordinary knowledge of a man of culture. Formerly men of business, statesmen, occupied themselves with philosophy; now, however, with the intricate idealism of the philosophy of Kant, their wings droop helpless to the ground. Hence it is with Kant that we first begin to find a line of separation which parts us from the common modes of consciousness; but the result, that the Absolute cannot be known, has become one generally acknowledged. With Fichte the common consciousness has still further separated itself from philosophy. . . . The public was through the philosophy of Kant and Jacobi

strengthened in its opinion . . . that the knowledge of God is immediate, and that we know it from the beginning and without requiring to study, and hence that philosophy is quite superfluous.[1]

How did philosophy conspire to in effect bring about its own demise? What was the influence of these developments on the philosophical outlook of the young Schelling, who began his career an admirer of both Kant and Jacobi? These are the topics of this chapter.

Kant was less than fortunate in the early reviews of the first *Critique*, although he found support and some understanding in the person of Christian Gottfried Schultz, the editor of the *Jenaische Allgemeine Literaturzeitung*, a journal in which Kant had occasionally published. Despite several well-meaning but more or less uncomprehending reviews which appeared in the *Allgemeine Literaturzeitung*, the general reaction of the learned public was accurately reflected in the preface to Karl Leonhard Reinhold's *Essay towards a New Theory of the Faculty of Representation*: "Never, with one exception, has a book been so wondered about, admired, hated, criticized, hounded and—misunderstood."[2] Reinhold's "Letters on the Kantian Philosophy," published 1786–87 in installments in the *Teutschen Merkur*, were the first interpretation of Kant to achieve any popular success.[3] In striking contrast to the later emphasis on the epistemological implications of the critical philosophy, Reinhold's "Letters" emphasized the moral and religious aspects of the first *Critique* and were written in a style almost entirely free of the ponderous scholarly jargon Kant favored. It is certainly hardly coincidental that it was to be precisely these Kantian teachings which were most grossly misrepresented and misunderstood, not least in Tübingen, a state of affairs Schelling later satirized in his "Philosophical Letters on Dogmatism and Criticism."

Reinhold's fame was secure after his "Letters" were publicly praised by Kant.[4] Beginning in the winter semester of 1787, Reinhold held an extremely popular *collegium publicum* at the University of Jena; several other professors, among them G. G. Schutz and K. F. C. Schmid, became interested in Kant around this time. "In this way Jena soon became a center for dissemination of the new doctrine and of the philosophical life in Germany in general."[5] The "classical era"[6] in Jena, where Fichte and Schelling were later to teach, had begun.

As I remarked above, Reinhold was initially attracted to the first *Critique* because of its guarantee of the unassailability of moral and religious beliefs. Yet by the time of the publication of the *Essay towards a New Theory of the Faculty of Representation* of 1789, the correctness of Kant's conclusions is no longer the central concern; Reinhold has discovered that Kant's philosophy still lacks a systematic scientific foundation and proposes to provide it. In his preface to the *Essay*, which first appeared in the *Teutschen Merkur* under the title "Concerning the Fate of the Kantian Philosophy," Reinhold speculates about the reasons why Kant's philosophy has not yet found wide acceptance and decides that the underlying reason has to do with Kant's inadequate explanation of his central concept of representation (*Vorstellung*).[7]

The task which Reinhold sets himself is the discovery and grounding of the premises upon which Kant's theory of representation rests, which in turn is the key to his theory of knowledge.[8] In Reinhold's view, that Kant himself did not do this is only natural: "That the actual premises of a science are first discovered after the science itself is nothing new, but rather is a necessary consequence of the analytical course that is prescribed for the progress of the human spirit by its own nature."[9] Recognition of the necessity of an original first principle for philosophy was regarded by Reinhold, as well as both his admirers and his critics, as his unique contribution to philosophy.

Inasmuch as it was the idea of the need for a first principle, not the details of the execution of Reinhold's elementary philosophy (*Elementarphilosophie*) which were of value, in Schelling's view, I will not examine it more closely here.[10] Schelling's appraisal of Reinhold's contribution is clearly stated in a letter written to Hegel in 1795:

> With respect to Reinhold's attempts to retrace philosophy to its ultimate principles, your suspicion that they would lead the revolution born of the Critique of Pure Reason no further has certainly not misled you. However, *that* too was one stage through which science had to pass, and I don't know whether or not it may be Reinhold we have to thank [for the fact] that we will so soon, as it must happen, according to my most certain expectations, be standing upon the highest point.[11]

What was this step? It was the contention that philosophy could not be a science until it rested upon a single principle, and the need to locate this principle in consciousness itself (although the two elements of this claim are not always clearly distinguished by Reinhold).

II. Jacobi and the Pantheism Controversy

A second extremely influential factor, which was eventually to dovetail with the concern for a single original principle of philosophy, was the complex of issues raised by the Spinoza renaissance, itself a result of the conflict between Jacobi and Mendelssohn and the publications connected with their feud. The significance of this event can hardly be overestimated in its significance for virtually every German thinker of the time.[12] Mendelssohn's *Morning Hours: Or Lectures on the Existence of God* and above all Jacobi's *On the Doctrine of Spinoza, in Letters to Moses Mendelssohn* (or the so-called *Spinoza-Büchlein*) made it possible for the all-but-forgotten Spinoza to achieve "universal historical influence . . . and soon, next to the *Critique of Pure Reason*, it became the fundamental intellectual power of the epoch."[13]

The Enlightenment under Attack

Jacobi's *Spinoza-Büchlein*, the first published result of his quarrel with Moses Mendelssohn, was unquestionably the beginning of the renewal of interest in Spinoza in the 1780s. In that work and in "David Hume on Belief or Realism and Idealism" (1787), as well as other shorter works, Jacobi developed his polemical interpretation of Spinoza. It became a general attack on all forms of rationalism, which in turn produced the extremely influential notion that all philosophical systems could be classified as one of two diametrically opposed types: realistic or idealistic. Finally, the notion that all philosophical systems had to belong to one of two utterly opposed types led to a heightened focus on the role of intuition in philosophy, for it was this, in Jacobi's view, that constituted the most fundamental difference between philosophies.

Jacobi used his views on rationalism, speculative philosophy, and the role of intuition in knowledge to criticize Kant, and all three elements of Jacobi's *Kantkritik* were widely discussed and influenced Kant's contemporaries as they struggled to come to terms with the critical philosophy. Today the understanding of all three has substantially changed from that of the late eighteenth century, and although it cannot be claimed that Jacobi himself was a philosopher of the first rank, he nevertheless formed the way the generation after Kant would understand their own philosophical task to a much greater extent than is now recognized.

It cannot be denied that the effort to find in Jacobi something approaching a characteristic philosophical standpoint leads to a certain sympathy with writers such as Ernst Cassirer, who see him as a polemicist or intellectual troublemaker, more gifted at criticizing others than at producing independent intellectual work. He was a "brilliant stimulus," although "between that which Jacobi is as a thinker and writer and the historical results which developed out of his teaching there exists a peculiar contradiction. . . . The movements he had called into life always after a short time grew beyond him, beyond his own basic intuitions, wishes, and inclinations."[14] Jacobi's defenders have usually claimed that he was ahead of his time; yet even among the more recent writers who are attempting to research and view Jacobi as a forerunner of *Lebensphilosophie*, it is not uncommon to find reservations. Gunther Baum's observation is to the point: "He who closely examines Jacobi's writings will soon begin to doubt whether it is sensible and justifiable to speak of Jacobi's philosophy."[15]

The renewal of interest in Spinoza occasioned by the pantheism conflict was, after the ferment stirred up by Kant, the most important philosophical movement of the late eighteenth century. Its significance for Schelling is hinted at in his often-repeated desire to be a "Spinoza in reverse"; to make it intelligible how a thinker born in 1775 could have nursed such an ambition after Spinoza had been ignored for almost a century requires an understanding of how "a seemingly provincial cultural-historical event"[16]—the public discussion of whether G. E. Lessing had been a Spinozist in the last years of his life—could have revived such widespread interest in Spinoza. The pantheism conflict is the first and clearest illustration of the singular antithetical effect Jacobi had on his contemporaries. That he, although a bitter opponent of Spinozism (which he identified with fatalism and atheism), had raised the issue of Lessing's Spinozism in order to refute pantheism in any form once and for all, only to produce an enchantment with Spinoza in comparison to which there has been "in recent cultural history no other event of comparable breadth of influence,"[17] is typical of this atypical thinker.

It is difficult to assess Jacobi's motives for publishing the *Spinoza-Büchlein*. At least three important factors are involved. On the personal level, Jacobi was almost certainly desirous of settling old scores with Mendelssohn, who had criticized his 1782 article "Something Lessing Said."[18] At the very least it should be remarked that the pattern of argumentation in the earlier controversy eerily prefigured that of the pantheism controversy, as Altmann has shown.[19] Less important than this, however, was the sense of mission informing Jacobi's crusade to expose the poverty and pernicious consequences of the Enlightenment worldview and at the same time advance his own solution to what he saw as the threat of rationalism.

Having heard through a mutual friend that Moses Mendelssohn was contemplating writing a biographical tribute to the recently deceased Lessing, Jacobi offered Mendelssohn his own recollections of several conversations he had had with Lessing as material for the planned biography. Through their mutual friend he hinted that Lessing had been a Spinozist, which at that time would have been understood to mean "crass atheist," "hypocrite," and "blasphemer," as Mendelssohn was later to express it in "To Lessing's Friends";[20] this too came in time to Mendelssohn's ears, as Jacobi had intended that it should, and a correspondence began between the two. As Jacobi began to suspect that Mendelssohn would publish something on Lessing and Spinoza without informing him, he quickly assembled their correspondence and published it, without Mendelssohn's knowledge or permission, in 1785; this was the original *Spinoza-Büchlein*. One month later Mendelssohn's *Morning Hours* appeared instead of the announced Lessing biography.

Without going too far afield into Lessing's own reputation, it can be said that he was one of the most prominent figures of the Enlightenment; therefore a profession of Spinozism would easily have been interpreted at the time as a betrayal of, or loss of faith in, the ideals of the Enlightenment of which he had seemed to be the ardent champion in such works as "Nathan the Wise."[21] Lessing was the perfect foil for Jacobi, for he could be used to achieve all three of Jacobi's purposes. Firstly, since Lessing had been a close friend of Mendelssohn's, the revelation of his Spinozism would be almost certain to shock and dismay Mendelssohn, both because of Spinozism's unsavory reputation and because Lessing had not confided his change of heart to him. Certain remarks in the

Spinoza-Büchlein to the effect that Lessing had felt that he dared not communicate his true views to Mendelssohn were doubtless included to this end, as well as Jacobi's asking Lessing "whether he had never told Mendelssohn about his own system [of philosophy]? 'Never,' answered Lessing, 'Only once did I mention to him that which attracted your attention in *The Education of the Human Race*. We could not come to any agreement, and I left it at that.'"[22]

Secondly, by focusing on the person of Lessing, Jacobi was able to dramatize the complete opposition of the Enlightenment worldview to his own and at the same time to avoid the necessity of presenting very much in the way of sustained argumentation, which had never been his forte. He had shrewdly guessed that it would not be the question of Lessing's Spinozism itself that would be the aspect of the controversy that would exert a lasting fascination; the conversations were reproduced from Jacobi's extensive notes so faithfully that agreement on the veracity of Jacobi's report was all but unanimous among those who had known Lessing. What was shocking was rather the implication that Lessing had rejected the values of the Enlightenment, as Mendelssohn had recognized when he set aside his planned Lessing biography to write the *Morning Hours*, and then what was to be his last work, the brief "To Lessing's Friends." When Mendelssohn suddenly died as the manuscript was still in the process of being printed, the sense that Jacobi was to blame extended far beyond just the circle of Mendelssohn's friends.[23]

Jacobi served his hidden agenda of calling the ideals of the Enlightenment itself into question by employing the fragmentary and anecdotal form of letters, letters supposedly concerned chiefly with the opinions of a single person. It was clearly Jacobi's intention to quarrel with the worldview of the Enlightenment in the person of Lessing when he recalled saying to Lessing, in what one imagines was a tone of the most plaintive sincerity: "It was the furthest thing from my mind, to find a Spinozist or pantheist in you. . . . I came in large part to seek your help against Spinoza."[24]

When it is recalled that Jacobi was at the time the comparatively unknown author of various articles, chiefly on political and theological topics, it is easier to understand why he might have been inspired to involve the famous and controversial Lessing as the central character in what turned out to be an intellectual morality play on that age-old theme, the quarrel of faith and reason. Thus it strengthened Jacobi's hand that Lessing's last work, *The Education of the Human Race*, had been greeted with puzzlement; moreover, his involvement as editor of the notorious *Wolfenbüttler Fragmente*, which contained biblical criticism similar in spirit to that of Spinoza's *Theological-Political Tractatus*, as well as attacks on the doctrine of the Trinity, had elicited considerable unfavorable reaction.

Thirdly, and least successfully, Jacobi appears to have used Lessing as at least indirectly endorsing his own views, insofar as Lessing is depicted as agreeing with Jacobi's interpretation of what Spinozism really meant: that there are only two possible philosophical positions, one based on faith and the other on reason. Ironically, Jacobi's own care in recording his conversations with Lessing may have betrayed him here, for it often seems clear that Lessing is not making the concessions that Jacobi assumes he has. Therefore it was not very difficult for Mendelssohn, among others, to take issue with Jacobi over how well he had actually understood what Lessing had said. As Altmann[25] and Allison[26] have shown, he attributed contradictory statements and extremely vague ideas to Lessing and did not always realize when he was being teased, all of which contributes to the impression that the *Spinoza-Büchlein* reveals more about Jacobi than it does about Lessing.

There is an additional irony, which can be fully appreciated only by understanding that Schelling, in his attempt to deal with the implications of the false dilemma of the choice between faith and reason Jacobi set up, turned to Leibniz's sophisticated theory of the development of rationality in order to escape it. According to Allison, in the *New Essays on Human Understanding*, Leibniz defended the idea that true ideas are often present in the soul in obscure form and may eventually be developed into rational concepts. In Leibniz, therefore, "there is no longer a radical opposition, as with Descartes, Spinoza, and again with Kant, between sense or feeling and reason, but only a difference in the degree of clarity with which the same fundamentally rational content is apprehended. Thus the obscure or pre-rational, that is feeling, is seen to contain an implicitly rational content . . . "[27] Allison also cites Kurt Hildebrandt to the effect that "Lessing was the first to grasp this aspect of Leibniz's thought and . . . the failure of others, like Kant, to do so, was one of the sources of the opposition between the advocates of pure reason and the champions of creative thought and intuition in German intellectual life of the 18th century."[28] Thus one means of resolving the dilemma the *Spinoza-Büchlein* creates could have been found in a more profound understanding of its nominal central figure, Lessing; but this avenue was to remain unexplored until Schelling developed his philosophy of nature.

In order to understand the impact of Jacobi's Spinoza interpretation, which equated Spinozism with rationalism and determinism in their most consistent possible form (i.e., as irrefutable by argument) *and* presented it as the final flower of a mystical pantheism with its roots in Plotinus and the kabbala, something of the view of Spinoza prevailing in Germany at that time must be sketched. When the Lessing of the *Spinoza-Büchlein* said: "People always speak of Spinoza as if of a dead dog,"[29] he was referring both to the assumption that Spinoza had been conclusively refuted by Wolff in his *Theologia Naturalis* and to his more general reputation as an atheist. Since Spinoza's works had become a bibliographical rarity early in the eighteenth century, Wolff and Pierre Bayle's *Dictionnaire* articles on Spinoza were almost the only sources of information generally available to the learned public. When Herder has Philolaus criticize Spinoza, he also shows him reflecting on the misfortune suffered by the great metaphysician at the hands of "that sprightly busybody, Bayle," especially since "so few read the obscure works of Spinoza, while all the world reads the manifoldly useful, varied and pleasant Bayle!"[30]

Since virtually all that was known about Spinoza was his supposed atheism, it was easier for Jacobi to make his interpretation seem convincing, particularly because the texts of Spinoza's works had become so rare. The *Spinoza-Büchlein* was widely thought to be "a thorough interpretation,"[31] incredible as that now seems. Fritz Mauthner included a cautionary observation with his 1912 edition of the Pantheism Controversy texts: "One ought not, in reading all these writings and letters, to forget for a moment that Spinoza was far less well known to the combatants and their supporters than he would be today to any ordinary candidate for a philosophy degree."[32] Jacobi himself was the major source of information about Spinoza for most of his contemporaries, even for Schleiermacher.[33]

What then were the main points of Jacobi's Spinoza interpretation? He seems most familiar with *The Ethics* and *On the Improvement of the Intellect*, although it is difficult to be certain because, as with most other authors he discusses, Jacobi vastly prefers extensive paraphrase to quotation. He stresses the identification of Spinozism with pantheism and of both with rationalism in its most extreme form in the first long letter he wrote in response to Mendelssohn's question about the manner and circumstances in which Lessing had supposedly divulged his Spinozism. Mendelssohn anticipates and tries to answer this line of argument in the sections of *Morgenstunden* in which he defends an "enlightened pantheism"[34] and concedes that Lessing may have been a pantheist in the sense that he held the existence of all things to be immanent in God. But such a "refined pantheism," Mendelssohn argued, could "very easily coexist with the truths of religion and morals"[35] because such subtle speculation would have no direct bearing on human conduct or happiness.

Mendelssohn was indirectly replying, with his championship of an "enlightened" Spinozism, to Jacobi's account of his conversation with Lessing, in the course of which he attempts to prove that all pantheistic systems are imperfect forms of Spinozism. Spinoza, according to Jacobi, was the most consistent of pantheists and rationalists, and his works reveal most clearly what pantheism and rationalism, properly understood, *must* imply—atheism and fatalism. When Jacobi depicts himself as saying to Lessing: "I believe I know him [Spinoza] as only very few have known him," he did not mean that he had discovered that Spinozism was atheism, but rather that it was Spinoza's *method* of rational demonstration which leads to atheism. "For the determinist, if he wants to be consistent, must become a fatalist."[36] That is, if rationalism is to be consistent (and Jacobi holds Spinoza's to have been the most consistent), it must be capable of explaining everything without exception. Once the mind sets itself to understand the universe and refuses to give up the principle *a nihilo nihil fit*, then it cannot rest until everything has a rational explanation. According to the argument of the *Spinoza-Büchlein*, because free will and a personal God cannot even in principle be rationally explained, they are denied any reality in Spinoza's system. Rationalism cannot allow "something out of nothing" to be postulated; it must deny "every transition from the infinite to the finite."[37] It can accomplish this only by means of a concept of being that possesses neither reason nor will, "a first cause, of an infinite nature ... [a] first, general, original stuff."[38] Jacobi concludes triumphantly: "Whoever can accept this fatalism cannot be refuted. He who cannot accept it must become Spinoza's antipode."[39] The gauntlet had been laid down—all philosophy must champion either faith or reason. It was here, in Jacobi's *Spinoza-Büchlein*, that the consequences of the opposition between faith and reason that Kant's philosophy had implied became crystallized in the form which engaged the attention of virtually every thinker of the time.[40]

Appended to the first (1785) edition there were six principles which were Jacobi's attempt to sum up his own position by emphasizing the unbridgeable gap between the orthodox concepts of divinity, which are based on revelation and faith, and the atheism to which every form of rationalism must necessarily lead.

1. Spinozism is atheism.
2. The kabbalistic philosophy, qua philosophy, is nothing but undeveloped Spinozism or a confused version of it.
3. The Leibniz-Wolffian philosophy is no less fatalistic than Spinoza's philosophy, to whose principles the persistent researcher will find it inevitably leads.
4. Every manner [of philosophizing that is based on the method] of demonstration ends in fatalism.
5. We can demonstrate only similarities; and every proof presupposes something already proven, the very first principle of which is revelation.
6. The fundamental element of all human action and knowledge is belief (*Glaube*).[41]

This is the essence of Jacobi's message, that the most fundamental question of all, that of the relation of the individual to the Absolute, can at bottom be answered in only two ways. The Enlightenment and everything it stands for has been shown to be not just deeply mistaken but pernicious, for the ultimate consequence of the use of reason is despair, fatalism, sterility, death; faith alone can maintain a vital, living connection with reality. The dilemma Jacobi presents is a false one, but it is thrust upon the reader with an unmistakably genuine urgency. I suggest that it had the influence it did in part because of its content: it succeeded in capturing the flavor of a growing disillusionment with the Enlightenment and the claims of reason rampant at the time. Yet the seductiveness of the form in which the opposition of faith and reason was presented ought not to be overlooked: the either/or, the mutually exclusive alternatives, had seldom if ever been stated in such starkly dramatic terms; the repercussions are still being felt today.

III. Faith or Reason?

It may seem peculiar at best that Jacobi thought that a book in the format of a lengthy correspondence would be the most effective way to showcase his interpretation of Spinoza's philosophy. The choice could be attributed to the great haste in which he had to prepare the manuscript in order to make his accusations public before Mendelssohn could publish a defense of Lessing; but it ought also to be borne in mind that the *Spinoza-Büchlein*, depicting Spinozism as the inevitable and catastrophic culmination of the dogmatic, rationalistic, and pantheistic thought of the Enlightenment, was but one expression of Jacobi's long-cherished anti-Enlightenment views, albeit the most influential. He had realized, like the other so-called philosophers of belief (*Glaubensphilosophen*),[42] J. G. Hamann and J. G. Herder, that since the Enlightenment was synonymous with an overemphasis on reason, it might be the case that a demonstrative rational argument would be the least effective way of revealing its weaknesses.

For all three thinkers the triumph of the Enlightenment meant a devaluation of what each of them held to be the center and foundation of human life: faith, feeling, and immediate intuitive connection to God, or the supersensible. The importance of challenging the most basic assumptions of the Enlightenment in a new way is illustrated at its most brilliant and excessive in Hamann's *Socratic Memorabilia* of 1759, which was an extended meditation, quarrel, act of provocation, and allegorical crusade against Kant, Hamann and Kant's mutual friend, Behrens, and the Enlightenment in general.[43] Neither the impact of its message nor its unique stylistic pyrotechnics can be summarized here; indeed, I can think of no philosophical work less amenable to summary. Yet the claim made by James O'Flaherty, echoing Hegel, to the effect that Hamann does not *have* a style, he rather *is* style through and through,[44] indicates that the unprecedented and idiosyncratic style of the *Socratic Memorabilia* is anything but unrelated to its anti-Enlightenment content.

Herder, a former student of Hamann's, most resembled his master in that he possessed a genuinely original turn of mind; however, the conclusions he reached in his published works were by no means always to Hamann's liking. His prize essay, *On the Origin of Language*, written for the 1770 competition of the Akademie der Wissenschaften in Berlin, contained a sophisticated argument for a naturalistic theory of language which was also an attack on the view that language is the creation and gift of God. If, Herder argued, language has a natural rather than a supernatural origin, it has a discoverable genesis and history, which can be studied. And since reason is expressed through language, it must also have a history and undergo change and development. This was the seed of Herder's concept of genetic method, a method which led him to stress the significance of social and historical factors in understanding any phenomenon, including the human race. Herder's contribution to the pantheism controversy is to be found in his *God: Some Conversations*, influential on all the post-Kantians, but it was not just the vitalistic theory of nature defended in that work which was an inspiration to Schelling; the genetic method was also to prove fatefully important.[45]

Jacobi was no Hamann in terms of intellectual ability or literary gifts, nor did he have Herder's wide-ranging erudition, but he does seem to have appreciated the difficulty of making his case against the Enlightenment by using the Enlightenment's own weapon of rational argument. Therefore I suggest that his fourth principle (above), according to which all demonstration leads to fatalism, be seen as a declaration of the bankruptcy of reason. The proof of the pernicious consequences of rationalism and the argument that Spinozism is the irrefutable (on rational grounds) final result of consistent rationalism were necessary presuppositions for Jacobi; if he had not insisted on the rational unimpeachability of Spinozism he could not have presented his own irrationalistic philosophy of belief as the only alternative.

Only this initially concealed purpose can explain the spectacle of Mendelssohn and Jacobi, both declared opponents of the archatheist Spinoza, publicly quarreling about the best method of refutation. Mendelssohn had attempted a speculative criticism of Spinoza along the lines of those offered by Wolff and Leibniz; but Jacobi could not give up his insistence on the impossibility of refuting Spinoza rationally, for he had no other way of forcing the issue of the unavoidability of his *salto mortale*, a nonrational leap of faith, as the only possible alternative to Spinozism. He later admitted as much: "My letters on Spinoza's doctrine were . . . written . . . in order to demonstrate the impossibility of overcoming Spinozism by means of the logical use of the understanding" (Jacobi 4:xxxvii). The complete opposition and irreconcilability of the rational and the irrational were the necessary presuppositions for Jacobi's conclusion that consistent rationalism can be overcome only by consistent irrationalism, which for Jacobi was Christian personalism, and his own emphasis on feeling and belief as the only means of unmediated access to reality.

However, the learned public had to wait until 1787, for "David Hume on Belief or Idealism and Realism," to learn more about Jacobi's philosophical ideas than the few hints that could be gleaned from the *Spinoza-Büchlein*, where Jacobi had insisted on the reality of belief and freedom on the grounds that the deterministic alternative was completely unacceptable: "It is impossible, that everything is nature and not freedom, because it is impossible that everything which elevates and ennobles man—the true, the good, and the beautiful—are only illusion, deception, and lies. This is the case, if there is no freedom" (Jacobi 2:3–4). That the polemical rejection of the consequences of rationalism, without suggesting anything in its place other than affirmation of a vague belief, was not enough to convince most readers was later acknowledged by Jacobi when he described the reaction to the *Spinoza-Büchlein*: "The claim made in the work on the doctrine of Spinoza by the author: all human knowledge arises out of revelation and belief, aroused general indignation in the German philosophical world" (Jacobi 2:3–4). Jacobi denies in the passages immediately following that he was "an enemy of reason" or that he had ever taught a blind belief, and announces "David Hume on Belief" as his answer to these accusations.

The dialogue explains, with the help of excerpts from Hume and Thomas Reid, Jacobi's concept of belief as the feeling of necessary connection to the real: a nonrational, immediate, intuitive conviction. At this point (at the latest) it becomes clear that Jacobi is not using the terms "idealism" and "realism" in any of their more familiar senses; for the appeal to belief, to intuitive knowledge, is also clearly an appeal to the real. Jacobi describes how he came to philosophy:

> As long as I can recall, it has been a part of my character that I could understand nothing of concepts whose outer or inner object I could not intuit through sensation or feeling. Objective truth and reality seemed the same thing to me, just as a clear representation and knowledge are. Every demonstration, which could not, proposition for proposition, be made graspable to me in this fashion; every explanation which could not be intuitively compared to an object, which was not genetic: to these I was blind and closed. (Jacobi 2:178)

Thus reason is for Jacobi always a means to an end and never superior to intuitive knowledge. Those systems which allow reason in the form of abstract ideas to reign over intuition are by their nature atheistic because their guiding force is the desire to explain everything. Several statements in the *Spinoza-Büchlein* are comprehensible for the first time against this background, especially the definition of philosophy's proper task:

> The greatest merit of the philosophical scholar is not to establish abstract conceptions nor to spin systems of them. His ultimate aim is pure absolute being; his greatest merit is to unveil and reveal that which can never be conceptualized, explained, deduced, in short to reveal the undissectable, the immediate, the simple.[46]

Jacobi's unwavering adherence to this basic insight also sheds light on his subsequent literary efforts, the philosophical novels *Allwills Briefsammlung* and *Woldemar*. According to George di Giovanni, Jacobi was the first to conceive of the idea of a philosophical *roman* and deserves to be compared with Kierkegaard in his innovative use of the form,[47] although there is ample circumstantial evidence that he may have been familiar with Herder's thesis in *Vom Erkennen und Empfinden* that the best understanding of life is to be found in literature.[48]

For Jacobi, to expose the speciousness and partiality of abstraction is implicitly to claim that another kind of approach to truth is more adequate. In his novels, his political writings with their profusion of historical illustrations, and of course in the letters which comprise the main body of the *Spinoza-Büchlein*, we see his strong attraction to the concrete and sensually graspable. Truth is most real when it comes to life in particular individual people and situations. Paradoxically, then, if there is to be any access to universal truth about the human condition, it will have to be found in the words and actions of individual people; but perhaps this is no more paradoxical than the fact that the universal desire to know is always and only instantiated in actual living persons. Thus it might be argued that for Jacobi, the novel is not just one perspective on the truth, but the closest it is possible to come to truth.

Herman Nohl finds Jacobi to have been "the most important philosophical critic of this [post-Kantian] generation"[49] precisely because he rejected the rationalism of the Enlightenment and insisted upon the fundamental role of experience, of feeling, and of faith. The terms rationalism and idealism appear to have been used interchangeably by Jacobi to characterize those systems not based on intuitive knowledge but depending to a greater or lesser extent on abstraction. The intuited is the undeniably real, the abstracted the ideal or rational.

Only the clear definition of these terms can make Jacobi's characterization of idealism as a "Spinozism in reverse" (Jacobi 2:10) understandable; what Spinoza and Fichte have in common for him is the desire to explain everything in terms of a single principle. Since such radical philosophies cannot succeed by appealing to intuition, they must both appeal to abstraction by means of concepts and are at bottom both speculative attempts to carry to its limits the principle *a nihilo nihil fit*. As Jacobi explained in a letter to Fichte:

> It is undeniably the spirit of speculative philosophy, and therefore has been from the very beginning its unceasing effort, to make the common man's originally *equal* certainty of these two principles: I am, and there are things outside of me, *unequal*. It must seek to subordinate one of these principles to the other. . . . In their basic thrust they [materialism and idealism] are in no way divergent, but rather gradually approach one another to the point of touching and commingling. The metaphysics of speculative materialism, in realizing its own consequences, must become transfigured idealism . . . (Letter of 3.3.1799, in Jacobi 3:10ff.)

Thus it can be seen that Jacobi's opposition of idealism and realism, despite his idiosyncratic definition of the terms, is of interest for the study of later idealists for two reasons. The *Spinoza-Büchlein* contained the earliest attempt of a contemporary author well known to Fichte and Schelling to set up an opposition between two *types* of philosophical systems,[50] which, by the fundamental nature of the choice between them, are at once mutually exclusive and incapable of refuting one another rationally. As can be seen in the letter cited above, Jacobi continued to uphold the thoroughgoing and necessary character of this opposition in his later writings. Still more important was Jacobi's insistence that one system can be seen to be superior to the other by virtue of the values it embodies; in the case of his "realistic" theory, freedom and a personal God.

Jacobi's *salto mortale* is the first "practical" solution to the difficulty of having to choose between mutually exclusive philosophical systems; rationalism is not rejected on theoretical grounds but rather because it denies freedom and the possibility of knowledge of a personal God. One must rescue oneself from these consequences, even if by means of an irrational "head-first leap."[51] Some of the implications of what it means to reject a philosophical view because of its practical or moral significance for the person who holds it were explored by both Fichte and Schelling; Jacobi was their model in this, not Kant.[52] After reading the second edition of the novel *Woldemar*, Fichte wrote enthusiastically to Jacobi, whom he had never met: "Yes, dear noble man, we are in complete agreement, and this agreement with you proves to me more than anything else that I am on the right track. You too seek all truth where I seek it: in the innermost sanctuary of our own being."[53]

Jacobi also seems to have been the first to employ the term "practical" to describe the unique advantage belief enjoys over reason when he claims "man must either participate in the divine nature or the divine must become flesh and blood. This practical way can neither be praised nor achieved by that impoverished reason which has decayed as it has become speculative."[54] Only with this background in mind can the ambiguous heritage of Kant's term practical reason be appreciated; it is by no means simply that reason which is not theoretical.

Practical reason is still more important for later thinkers than it was for Kant. Schelling goes so far as to assert that "no system can be completed other than *practically*," and that "no man can convince himself of any system except pragmatically, that is, by realizing the system *in* himself" (1:304). He finds awareness of the living reality of freedom to be the sine qua non: whether we choose the system of dogmatism or criticism "depends on the freedom of spirit we have ourselves acquired" (1:308). Fichte echoes this sentiment two years later in what is probably the best known and most frequently quoted statement of the position:

> What sort of philosophy one chooses depends, therefore, on what sort of man one is; for a philosophical system is not a dead piece of furniture that we can accept or reject as we wish, it is rather a thing animated by the soul of the person who holds it. (1:434)

In the final analysis, the choice of philosophical system rests on something preconceptual and fundamental in each of us. This has two vital implications: reason has been dethroned, in the sense that rational argument has been exposed as inadequate to compel agreement; and we realize that we have been rudely awakened from the dream that progressively increasing rationality will ultimately reveal universal truth, which was the central myth of the Enlightenment.

2

The Knowledge of Reality

I. The Problem of the Thing in Itself

Jacobi is justly, if misleadingly, famous for his complaint that without presupposing the thing in itself, he could not get into the *Critique of Pure Reason*, but with the thing in itself, he could not remain in it (Jacobi 2:304). But what does this objection really mean? At bottom Jacobi is reflecting the widespread concern of his time with the question of the possibility of knowledge of reality. Both Kant's admirers and his detractors saw as problematic the *Critique* and its claims to have demarcated the limits of human knowledge, and Jacobi's objections went to the heart of the matter: simultaneously to name an ultimate reality (the thing in itself) and to declare it unknowable betrays an unresolved ambivalence concerning the powers of human reason. Do we know reality—or only that we do not know it?

This also helps to explain Jacobi's seemingly contradictory attitude toward Spinoza. He combines veneration for him as a great man and a profound thinker[1]—indeed the greatest of the dogmatists—with strenuous attempts to show his thought to have had the most unholy and pernicious implications. Jacobi admires Spinoza most for his uncompromising honesty and willingness to follow his argument wherever it might lead. "I love Spinoza because he, more than any other philosopher, has led me to the firm conviction that certain things cannot be explained: one must not on that account close one's eyes to them, but rather must take them as one finds them."[2] He even claims to be following Spinoza's example in going beyond skepticism, indeed beyond all philosophy, following "the light of which Spinoza says that it illuminates both itself and the darkness."[3] Jacobi's self-assigned role as defender of the faith in an increasingly godless time did earn him a large following and a growing reputation, leading many to regard him by 1809 as "almost the Pope of philosophy."[4] This is to get ahead of the story.

Jacobi's interest in Kant had been awakened as early as 1762 by Kant's "The Only Possible Proof for a Demonstration of God's Existence," which Jacobi found a welcome aid in his struggle to preserve his religious views against the assaults they had suffered during his study of the materialist and determinist ideas of the philosophes. Jacobi was also in agreement with Kant's insistence on the recognition of the limits of reason in the first *Critique*. Still, when in the *Spinoza-Büchlein* Jacobi characterized passages of the first *Critique* as "entirely in the spirit of Spinoza"[5] and used the concept of transcendental apperception to explain Spinoza's concept of substance,[6] he found himself sharply criticized by Kant in "What Is Orientation in Thinking?" Surprised and taken aback, Jacobi hastened to further develop his interpretation of Kant in "David Hume" and "On Transcendental Idealism." There is therefore much in his *Kantkritik*, as Verra and Timm have noted,[7] which should be attributed to Jacobi's desire to defend himself rather than to a desire to provide a careful assessment of the critical doctrines on their own merits.

However, I am concerned here only with Jacobi's influential view on the role of intuition in knowledge. In "On Transcendental Idealism," Jacobi quotes at some length those sections of the *Critique of Pure Reason* in which Kant argues for the transcendental ideality of time and space and says that we only understand that which we have constructed after a plan of our own; for example, the regularity and order in nature. Jacobi then points out that for Kant it is contradictory to speak of objects outside our representations which in some sense bring those representations into being: "for according to the Kantian doctrine the empirical object, which is always only appearance, cannot be present outside us and yet be something other than a representation" (Jacobi 2:302).

Yet Kant cannot simply do away with the presupposition of objects outside our representations, for then his understanding of empirical intuition as receptive would be endangered.

> However much it may be opposed to the spirit of Kantian philosophy to say of objects that they make impressions upon the senses, it nevertheless cannot be understood how, without this presupposition, even the Kantian philosophy could find a starting-point for itself. (Jacobi 2:302)

This was the contradiction which led Jacobi to maintain that he had needed to begin the *Critique* over and over again, "because I always became confused by the fact that *without* this presupposition I could not get into the system, and *with* this presupposition could not remain within it" (Jacobi 2:304). Kant's philosophy leaves unexplained the most evident and convincing objective real determinations and reduces them to subjective appearances. Jacobi concludes that contrary to Kant's claims, he has in fact shown that with respect to the "way and manner in which we are affected by objects, we are totally ignorant" (Jacobi 2:306).

The significance of this conclusion may become more understandable in the light of the discussion of Jacobi's view of idealism and realism. "Idealistic" philosophers who deny immediate intuitive knowledge of objects and claim that passive perceptions are actively synthesized through the understanding, as Kant does, can never attain real knowledge of objects. All knowledge is indirect, because it is conditioned by the understanding, and the discursive understanding only produces representations. Since no representation can be produced that is adequate to the idea of God or of freedom, these ideas are declared to be inaccessible to us, which was the most damning consequence of idealism, in Jacobi's view.

If the presupposition of the thing in itself is necessary for Kant's theory of empirical intuition, according to Jacobi, then we have no possibility of proving that our representations correspond to real things outside us. "The transcendental idealist must therefore have the courage to maintain the strongest idealism that has ever been taught, and not fear even the reproach of speculative egoism, for he cannot maintain himself in his system if he so much as attempts to rid himself of this last reproach" (Jacobi 2:310).

A great deal more could be and has been said about Jacobi's *Kantkritik*.[8] Of particular interest here, however, is Jacobi's complaint that Kant is not being consistent in claiming that there are two sources or elements in knowledge, and that Kant's account of empirical intuition cannot ultimately be reconciled with his insistence on the understanding's law-giving capacity. Consistent idealism (in Jacobi's sense of the term) must make the mind the source of all knowledge; the only other possibility is the recognition that knowledge of the real is based on an original intuition thereof: a concrete, sensual, individual experience. This, of course, is his own "realistic" theory, to be distinguished from empiricism by the recognition that experience itself is the highest form of knowledge, not an element or part of some mind-created or -controlled reality. Jacobi later formulated the essence of his doctrine of the primacy of intuition as the simplest possible statement of the fundamental insight that "true being . . . is recognized in feeling alone" (Jacobi 2:105).

II. Fichte: The Self as First Principle

In Jacobi's call to make feeling the standard and foundation of reality, the voice of Romanticism is loud and clear. Jacobi's claim that the richness of experience cannot be grasped by philosophy (by which he appears to have meant any form of discursive reasoning) was anything but discouraging to Fichte. On the contrary, he seems to have relished the challenge of bringing into being a new, vital philosophy, one which appealed to the heart as much or even more than it did to the mind. The essential and characteristic change Fichte made was simultaneously to proclaim the self as the first principle of philosophy and the activity of the self as ultimately the ground of all reality—the most basic feeling being self-consciousness itself.

Both Fichte and Schelling are confident and unapologetic about their use of the self as the highest principle of philosophy. Since Schelling gives no satisfactory account of how he arrived at the conviction that the self is central in this way to philosophy, and because Fichte was the first to publish works using the term as the first principle, it will be of interest to retrace the steps which led him to this innovative and fateful change. Hegel would have us believe that Fichte is a simple extension of Jacobi, but the actual development of his thought is considerably more circuitous.[9]

Though the beginning of Fichte's study of Kant is reliably established to have been during the summer of 1790, there is no evidence of an interest in or familiarity with Reinhold until September 1792.[10] Initially excited by the conviction that Reinhold was also aware of the problem of bringing systematic unity to the critical philosophy, Fichte was complaining of dissatisfaction with Reinhold's theory as early as February 1793, and does so with specific mention of doubt concerning the first principle of philosophy:

> I had always held the critical philosophy for an impregnable fortress, in its spirit, that is, which neither Kant nor Reinhold has portrayed, and which I am only beginning to understand ... until recently, in conversation with an independent spirit [*Selbstdenker*], I fell prey to a doubt concerning nothing less than the first principle ... which, were it not laid to

rest, would destroy the whole of philosophy, and set in its place the most soulless skepticism.[11]

In November and December of 1792, Fichte put in weeks of work on a review of G. E. Schulze's provocative attack on Reinhold, commonly referred to by the pseudonym of the author as "Aenesidemus." Schulze attacks Reinhold's elementary philosophy as well as the critical philosophy by arguing that neither has adequately responded to Hume's skepticism.[12] The result of this period of intensive study of Reinhold's system was to make Fichte even more aware than he had been that neither Kant nor Reinhold had succeeded in making philosophy entirely scientific and secure against the attacks of skeptics. Though he is not as harsh in his judgment of Reinhold in the published review, the true extent of the change in his views is revealed in a letter:

> Have you read Aenesidemus? He had me confused for quite some time, has toppled Reinhold in my regard, made Kant suspicious to me, and completely upset my own system, down to the foundations. But it is impossible to live without a roof over my head! There was no help for it; it had to be rebuilt. And this I have been steadfastly doing for about six weeks.[13]

This letter has been variously dated as having been written in November or December of 1792, or during the time Fichte was at work on the "Review of Aenesidemus."

Fichte's growing dissatisfaction with Reinhold and his first principle of consciousness finally led him to an open admission of his objections in March 1794. In a letter to Reinhold he says that although he feels that they are in complete agreement about the need for a first principle, he "cannot recognize it to be [Reinhold's principle of consciousness, for] . . . in my view that is a subordinate principle, which is determined and proven through higher principles."[14] What are these higher principles?

How did Fichte arrive at his central insight of the self as the highest principle?

Perhaps it suits our understanding of Fichte's famously volatile and passionate temperament to imagine the discovery occurring in a sudden and solitary flash of insight, and this was a view Fichte himself seemed to have encouraged. According to his grandson, Fichte had often spoken of the time when he was originally wrestling with the problem, and said that he used to "meditate long and perseveringly about the highest principle of philosophy [and] was suddenly seized by the thought, as he stood by the warm winter oven, that only the self, the concept of pure subject-objectivity, could serve as the highest principle of philosophy."[15]

Although it is less romantic, there exists a detailed report of a conversation between Jens Baggesen and Fichte which gives a more mundane indication of the background and genesis of Fichte's insight into the nature of the self. Baggesen had just been criticizing Reinhold by saying that to distinguish (*unterscheiden*), to represent (*vorstellen*), and to relate (*beziehen*) are all both indeterminate and derivative concepts, not original, as Reinhold claims. Fichte replied:

> Allow me, I said, I see—or rather suspect, only one possibility of going deeper.... I go back as far as I can to the first form of philosophy and retrace the course taken by the first principles of those who have progressed in it or made reforms. I find immediately that their work consisted of... simplification—one cut away a piece—the next another—his successor another—because he found it heterogenous, superfluous, impure, or rotten.
>
> Therefore Aristotle cut away a good bit—and Cartesius so much that he retained only the *Cogito*. I THINK means: *I combine representations*—then came Reinhold and cut away still more, in that he said: *I represent*, and in this way came as close as possible to the

generic principle—I confess that I do not see how more than representation could now be cut away, and if it is cut away nothing remains but the *self!*

Exactly! Precisely! Completely! he cried.[16]

Baggesen then asks whether this is the new principle for philosophy which Fichte had been working toward, and Fichte confirms that it is, although he adds that the self must be conceived of as active.

Fichte's dissatisfaction with his predecessors, then, paved the way for what he later enjoyed recalling as a "sudden" inspiration.[17] Daniel Breazeale has arrived at a similar conclusion after investigating the contents of Fichte's 1792–93 unpublished manuscript "Personal Meditations on Elementary Philosophy," which is less a defense of Reinhold against Schulze's skepticism than an attempt to establish the foundations of his own philosophy.[18] In either case it is he who must be given credit for explicitly introducing the self as the highest principle of philosophy; and inasmuch as he also claimed intellectual intuition was the characteristic activity of the self, it will be illuminating to look at his concept of this controversial activity.

The first step toward understanding what Fichte meant by intellectual intuition has to be sought in the process by which, I have argued, he arrived at his concept of the self—the process of criticizing Reinhold. The reason why Fichte could praise Reinhold's insight, especially with respect to the latter's insistence on the establishment of a single original principle for philosophy, yet be so dismissively critical of virtually every feature of his theory, was that he thought he had discovered where the fundamental error lay. Reinhold had mistakenly assumed that the highest principle of philosophy must rest upon a single original fact. Fichte had concluded in the "Review" that any object of consciousness, to be an object, is already conditioned by the forms of intuition (i.e, it must be in space and time, etc.) and hence can be no more than the product of empirical consciousness and necessarily abstract. That which is abstracted from empirical consciousness can produce at best a formal principle, whereas the principle philosophy requires must be real and not merely formal. Such a principle would have to be based not on a fact (*Tatsache*), but an act (*Tathandlung*).

Fichte's "Second Introduction to the Science of Knowledge" tells us that "the Science of Knowledge sets out from an intellectual intuition, that of the absolute self-activity of the self" (Fichte 1:471). Intellectual intuition correctly understood is

> the intuiting of himself that is required of the philosopher, in performing the act whereby the self arises for him. . . . It is the immediate consciousness that I act and what I enact: it is that whereby I know something because I do it. We cannot prove from concepts that this power of intuition exists, nor evolve from them what it may be. Everyone must discover it immediately in himself, or else he will never make its acquaintance." (Fichte 1:463)

For Fichte, intellectual intuition is the capacity of the self to be aware of its own activity, which is its first and highest reality. Fichte undeniably developed his theory of intellectual intuition in directions Jacobi never would have sanctioned, yet he retained Jacobi's emphasis on the immediacy and simplicity of this original intuition and insisted that it was the necessary basis for philosophy properly understood (Fichte 1:466–67). It is less often remarked upon that Fichte also adopted Jacobi's stress on the ultimate incommunicability of this most basic feeling.[19]

Given the major role that the concept of intellectual intuition plays in Schelling's early theories of the self, two things about the thought of the early Fichte on the self will immediately attract notice. First, it is curious that although Fichte employed the term 'intellectual intuition' before Schelling did (in the "Review of Aenesidemus" of 1792), he does not use it in the 1794 *Science of Knowl-*

edge, the most complete statement of his system before 1798; in fact, he does not refer to it at all between the "Review" and the "First Introduction to the Science of Knowledge" of 1797. The second and more significant difference between Fichte and Schelling concerns their views on the concept of the absolute self. This difference is most pronounced in the dissimilar uses each makes of what they both call intellectual intuition.

Here the question of Fichte's influence on Schelling must give way to the undeservedly neglected question of Schelling's influence on Fichte, or more accurately, the influence of his 1794 article "Of the I" on the popular reception of Fichte's *Science of Knowledge*. As Xavier Tilliette reminds us, the publication of the *Science of Knowledge* was one of the great philosophical events of its time—much more so than even the publication of the *Critique of Pure Reason* had been—but as was the case with the *Critique*, the early reaction was far from universally positive.[20] The criticism of Fichte's contemporaries centered on the concept of the self, as is reflected in the letters of Hölderlin, Wieland, Herbart, Novalis, and Friedrich Schlegel, among others. The latter two specifically mentioned turning to "Of the I" as an aid in their struggle to understand Fichte. Tilliette relates how the greater emphasis placed on the concept of the absolute self in "Of the I" earned Schelling the label "town crier of the self" [*Marktschreier des Ich*].[21]

> It can hardly be doubted that it was the blaring of the Schellingian trumpet which placed the weight, the emphasis, on the self.... Fichte was from the start convinced that his self was a supra- and inner-individual self ... yet astonishingly Fichte does not say how the original action, the pure energy, with which the being of the self coincides ... comes into consciousness or is known. Here Schelling contributes a theory of intellectual intuition which stirred the interest of many.[22]

Tilliette's comments confirm my suspicion that the resemblances of Fichte's and Schelling's theories are due at least in part to Schelling's indirect influence on Fichte, rather than to Fichte's direct influence on Schelling.

A brief examination of Fichte's earlier theories of the self and intellectual intuition will suffice to illustrate their important differences. Fichte's first use of the expression "intellectual intuition" occurs in the "Personal Meditations on Elementary Philosophy" of 1792–93. The editors of the historical-critical Fichte edition describe it as follows:

> [I]n the following hand-written manuscript we find the train of thought which Fichte followed, with "pen in hand" in the attempt to systematize Reinhold's doctrine of the elementary, to the point of view of the Science of Knowledge; one might dub it a science of knowledge in *statu nascendi*, . . . the significance of the Personal Meditations for the evaluation of the Science of Knowledge ought not to be underestimated.[23]

A careful reading of the "Personal Meditations" strongly suggests that Fichte was experimenting with a defense of Reinhold's principle of consciousness against Schulze's criticisms, and that this was the original source for his first concept of intellectual intuition. Reinhold had declared in *On the Foundation of Philosophical Knowledge* that his new philosophy would "have as [its] object the forms [of representation] themselves as the original a priori unknowable."[24] These forms were accessible, according to Reinhold, by means of an unmediated reflection, which is first called intellectual intuition in an appendix to *Essay towards a New Theory of the Faculty of Representation*.[25] Without going into great detail, it may be said that Reinhold's theory is circular, as has been thoroughly demonstrated by Jürgen Stolzenberg.[26] His intellectual intuition is explained as offering unmediated access to the forms of representation, which are differentiated from the representations themselves. However, even the forms of representation must somehow be capable of representation, or they would not be present to consciousness. Hence it appears that Reinhold is claiming both that the forms of representation (sometimes also called facts of consciousness (*Tatsachen des Bewusstseins*)) are necessary for representation to occur, and that these forms themselves are capable of being represented.

The clumsiness and circularity of Reinhold's theory became increasingly apparent to Fichte in the course of writing the "Personal Meditations." Stolzenberg concludes: "'Intellectual intuition' is, for Reinhold, nothing other than a theory of immediate inner experience . . . "[27] Fichte, however, after evaluating at length the differences between thought and intuition, discards Reinhold's emphasis on intellectual intuition of the forms of representation. The only object of unmediated knowledge is the self: "Everyone is immediately certain of *his* self; for he can intuit only it. To show how the conviction of the existence of external things, and through them also of intelligent beings external to us arises is precisely the goal of an elementary philosophy."[28]

Beginning with this new restriction on what he most often calls "original intuition" of the self, Fichte proceeds to observe that the self becomes aware of itself by opposing itself to a not-self, or distinguishing itself, for itself, from all that is not-self.[29] Fichte replaces Reinhold's forms of representation with references to "acts of the human spirit."[30] Reinhold had claimed that it was possible to intuit the forms of representation. Fichte reinterpreted this as an "original intuition" of the "activities of spirit," which, in the course of Fichte's attempts to work out a satisfactory principle of the self, became laws of spirit. Near the end of the "Personal Meditations" he arrives at a conception of the self and its laws which appears to provide the best solution: "[It is] *practical*, self-legislating, and to that extent entirely determined through itself: it itself *determines*, and determines *itself*. It is at once actor and that which is acted upon."[31]

Ultimately, Fichte's intellectual intuition is practical; as his subsequent works were to demonstrate, the laws and logic of the opposition of the self and not-self are to be understood only in the light of practical reason. One of the central concepts of the *Science of Knowledge*, that of striving, is also introduced here, significantly in connection with the second and final mention of intellectual intuition:

> . . . if the self of intellectual intuition *is, because* it is, and *is, what* it is; then it is insofar as it *posits itself*, absolutely self-sufficient and independent. . . . But since the self cannot relinquish its character of absolute self-sufficiency; there arises a striving to make the intelligible dependent on it, in order to bring the representing self into unity with the self-positing self. And this is the meaning of the expression: *reason is practical.* (Fichte 1:22)

III. The Early Schelling's Concept of the Self

The traditional view of the early Schelling as little more than a disciple of Fichte is inaccurate; I have argued that the similarities in their early writings are best explained as a result of their shared fascination with Kant's ambiguous legacy. The early Fichte, as I demonstrated in the previous section, was above all concerned with the problem of finding a first principle for philosophy, a problem initially formulated by Reinhold. The early Schelling, by contrast, took his chief inspiration from issues raised by the Spinoza renaissance of the 1790s and F. H. Jacobi, as discussed in chapter 1. This section will be devoted to an examination of Schelling's first concept of the self and its dependence on Spinoza.

Schelling thinks that his intentions in writing "Of the I as the Principle of Philosophy" (1795) should be perfectly clear to anyone who truly understands what philosophy is; but for the sake of the uninitiated reader, he is careful to explain himself in the preface:

A philosophy which is based on the nature of man himself could not aim at dead formulae, which would function as just so many prisons of man's mind, nor could it aim at being a philosophical artifice which, by deducing current concepts from apparently superior ones, would bury the living work of the human mind in dead mental faculties. If I may say it in the words of Jacobi, philosophy seeks to unveil and reveal that which is [*Daseyn*], so that the nature and spirit of philosophy cannot lie in any formula or letter; its highest topic must be what is immediate in man and present only to itself. . . . The aim of philosophy is no mere reform of its discipline but a complete reversal of its principles, that is, a revolution which one can view as the second possible revolution in its field. (1:156)

The allusions to Kant illustrate Schelling's view of Kant's weakness—the architectonic which buries the living work of the mind in dead mental faculties—and his positive achievement of having brought about the first revolution in philosophy. Like Fichte, who maintained as late as 1797 that his system was nothing other than "Kantianism properly understood,"[32] Schelling claims that the aim of his essay is to explain the higher principles which Kant's system presupposes (1:155). The allusion to Jacobi may be understood as the first dawning of Schelling's awareness that Kant's ends (or what he understands them to be) may not be achievable by strictly Kantian means. The highest principle is the self, and though it is not explicitly stated, it is implied that an adequate understanding of the nature of the self would both illustrate the insufficiencies of Kant's faculty psychology (and the resultant estrangement of theoretical and practical philosophy) and yet confirm the correctness and revolutionary nature of Kant's insight into the contribution of the knowing subject to knowledge.

We see Schelling bypassing the route chosen by Reinhold in his dismissive remarks concerning the insufficiency of any analysis of consciousness or axiom of consciousness as a first principle for philosophy: "To be sure, the act that appears to the philosopher first (as far as time is concerned) is the act of consciousness, but the condition of the possibility of this act must be a superior act of the human mind itself" [*höherer Akt des menschlichen Geistes selbst*] (1:100).

Schelling's hints about the all-important role to be played by some form of preconscious activity of the self remain vague in "On the Possibility"; the only positive characteristic given is that this preconceptual insight is uniquely human (1:112). In "Of the I" he is much more definite. The self cannot be given by a concept. As Kant has proved, there can be concepts only of objects. Since the self is that which makes concepts possible in the first place, it cannot itself be the object of any concept, for by its nature it is not an object at all, but a subject.

> An object receives its existence from something outside the sphere of its mere conceivability. In contrast, the self is not even conceivable unless it first exists as a self. If it does not so exist it is nothing at all. And it is *not at all thinkable except insofar as it thinks itself*, that is, *insofar as it is*. (1:168; emphasis in the original)

The absolute self, for the Schelling of the early essays, is the "One Unconditionable . . . the absolute all-comprehending reality" (1:176), or that which produces itself as an absolute reality (1:206–7). The Spinozistic inspiration of this concept of the self is apparent from the beginning of "Of the I": "The last ground for all reality is something that is thinkable only through itself, that is, it is thinkable only through its being; it is thought only inasmuch as it is. In short, *the principle of being and thinking is one and the same*" (1:163; emphasis in the original). That which is thinkable only through itself, whose principle of being and thought coincide, is *causa sui*, as unmistakably as Spinoza's God or substance is.[33]

Higher than all abstraction, beyond conceptualization, the living essence of philosophy—these are the characterizations of the absolute self. Schelling's idea of the absolute self cannot be understood apart from his concept of intellectual intuition, the only means of access to the absolute. The absolute self exists only through the identity of its self-intuition (*Einheit seiner Anschauung*) (1:219). We are aware of it only insofar as we know ourselves as selves, which Schelling speaks of in some contexts as knowing the absolute in ourselves:

> I wish I had Plato's gift of language or that of his kindred spirit, Jacobi, in order to be able to differentiate between the absolute, immutable being and every kind of conditional, changeable existence. Yet I see that even these men had to struggle with their own language when they attempted to speak of the immutable and supersensuous—and I believe that this absolute in us cannot be captured by a mere word of human language, and that only self-attained insight into the intellectual in us can come to the rescue of the patchwork of our language. (1:216)

These references to the "unity of self-intuition" and "the intellectual in us" are reminiscent of Kant's statement in the first edition of the *Critique of Pure Reason*: "This much, then, is certain, that through the 'self' I always entertain the thought of an absolute, but logical unity of the subject" (A356) as well as his concept of the transcendental unity of apperception in the B deduction (B138–39). That Schelling took his understanding of the self as a unity of self-intuition from Kant is further supported by his claim near the end of "Of the I": "Kant was the first to establish the absolute self as the ultimate substratum of all being and identity (though he established it nowhere directly but everywhere indirectly)" (1:233 n). Whether or not Kant would have agreed with this assessment is here beside the point. Schelling is arguing that Kant's transcendental unity of apperception could not originally have been conceived (and cannot properly be understood now) without a concept of the absolute self he feels certain Kant must have presupposed.

The fatal weakness in the *Critique*, according to Schelling, was that Kant did not go beyond the empirical, merely thinkable, I; since it is possible to conceptualize it (as *das reine Ich denke*), it is still empirical and conditioned. Schelling argues at length that the empirical self is comprehensible only as arising (though it is by no means clear how) out of the unity of an absolute self: "For if there were no absolute self one could not comprehend how a not-self could produce a logical self, a unity of thinking, nor could one comprehend at all how any not-self could be possible" (1:207).

The references to the impossibility of deriving a not-self without presupposing an absolute self are similar in form to some of Fichte's arguments, and the possibility that Schelling borrowed them virtually unaltered from Fichte is not to be dismissed out of hand. Still, it is my contention that Schelling's ideas of the absolute self sprang first and foremost from the deficiencies he thought he perceived in Kant's system, and that he sought to remedy these deficiencies with a concept of the absolute self strongly resembling Spinoza's substance.

As will become increasingly evident in what follows, Schelling believed himself to be working toward the same goal as Fichte, and this may have predisposed him to some degree to uncritical acceptance of Fichte's formulations of their supposedly common interests; to the extent that Schelling does accept Fichte's view it will be shown that he repeatedly encounters paradoxes which forced him to modify or abandon his early positions. That even at this early stage Schelling's concept of the absolute self owes more to Spinoza than to Fichte is evidenced by his description of it as absolute power (1:195), absolute causality (1:167), and as the only true substance (1:193).

The concept of intellectual intuition, that which makes access to the absolute self possible, is related to Jacobi's *Glaube*, Spinoza's *vis intuitiva*, and possibly to the term as employed in Fichte's "Review of Aenesidemus." Both Fichte and Jacobi were instrumental in forming Schelling's view that philosophy ought to be a revelation of the living and essential in man rather than an arid manipulation of concepts and abstractions; the question of the extent to which Fichte may have been influenced by Jacobi will not be entertained here.

The absolute self has been characterized as cause of itself, as preconscious self-activity, and as accessible only to intellectual intuition. Yet despite its centrality in "Of the I," even if the most is made of the obvious parallels to Spinoza's thought, Schelling's concept of the absolute self remains vague and inadequately defined. The lack of a sufficiently clear concept of intellectual intuition is a related failing: Schelling is caught in the dilemma of maintaining both that we know the absolute in ourselves through intellectual intuition *and* that the absolute self is the necessary precondition for the existence of the empirical self or consciousness; but the empirical self cannot know the absolute self, because it does not appear in consciousness. Schelling does not shy away from the paradoxes this view implies, and even reprimands the reader:

> Are you considering in any way that the self is no longer the pure, absolute self once it occurs in consciousness; that there can be no object at all for the absolute I; and moreover, that the absolute self can never become an object? Self-awareness implies the danger of losing the self. (1:180)

Thus the attempt to either refute or establish the absolute self from the viewpoint of consciousness is doomed to failure (1:182–84). At this early stage, Schelling does not yet recognize that this renders the nature of the connection between the empirical and absolute self mysterious at best.

In "The Philosophical Letters on Dogmatism and Criticism," Schelling takes a fateful and decisive step when he shifts his perspective from the viewpoint of "Of the I," where the finite self was in search of the absolute, to the assumption of the absolute as the only unquestionable reality. This shift is another illustration of how, when faced with fundamental difficulties, Schelling turns to Spinoza for an indication of the way in which the difficulty must be resolved. Since the transition from the finite to the infinite cannot be made comprehensible, the solution must after all lie with the nature of the infinite. It is evident to Schelling that Spinoza was primarily concerned not with the theoretical proofs which constitute his system but with the highest problem of philosophy, "the riddle of the world, the question of how the absolute could come out of itself and oppose to itself a world?" (1:310). It was Spinoza's awareness of the absolute or unconditioned which forced him to pose this question, according to Schelling, and his answer in *The Ethics* is in its essentials correct—except for the lack of an adequate explanation of the relation between the finite self and the absolute. They must, for Schelling, have an original ground of unity Spinoza nowhere admits to, or the freedom of the self is an illusion, for without such it would be utterly dependent on an absolute in every respect heterogenous, foreign, and opposed to it.

Perhaps the change from the view of "Of the I" and allowing the "riddle of the world" to be posed by the archdogmatist Spinoza can be traced to the unsatisfactoriness of the answers reached there. The two key concepts, intellectual intuition and the absolute, were described largely negatively, that is, in terms of what they were not. More significantly, Schelling apparently faced one of the consequences of his argument that the absolute is completely indeterminate and concluded that it was not possible to characterize the absolute as an absolute self. This is more consistent than the assumptions of either "Of the I" or Fichte in the *Science of Knowledge*, for that which is not an object cannot be known or determined *in any form*. Therefore intellectual intuition, as the only means of access to the absolute, must be "an experience which admits of two interpretations: either he [Spinoza] had become identical with the absolute, or else the absolute had become identical with him" (1:319). The position of the "Letters" is an advance beyond "Of the I" insofar as it is no longer simply assumed that the absolute is an absolute *subject*. The original indeterminacy of the absolute can be emphasized, and criticism, if it is to triumph as the best system, must do so on practical grounds.

Schelling has in effect abandoned his attempt to argue for the superiority of criticism on theoretical grounds. He has recognized that even if it were possible, it would be undesirable, because our acceptance of a flawless theoretical demonstration neither implies nor requires freedom. The insistence in "Of the I" that all reality comes through freedom and that "the beginning and end of all philosophy is freedom!" (1:177) has in the "Letters" evolved into a very modern-sounding emphasis on the all-important role of individual practical choice. Reality is created through freedom, in the sense that "no man can convince himself of any system except *practically*, that is, by realizing either system *in* himself" (1:306). We determine whether all our action points toward a submersion of the self in the absolute, as Spinoza advocated, or constitutes a striving for absolute freedom, the subordination of all things to oneself. This makes more intelligible in what sense dogmatism and criticism are opposites. If, as Schelling now insists, "the main task of philosophy consists of solving the problem of the existence of the world" (1:313), then the only possible views of the relation of the self to the absolute are the two described above, and dogmatism and criticism are, properly understood, grappling with the same problem.

The choice between dogmatism and criticism cannot be made by means of the arguments Schelling employed in "Of the I." "Which of the two we choose depends upon the freedom of the spirit we have ourselves acquired" (1:308), declares Schelling, in his influential statement of the connection between freedom and philosophy. The extent to which Fichte's "Attempt at a New Presentation of the Science of Knowledge" and "Second Introduction to the Science of Knowledge for Readers Who Already Have a System of Philosophy" were intended as replies to Schelling's early works is a question which cannot be considered here; still, there is a general consensus[34] that Fichte was inspired by Schelling to make his famous claim about the role of choice in the "First Introduction to the Science of Knowledge" of 1797: "What sort of philosophy one chooses depends, therefore, on what sort of man one is; . . . it is necessary to be born, raised, self-educated as a philosopher" (Fichte 1:434–35).

Reality is created by the choice of a system. Schelling reasons that dogmatism and criticism are equally inept at answering the question of *why* there is a realm of experience, for every answer that either can offer already presupposes the existence of a world of experience. Therefore reason is forced to leave the bounds of knowledge and itself produce the ground upon which it stands. This transition from theoretical to practical Schelling calls the change from a "merely cognitive" to a "creative reason" (1:311).

This formulation of the difference between the two types of reason makes it clear that Schelling is *not* employing the term "practical" reason in the same sense that Fichte did, for Schelling's argument for the necessity of a practical decision in favor of one of the two possible systems forms the background to the final redefinition of the problem of all philosophy given in the seventh Letter. Schelling again refers to Spinoza for his illustration: "When Lessing asked Jacobi what he considered the spirit of Spinozism to be, Jacobi replied: it could be nothing else than the old *a nihil fit* . . . he found that the notion of anything emerging within the non-finite posits *something* from nothing" (1:313). Realizing the absurdity of this conclusion, he consistently rejected any and all possible transition from the infinite to the finite. Spinoza's system represents the only correct response

(1:314). There can be no creation from nothing, no transition. Yet Schelling was also committed to the view that it is the essence of reason to demand the unconditioned. Therefore, Schelling concludes, the only possible transition is from the finite to the infinite; the demand of the finite, for the infinite, unrealizable though it may be, is the source of all practical striving.

Thus when Schelling speaks of realizing a system in practical action, he is appealing not to moral consciousness as it was understood by Kant and Fichte but rather to a pretheoretical and immediate striving of reason. He does call it practical reason, but he does so in part from conceptual confusion (since he is thinking of creative reason, and moral action is self-constitutive activity, as he understood it), and in part to distinguish it unmistakably from theoretical reason.

In order to *be* what we call ourselves theoretically, "nothing can convince us of being that, except our very *endeavor* to be just that. This endeavor brings to pass our knowledge of ourselves, and thus this knowledge becomes the pure product of our freedom. . . . Man cannot get there by arguing, nor can others argue him up to that point" (1:308). This rather Aristotelian-sounding insistence that we are what we have made ourselves reappears in a more mature form in the theory of character developed in *Of Human Freedom*; here Schelling is taking a hint from Jacobi in his insistence that theoretical reason alone cannot reveal the essence of the human. The German is "'hinaufvernünfteln' kann sich der Mensch nicht, noch durch andere dahin vernünfteln lassen," and remarkably similar to Jacobi's "Man cannot . . . reason himself into wisdom or virtue: he must be *moved* to be so elevated and move himself."[35] When Schelling then concludes that the choice between dogmatism and criticism depends on "the freedom of spirit which we have ourselves acquired" (1:308), he is very close to the spirit of Jacobi's historicizing of theoretical reason: "the actions of men should not be derived from their philosophy, but their philosophy from their actions; their history does not arise from their manner of thought, but rather their manner of thought from their history."[36]

IV. How Is Knowledge of Reality Possible?

Between November of 1796 and the summer of 1797 Schelling contributed eight installments of what was originally intended to be an extended book review to his friend Immanuel Niethammer's new *Philosophisches Journal*.[37] It appeared under the title "General Survey of the most Recent Philosophical Literature"; however, when Schelling reprinted these essays in the first volume of his collected works in 1809, he called them "Treatises Explicatory of the Idealism in the *Science of Knowledge*," and it is as the "Treatises" that I will refer to this curious work here. In it Schelling's understanding of idealism can be seen expanding and growing from one installment to the next.[38]

The question presented as the central question of philosophy in the "Treatises" is the question of how knowledge is possible: "The problem, then, is as follows: to explain the absolute correspondence of the object and the representation, of being and knowledge" (1:365). This concern with the reality of knowledge might seem a far cry from the preoccupations of Schelling's earlier works, in which the discussion had revolved around the absolute, intellectual intuition and the relationship between the finite and the infinite. It is true in one sense that Schelling's overriding concern in the early works, namely, to achieve an understanding of the relation of the *self* to the absolute, has in the "Treatises" retreated into the background, for the language of the opposition between the (finite) self and the (infinite) Absolute is seldom employed. It has been replaced and improved upon in the form of a question about the relationship of the *world* of nature to the absolute (where the world of nature is understood to have just such a structure as to be capable, at its highest level of development, of giving rise to the individual conscious self).

An evolution of Schelling's thought has become evident: the sheerly unconditioned absolute of "Of the I" (1794) stood in complete opposition to the finite self; the absolute of the "Letters" (1796) could be known only as the goal of the practical striving of the finite self aware of and determined by its freedom; finally, in the "Treatises" (1796–97) this "practical" self-determination of the finite self is shown to be the key to the understanding of nature, and indeed as the only way in which a nature which includes life and consciousness can be understood.

The view Schelling had defended in the tenth and final "Letter" was that there could be no transition from the infinite to the finite (thereby abandoning the standpoint of "Of the I"). The only transition possible, then, was that from the finite to the infinite, through practical realization. This is equally true for dogmatism and criticism, since all theoretical philosophy presupposes conflict between subject and object, which is precisely what is denied in the very possibility of transition between the finite and the infinite. "Therefore nothing is left for both systems except to make the absolute, which could not be an object of knowledge, an object of *action*, or *to demand the action* by which the absolute is realized" (1:333).

Convinced that the relationship of the self to the absolute had been adequately defined (an original tendency toward the absolute is implied in the freedom of the finite self), Schelling proceeded to demonstrate that only critical philosophy was compatible with human freedom. Of course, dogmatism cannot be refuted theoretically, because "it leaves the theoretical realm to complete its system *practically*[; therefore] it is still irrefutable for him who is able to realize it practically, for him who can bear the thought of working at his own annihilation" (1:339). Even the archdogmatist Spinoza was mistaken in thinking that he had succeeded at this impossible task, for he did not submerge himself in God but rather put his own ego in the place of the Deity (1:315–19).

Therefore, having shown, at least to his own satisfaction, that dogmatism cannot provide a practical solution to the question of the relation of the finite self and the absolute (for in the very attempt to give up one's identity, one necessarily reaffirms it), Schelling feels that the time has come to turn his attention to other problems. Near the end of the "Letters" he announces:

> Let us rejoice in the conviction of having advanced to the last great problem to which any philosophy can advance. We feel freer in our spirit, if we now return from the state of speculation to the enjoyment and exploration of nature.... The ideas to which our speculation has risen cease to be objects of an idle occupation that tires out our spirit all too soon; they become the law of our life, and, as they themselves change into life and existence and become objects of experience, they free us forever from the painful enterprise of ascertaining their reality by way of speculation a priori. (1:341)

In the "Treatises" Schelling identifies as a further deficiency of dogmatism (and to some extent of criticism) that neither can explain the workings of the world of nature other than by the "painful enterprise of ascertaining their reality by speculation a priori." What this brief review of the development of Schelling's early thought reveals is the growing significance of his stress on the connection between the characteristic flaw of all previous philosophy—the inability to provide a unified theory of the self—and their inadequate and inappropriate theories of nature.

The problem of grasping the relationship of the world to the absolute is a recurring theme, because of the urgency and importance of understanding how it is that the human mind has contact with reality. In the language of "Of the I," it is the task of philosophy to unveil and reveal what is; here Schelling deliberately invokes Jacobi, by using one of his signature terms, *Daseyn* (1:156). The only way to accomplish this is by means of a complete science of the living self (1:238 n). Were this completed, it would be seen that "the ultimate goal of the self is to turn the laws of freedom into the laws of nature, to bring about *nature* in the self, and the *self* in nature" (1:199 n). This description could easily stand as a concise statement of the goal of Schelling's philosophy of nature.

It remained an unrealized dream in the "Treatises," but it is clear that for Schelling, the will is *originally* explicable as a will to have unified cognition, or to grasp philosophically the world of experience as it appears to the knowing self. This is the problem attacked in the "Treatises," but before Schelling feels truly free to turn to the philosophy of nature, he wants very much to dispense with what he regards impatiently as the lingering misconceptions which are hampering the progress of philosophy.

The first of these concerns the widespread misunderstanding and abuse of Kant's concept of an interest of reason. Schelling takes Karl Heinrich Heydenreich's *Letters on Atheism* to task as an example of the common tendency to misconstrue the concept of an interest of reason so crudely that it becomes something which occurs in a vacuum, detached and independent of all other interests. In particular, the idea that there exists a "special moral awareness" [*besondere moralische Stimmung*] (1:350) is ridiculed. All interests, whether of reason or not, are culturally conditioned, Schelling points out (how else could the concept of interest itself, since it implies an object, remain coherent?); this early, undeveloped rejection of the concept of a moral necessity grounded in human nature shows parallels to Hamann and Herder's rejection of the claims of the Enlightenment with respect to objectivity and the authority of reason itself (early and insufficiently appreciated critiques of "the view from nowhere").

So much for Schelling's negative criticisms. From the heart of his basic disagreement with Kant, which echoes Jacobi's insistence that intuition be considered not the lowest, but the highest in our knowledge, emerges a theory of the priority of intuition which is of the utmost importance for Schelling's subsequent development. In a charming display of wishful thinking, Schelling appears to have believed that Kant thoughtfully left various clues lying about in his system in order to lead the way to what Schelling calls "the last—that is highest, problem of reason": "He [Kant] intentionally left something unresolved here, which only later was to appear as the last, highest problem of reason" (1:355). The "something" so tantalizingly left out of Kant's philosophy was the answer to the question of the origin of the affection of our senses. Schelling variously expresses this as "What is the reality that inheres in our representations?" and "Where does all our knowledge come from?" (1:353); this is the question with which the "Treatises" begin.

Schelling also employs these questions as a way of demonstrating the incompleteness of Kant's and Reinhold's theories. Kant does not recognize that all reality in our knowledge must ultimately be traced to intuition. For Schelling, intuition is "the highest in the human spirit, that from which all our other knowledge derives its worth and reality" (1:355). Although Kant admitted that intuition is "the first in our knowledge," he mistakenly held that it is also "the lowest level of knowledge" (1:355). This misconception, combined with Kant's failure to explain adequately the origin of the affection of our sensibility (which is intuition), leaves the nature of the connection between being and thought entirely mysterious.

Fortunately all the elements of a solution are already present in Kant's system. Schelling finds an especially promising indication of a way out of these difficulties in Kant's theory of the synthesis of imagination in intuition, for it is essential to the theory that it is the *action* of the imagination which makes knowledge possible. Also, space and time are not pure original intuitions, as Kant maintains, argues Schelling; they are themselves evidence of the original activity of spirit. They cannot exist apart from one another yet are entirely opposed in principle, space being completely indeterminate (Plato's *apeiron*) and time completely determinate (*peras*). Schelling concludes: "Therefore, since space and time are conditions for intuition, it follows that intuition is, in general, only possible by means of two absolutely opposed activities" (1:356).

This conclusion will prove to be decisive for the philosophy of nature, for formally speaking, Schelling's explanation of the structure and dynamic of the various levels of nature will be shown to consist of increasingly complex opposed activities seeking equilibrium. This is the formal principle of all of nature, from matter itself to organic life—indeed of all reality, which will have revolutionary implications for Schelling's theory of evil. It will be the business of the *System of Transcendental Idealism* to demonstrate the affinities of this formal structure to the structure of consciousness, which is what makes genuine knowledge of nature possible. The way in which Schelling initially makes the connection is to argue that if it is established that the highest level of knowledge, its connection with reality, is intuition, and if intuition properly understood proves to consist of opposed activities (one positive and one negative), we must ask ourselves:

> The latter [negative], what could it be other than that which Kant refers to as the activity affecting us from *the outside*? The former, then obviously is the one which is assumed as active in the synthesis of intuition, that is to say, the original activity of the spirit. And so it is shown, clear as the light of day: the object is not something given to us from the outside and *as such*, but rather is strictly the product of the original, spontaneous activity of the spirit. (1:357)

This original activity of spirit, says Schelling, is correctly attributed by Kant to the imagination, for the imagination is the only activity which is passive and active in equal measure: that which brings forth objects as we know them is the *transcendental synthesis of imagination*. If only the true meaning of this term had been understood, Kant's critics would not have been able to create the controversy they did concerning the meaning and possibility of things in themselves. Kant's teaching is simply that no thing can be an object of our knowledge which we do not in some measure produce or make the thing that it is. There can be no things that are not known by a mind; conversely, there is no consciousness that is not consciousness *of* something (as will be explained in much greater detail in the philosophy of nature, the parallel orders of external things and of thought can be traced to the self's ability to grasp the other as it does itself).

> For the very essence of the spirit involves an original conflict in self-consciousness resulting in the creation of a real world outside the spirit in intuition. That is why there is no world unless a spirit knows it, and conversely no spirit exists without a world outside of itself. (1:358)

Schelling's search for reality in the earlier works had yielded concepts of the absolute which were incompatible with self-consciousness, although they were described in terms appropriate to subjects. Now, after examining more closely the conditions necessary for knowledge, he returns to the insight that no consciousness is possible without an object. This fundamental insight into the synthetic nature of consciousness can be pursued in the Fichtean manner: all being is being-for-the-self and thus dependent on the self as the primary reality. Or it can be understood as I will suggest that Schelling understood it: the worlds of nature and consciousness arise out of one another and are inextricably interdependent; from different points of view one will appear more primary than the other. Our knowledge of the world will have reality when there is perfect agreement between the object and our representations of it, when being and knowledge coincide (1:365). Schelling wants to go still further and explain the *necessity* of the world for the self: "It is obvious that not only the *possibility* of a representation of external things in us, but also its *necessity* must be explained" (1:365). Hand in hand with this question goes its metaphysical counterpart:

how, given the original identity of the world and of consciousness, did any division between the two become possible? (1:362).

V. Genius: The "Sunday's Children" Problem

To emphasize intuition as the source of all knowledge renders a theory vulnerable to having the same defect that any appeal to prerational experience leaves itself open to: an inability to answer the objections of those who claim not to know what you are talking about. And indeed Jacobi's claims about the immediacy of our knowledge of God, an insight he called *Glaube*, were easy for Hegel to criticize for their lack of rigor:

> ... what Jacobi calls faith, namely, that God—being in-and-for-itself, the absolute as such, the unconditioned, and so forth—cannot be demonstrated, because demonstrating or conceiving means discovering the conditions for something, deriving it from conditions. A derived absolute or a derived God would not be an absolute or something unconditioned, would not be God but a creature.... Since Jacobi's time everything said and even written by philosophers such as Fries, and by theologians, amounts to the contention that what we know of God we know immediately through intuition—primordial intuition, intellectual intuition, or immediate knowledge of the spiritual." [39]

In short, the claim of intuitive access to the truth, which was to have provided an answer to that most alarming of the consequences of the critical philosophy, the claim that it is impossible in principle for human beings ever to know reality, proved to be a cure which was more deadly than the disease. For as Hegel clearly recognized, Jacobi and many of his successors could claim an immediate intuition as the warrant for any of their many so-called insights and discoveries. "In their sense of philosophy all believe themselves to be philosophers and to be capable of judging philosophy, because they all have within them the same measuring stick."[40] As early as 1802, in *Faith and Knowledge*, Hegel had claimed in his discussion of Schleiermacher, whose *Speeches* he regarded as the highest point to which "the Jacobian principle" had risen, that intuition was too particular and subjective a basis on which to establish the religious community.[41]

However, Jacobi, Fries, and other minor figures were of little real concern to Hegel. What he found by far the most alarming was the central role played by the concept of intellectual intuition in Schelling. Schelling's intellectual intuition involved above all the ability to posit thinking and being as a unity, and this idea, as Hegel saw it, carries with it the consequence that "philosophy thus appears as an artistic talent of genius that comes only to 'Sunday's children.'"[42] Thus it is evident, in Hegel's view, that the philosophy of Schelling is willing to abdicate the claim to be universal, inasmuch as it depends upon a special power of imagination.

> [S]ince the immediate presupposition in Philosophy is that individuals have the immediate intuition of this identity of subjective and objective, this gave the philosophy of Schelling the appearance of indicating that the presence of this intuition in individuals demanded a special talent, genius, or condition of mind of their own, or as though it were generally speaking an accidental faculty which pertained to the specially favored few. For the immediate, the intuitively perceived, is in the form of an existent, and is thus not an essential; and whoever does not understand the intellectual intuition must come to the conclusion that he does not possess it. Or else, in order to understand it, men must give themselves the trouble of possessing it; but no one can tell whether he has it or not—not even from understanding it, for we may merely think we understand it.[43]

Here Hegel has in very few words precisely located the most important difference between himself and Schelling. I have discussed the genesis and development of Schelling's concept of intellectual intuition at length elsewhere.[44] Certainly the respectful treatment accorded Jacobi in the very early essays, where he is mentioned in the same breath with Plato, gives an indication that Schelling has taken to heart Jacobi's definition of the philosopher as one whose task is to reveal *Daseyn*. It is also clear that this task calls for a certain kind of man: "He who feels and recognizes nothing real outside himself—he who lives only in concepts, and plays with concepts—he who takes his own existence to be nothing more than a lusterless thought—how can such a one speak of reality?" (1:353). Therefore it is obvious that philosophy "is not for everyone. It contains even in its first postulates something that shuts out certain people from it forever" (1:417).

To gain an appreciation of how Schelling understood the nature and source of the talent for philosophy, it may be helpful to turn to the "Lectures on the Method of Academic Study,"[45] which were delivered in 1802–3; thus, after Schelling and Hegel had ceased to collaborate as editors in 1802 but before the publication of the *Phenomenology* in 1807. In the first lecture, "The Concept of Absolute Knowledge," Schelling stresses the underlying unity of all that is worthy of the name of knowledge. The second lecture considers the practical question of "the scientific and moral functions of the university," that is, "what should be done within the actual structure of our universities today, in order that the unity of the whole may re-emerge amid the wide-spread specialization?" (5:228). We will never have a university that is a genuinely scientific institution, in Schelling's view, unless, to paraphrase Plato, its professors become philosophers or philosophers become professors. The ability to transmit knowledge depends upon the one's imaginative grasp of the knowledge, and this, in the final analysis, is a question of genius:

> to transmit knowledge intelligently one must be able to understand the discoveries made by others. . . . Many of them are of a kind whose inner essence can only be grasped by a kindred genius, through a rediscovery in the literal sense of the word. A teacher who merely transmits will often give a radically false version of what he learned. . . . A man incapable of reconstructing the totality of his science for himself, or reformulating it from his own inner, living vision, will never even be able to rise to the level of giving a mere historical exposition of the science. (5:233).

The enormous influence of this vision of the special educational role of genius has been documented by Elinor Shaffer, who argues that the special connection between research and teaching implied by Schelling's views was reflected in the founding documents of the Humboldt University of Berlin and German higher education more generally.[46]

Yet even if a reverence for genius and a sense that the acquisition of knowledge is an active, not a passive, process are undeniably valuable aspects of Schelling's views, the lectures as a whole, especially lecture 6, "On the Study of Philosophy," show that Hegel was correct in accusing Schelling of in some sense identifying the ability to grasp the absolute with the talent for philosophy itself:

> An emanation coming from the inner essence of the absolute, which is the eternal unity [In = Eins = Bildung] of the universal and the particular, manifests itself at the phenomenal level as reason and imagination. . . . Those equipped with nothing more than a dry and barren understanding might be astonished to hear that imagination is required in philosophy. (5:267)

It is very revealing that Schelling speaks in the same passage of the "poetry of philosophy." The reference to imagination and the comparison of the poet and the philosopher provide a provisional answer to Hegel: Schelling holds it to be just as unlikely that everyone has the talent for philosophy as that everyone is a poet. Yet the rarity of the poetic and philosophical gift does not detract from its importance in the way Hegel implies, for the fact that only a few are capable of *creating* poetry or philosophy does not make the message of the poets and philosophers any less universal.

Schelling's dependence on the immediate seems to tie his thought to that which is existent, and therefore individual. Hegel, in sharp contrast, requires that anything worthy of the name of philosophy be concerned with the universal and essential, for "its groundwork is thought, and it is through thought that man is man."[47] Is Schelling really admitting that he is willing to renounce any claim to universality when he says, "philosophical knowledge is not for everyone, and that cannot be changed, even with the best will in the world" (5:219)? The philosopher seems to have indeed become an explorer in a distant and fabulous country, one who understandably has difficulty in communicating with lesser lights in Schelling's description:

> Those who do not have intellectual intuition cannot understand what is said of it, and for this reason it cannot at all be given. A negative condition of its possession is the clear and sincere insight into the nothingness of all merely finite cognition. One can develop it within oneself; in the philosopher it must become, so to speak, one's character—a constant organ, a skill for seeing everything only as it presents itself in the idea. (5:256)

The development of the philosophy of nature and the new understanding of what it is to be a scientist which arises out of these efforts reveal the directions in which Schelling is beginning to grow beyond Hegel and Enlightenment concepts of nature and humanity's place in it.

3

The Philosophy of Nature

I. The Essential Role of the Philosophy of Nature

Schelling's philosophy of nature in particular and *Naturphilosophie* in general have suffered a great many critical slings and arrows; yet it must be admitted that both presented their foes with an inviting target. Most scholars agree that Schelling's philosophy of nature had its greatest influence in almost all areas of science, but especially medicine, between 1800 and 1830.[1] Although Schelling's views were never without their critics, these first gained the upper hand only among the next generation of scientists, who rejected *Naturphilosophie* as passionately as it had once been embraced. By 1840 Justus von Liebig could speak of *Naturphilosophie* as the "insane sister" of true philosophy, "the activity and influence of which were the pestilence and the black death of the century."[2] Fortunately, all "their efforts have turned to dust, for they were from the beginning dust, and from all their labors the state, life itself and science has not been able to make the smallest use."[3]

Many of the descriptions of *Naturphilosophie* employed by present-day historians of science are nearly as negative; Timothy Lenoir calls it "that strange and nearly impenetrable offshoot of the Romantic movement"[4] and devotes a book to the proposition that it was not as influential and significant as many historians of science have thought.[5] Barry Gower argues that "*Naturphilosophie* may be novel and even interesting in some contexts, but as a contribution to philosophical debate it has been, and can be, safely ignored. Certainly it would be a mistake to think that philosophers who credit science with metaphysical foundations in one sense or another have anything so insubstantial as Schelling's speculative physics in mind."[6] Even such a sympathetic reader of Schelling as Joseph Esposito could say in 1978 that "outside of Germany it has been regarded as a paradigm of bad philosophy, serving neither philosophy nor natural science very well."[7]

Yet the recent past has produced an impressive variety of reassessments and praise for Schelling's *Naturphilosophie*.[8] A striking number of these authors argue as follows: it is a commonplace of the history of science that as a reigning theory grows old, its ability to encompass new phenomena and discoveries is increasingly impaired, until, baroquely ornamented with exceptions and caveats, it must give way to the new. In a scientific moment such as the present, caught between pressing practical difficulties (many caused, at least in part, by assuming that man is not a part of nature), on the one hand, and a theoretical drive toward grand unified theories, on the other, *naturphilosophischen* insights may provide precisely that fresh perspective that scientists and philosophers alike will draw upon to give birth to the next incarnation of science.

The debate over the enduring significance of Schelling's philosophy of nature cannot be my focus here,[9] for I wish to restrict my inquiry to consideration of the impact that Schelling's philosophy of nature has had on his idealism. In one sense his scientific interests were a clear signal of his growing distance from Fichte, for to take nature seriously is to acknowledge that the natural world "is not a board nailed together by the Absolute Self" that it might have something to bounce off, but a "ladder upon which the spirit ascends to itself."[10] In the introduction to the *Ideas for a Philosophy of Nature*[11] of 1797, Schelling has already moved beyond the standpoint of the "Treatises," which was that the philosophy of nature is possible; in the *Ideas* it is declared to be necessary. We can almost see Schelling thinking aloud as he accomplishes three very important things: he declares the philosophy of nature to be an essential part of philosophy, without which philosophy could not achieve systematic unity; he distances himself from Fichte and moves closer to Spinoza, who was especially influential on his concept of the absolute; and there is further development of the view of the world of nature as an organic, living system, an idea which first appeared in the "Treatises."

Schelling makes it clear that he does not intend to apply philosophy to existing empirical science. Hamann's description of the proper approaches to nature as interpretive and imitative may have been an influence: "In nature we have nothing but a confusion of poems . . . the scholar's task is to collect them; that of the philosopher, to expound them; the poet's humble part is to imitate them or perhaps even more audaciously to bring them into order."[12] The philosopher is first and foremost an interpreter:

> My purpose is to first let the philosophy of nature arise philosophically, and my philosophy is itself nothing other than the science of nature. It is true that chemistry teaches us to *read* the *letters*, physics the *syllables*, and mathematics *nature*; but it should not be forgotten that it is for philosophy to interpret that which is read. (2:6)

The connection between philosophy and natural science can be found by carefully considering what philosophy is—true philosophy is the product of freedom (2:11). We are led to freely ask ourselves about the origin of the world; in fact, it is "the first step to philosophy" (2:13). Freedom produces philosophy in the form of the original question about nature: "How a world outside us, how nature and with it, experience, are possible[;] we have philosophy to thank for this question or rather, with this question was philosophy born" (2:12).

This separation between the self and the external world of nature is the beginning of reflection, which aims at the separation of what nature had united: the object from the intuition, the concept from the image, and finally the self from itself. If the artificiality of the standpoint of reflection is maintained, Schelling adds, it becomes a spiritual sickness (2:13); in fact, this is the malady which Schelling will later conclude afflicts Hegel—intoxication with concepts. Among the most salient consequences of this affliction is that it renders it impossible to grasp life and the living adequately.

In Schelling's view, what reflection has put asunder, namely, objects and their representations, is what true philosophy attempts, through freedom, to reunite. This is a more sophisticated reaffirmation of the argument of the "Treatises," that being and thought must be identical. Here, the connection to freedom is central. He who first remarked upon his ability to differentiate himself from external objects and thereby differentiate his representations of the objects from them was the first philosopher (2:15). Therefore, given the origin of philosophy (the recognition of oneself as distinguishable from all else), both the objects and their representations must be investigated by philosophy.

II. Arguments against the Mechanistic Model of Nature

This view of the origin of philosophy explains the genesis of the concepts of both nature and spirit. For

> in asking: How does it come about that I have ideas? I raise myself *above* the idea and become, *through this very question*, a being that feels itself to be free *ab origine* with respect to all ideation, who surveys the ideation itself and the whole fabric of his ideas *beneath* him. Through this question I become an entity which, independent of external things, has *being in itself*. (2:16)

Two distinct realms are established, and their connection, if any, appears incomprehensible. Insofar as the self elevates itself above the objects and inquires about the nature of their connection, it shows itself *not* to be a thing; the view which holds that even representations of the self are the result of a variety of influences, that is, are mechanically produced, is false, for "that which is sustained in mechanism cannot step out of it and ask how the entire [mechanistic] system becomes possible" (2:17), as Fichte was also fond of pointing out.[13]

This depiction of the origin of philosophy hearkens back to Schelling's original division of philosophy into dogmatic and critical, with a tacitly understood division also drawn between all the various mistaken interpretations of criticism and true criticism. True criticism in the early works was that philosophy based upon the self; here it has as its most fundamental concept the self which knows itself as both subject and object through freedom.

> He who is nothing for himself save what things and circumstances have made of him; who is powerless with respect to his own representations of causes and effects, and swept along in their train, how is he then to know where they come from, where he is going, and how he has become that which he is? Does the wave tossed by the storm know? He does not even possess the right to say that he is the result of the combined effects of external things; for in order to say this, he must presuppose that he knows *himself*, that is, that he is also something *for himself*. But he is not. (2:18)

Schelling invokes Leibniz, Plato, and Spinoza as examples of great thinkers who "elevated themselves above the course of nature," where the "leaden wings of the [ordinary] imagination are incapable of carrying average people" (2:19). It is significant that Schelling links philosophical insight and knowledge of the self with the ability to break through the reign of mechanism, and derides prephilosophical and dogmatic thought as mechanical. The crucial next step, here presented only sketchily, is that since we only understand what we make after a plan of our own, the proper understanding of nature must be organic and teleological, for this is the way in which the self comes to know itself. This argument will be returned to below in the context of its debt to Hume and Kant.

Here, Schelling is content to point out that Spinoza was the first to do what ancient mythology and religion as well as Plato had failed to do: grasp the essence of the connection between nature and spirit.

> The first to regard spirit and matter with full consciousness as one, thought and extension as only modifications of the same principle, was Spinoza. His system was the first bold sketch of a creative imagination, in which the idea of the infinite, purely as such, directly grasped the finite, and recognized the latter only in the former. (2:20)

Spinoza's philosophy provides the clue: the only possible solution to the apparently unbridgeable gap between spirit and matter is a primordial unity. Only in this fashion can the finite and the infinite be related to one another. It will be recalled that in the "Treatises," Schelling argued that the infinite and the finite were originally united only in a being of a spiritual nature (1:369). Here this "being of a spiritual nature" is directly linked with Spinoza's original unity. This clearly implies that the world, and especially the opposition of matter and spirit, cannot be understood other than as an ultimate unity; and the argument immediately preceding strongly suggests that it will not be a mechanistic unity, but one accessible only to the free self.

Yet Spinoza made one fateful error, which Schelling discusses here in the same manner, though with different terms, as he employed in the "Philosophical Letters." It is Spinoza's explanation of the necessity that both an ideal and a real world exist for us that is mistaken:

> Instead of descending into the depths of his self-consciousness and from there attending to the cre-

The Philosophy of Nature

ation of two worlds in us—the ideal and the real—he surpassed himself; instead of explaining out of our nature how the finite and the infinite, originally united in us, arise out of one another, he at once abandoned himself in the idea of an infinite outside us. (2:36)

Spinoza was correct in his recognition of the ideal and real worlds as inseparably united in human nature—but for Schelling the ultimate unity cannot be outside us. A modified form of Schelling's argument against mechanism and dogmatism can be applied to Spinoza: if the self has its ground in an infinite ultimate reality outside itself, then "I am but a thought of the Infinite or rather only a constant succession of representations. But Spinoza is not able to explain how I become aware of this succession" (2:36). To put it in somewhat more contemporary terms, Schelling is criticizing Spinoza for taking the position of a privileged observer; the "view from nowhere" was no more defensible in the seventeenth century than it is today. As always, the experience of the self recognizing itself as somehow distinct from its representations is the touchstone of experience; no philosopher who fails to do justice to this essential insight is wholly acceptable to Schelling.

It is a measure of how close Schelling has moved to Spinoza that he is able to suggest in so few words how Spinoza's system could be remedied. Spinoza's understanding of the relation of the infinite and the finite is, Schelling believes, the only true one—but what Spinoza describes as happening outside the self Schelling locates within it. The infinite and the finite are originally united in us, and it is

> precisely upon this original union that the nature of our spirit and our entire spiritual existence rests. For we know immediately only our own essence, and are only comprehensible to ourselves. How affections and determinations are and can exist in an Absolute

> external to me, I cannot grasp. But I do understand that even within me there could be nothing *infinite* unless there were at the same time a *finite*. For that necessary union of ideal and real, of the absolutely active and the absolutely passive (which Spinoza displaced into an infinite substance outside me) exists *within me* originally without my co-operation, and that is just what *my* nature consists in. (2:37)

Thus Schelling's negative argument against mechanism as a model for nature may be summarized as the view that any philosophy unable to account for the existence of the philosopher who thinks it (the knowing self) is deficient, or at the very least, incomplete. However, there are also arguments from the significance of organic causality and the purposiveness exhibited by organic nature which are equally effective in illustrating the incompleteness of mechanistic theories of nature.

Every organized product of nature, no matter how simple, confronts us with a concept: firstly, because its parts bear a definite relationship, not dependent on us, to the whole of which they are a part, and secondly, because it organizes itself according to a concept, from which it cannot be separated. This concept is not imposed from without, as the artist imposes a vision on his product, but rather is integral to the existence of the organic product itself. Schelling stresses that because in this kind of organization "the form cannot be separated from the matter... the origin of an organization can be explained mechanically just as little as the origin of matter itself (2:41). That is, the purposiveness of the organic points toward a higher unity in nature than mechanism could ever reveal.

III. Development of the Concept of Matter

One might say that Schelling finds that the superiority of his philosophy of nature is most evident at the lowest level (the nature of material reality or matter) and at the highest (the all-embracing vision of the whole). Matter ought to be "the first foundation of all experience" (2:22), and so indeed it seems to be from the point of view of intuition. However, when reflection tries to get at the essence of matter, it fails, and worse yet, appears to contradict the picture of reality intuition gives us. Schelling mocks then popular theories of matter:

> Matter is not insubstantial, you say, for it has original *forces*, which cannot be destroyed by any subdivision. "Matter has forces." I know that this expression is very common. But how? "Matter has"—therefore, it is presupposed a something which exists for itself and independently of its forces. Therefore the forces were only accidental to it? Because matter is present *outside you*, it must owe its powers to an external cause. Perhaps they are, as some Newtonians say, planted in it by a higher hand? (2:23)

Schelling's point is that the *essence* of matter is force; the dogmatist, with his nondynamic concept of matter as inert stuff, has gone wrong on two counts. He cannot explain how matter has force(s), despite the fact that he bases his entire physics on the idea that forces act on each other. More seriously still, Schelling claims, the dogmatist cannot even explain how he is able to know a force independent of himself.

The form of this argument is by now familiar: Schelling finds the dogmatic theory of matter remiss for failing to acknowledge the role of the self. "Force in general is announced merely by means of your feeling [it]" (2:23). A force or forces not recognized by feeling must be discovered empirically, but the empirical cannot be the basis for a world system. In short, Schelling must reject any concept of matter which could not be a principle in a world system, which, he reminds us, is an idea. Although the bulk of what Schelling has to say about matter in the introduction to the *Ideas* is criticism of other theories, he shows both familiarity with, and respect for, Kant's *Meta-*

physical Foundations of Natural Science in the section "Basic Principles of Dynamics" in the *Ideas* proper.[14]

Kant had argued that matter does not occupy space "by its mere existence, but by a special moving force,"[15] and he explained the necessity of this assumption: "Only when I attribute to that which occupies a space a force to repel every external movable thing that approaches it, do I understand how a contradiction is involved when the space which a thing occupies is penetrated by another thing of the same kind."[16] This force is the repulsive force; it is counteracted by an equally powerful attractive force. The attractive force is a fundamental requirement for the existence of the material world, for if only the repulsive force were active, "matter would . . . disperse itself to infinity."[17] Yet while Kant does not go beyond arguing that the attractive and repulsive forces are the conditions for the possibility of matter, Schelling thinks he can justify the claim that "attractive and repulsive forces constitute the *essence* of matter itself."[18]

In the detailed deduction of matter in the *System of Transcendental Idealism*, Schelling describes three stages or dimensions in the construction of matter, founded upon the three basic forces. The first is the union of two opposed forces, the positive (or expansive) and the negative: these provide the first dimension of matter, length, and are represented in nature in the phenomenon of magnetism. The second consists of the state of separatedness of the two forces: this separation must be expressed in two dimensions and thus adds breadth to length; it is repeated in nature as electricity, which occupies whole surfaces and is not merely linear. The third stage provides the possibility of reconciliation and mutual interpenetration of the first two, which gives rise to impenetrability and the third dimension, thickness: in nature this is the chemical process. Since transcendental philosophy "is nothing else but a constant raising of the self to a higher power" (3:451), Schelling claims that the construction of consciousness can be shown to follow the same pattern: the two opposed forces are the subjective and objective activities which in equilibrium constitute the self.

The details of this parallelism need not further concern us. It is the intention which is significant: the intention to show "that the three stages in the construction of matter really do correspond to the three acts in the intelligence" (3:453). Thus it can be seen, declares Schelling triumphantly, that it is this identity which underlies what he calls "the idealism of Leibniz: 'When Leibniz calls matter the sleeping state of monads, or when Hemsterhuis speaks of it as congealed mind, there lies in these statements a meaning very easy to discern from the principles now put forward. Matter is indeed nothing else but mind viewed in an equilibrium of its activities'" (3:453). Among the many benefits of this view, Schelling is especially eager to emphasize the elimination of the puzzles of interaction common to dualistic theories, and says that this view preserves "far more elevated notions of the nature and dignity of matter" (3:454).

IV. Necessity and Scientific Objectivity

The "Treatises" introduced the idea of philosophy as the history of self-consciousness and the argument that "it belongs to our essence to make representations in general (1:369, 380, 383). Here in the introduction to the *Ideas* the argument has been refined to the claim that it is the representation of the natural world which is essential to the self: "For it will be presupposed as undeniable that the representation of a succession of causes and effects outside us is as necessary to our spirit as if it belonged to its being and nature. To explain this necessity is the chief problem of philosophy" (2:30). Anticipating later developments, specifically in the *System of Transcendental Idealism*, may be helpful for the understanding of the argument presented here for the first time in a meandering and confused fashion: Schelling will argue that it is of the essence of the self to be able to come to understand itself only through nature, and that it must go beyond mechanism in order to come to know itself non-mechanically (although this is not possible for everyone). The causality of the self will be seen to be increasingly accurately mirrored as the scale of complexity in natural organization is ascended.

When we consider the origin of the succession of representations we call the course of nature (*Naturlauf*), Schelling argues, two things are immediately apparent to us: we are aware of a feeling of constraint: we feel ourselves compelled to experience the succession—that it must be so and not otherwise; and we are aware of a subjective necessity in the order of our representations, and that they cannot be separated from the succession. Although there is certainly some ambiguity with respect to this distinction between "the succession" and "our representations of the succession," if the point is conceded for the moment that we *are* capable of distinguishing the two, Schelling proceeds to claim that if the succession and our representations of the succession are inseparable in the manner described above, then there are only two possible ways of accounting for this:

Either the succession and the representations both arise at the same time and inseparably *outside* us.

Or the succession and the representations both arise at the same time and inseparably *within* us. (2:30–31)

The first alternative he identifies with "the common understanding"; it could be designated passive dogmatism. Referring to it he remarks: "In this system the things in themselves follow one another, we are merely observers; but how the representation of them comes to be in us is a question far beyond the range of this system" (2:31). The question is not how a succession outside us is possible but rather how this *particular* succession appears to us as it does with such necessity. All dogmatic systems have in common that they not only do not answer this question but they do not even raise it.

The Philosophy of Nature

The second alternative is described as the one all philosophers have accepted: "succession is something which cannot be conceived at all apart from the presentations of a finite mind" (2:32). This statement, too, admits of two meanings: either the things exist independently outside of us, and our sense of necessity in connection with their succession is an illusion, or both things and their representations must arise in us. Clearly, remarks Schelling, only the second alternative could be true. He characterizes the idea that things outside us affect us as "giving rise to the most fantastical system that has ever existed" (2:32). Echoing Jacobi, Schelling points out that if we divest these alleged external realities of every characteristic which could be traced to the peculiarities of our faculty of representations—succession, cause and effect, extension, duration, there is less than nothing left:

> If we speak of them, we must have an idea of them, or else we speak as we should not. One has, indeed, an idea even of nothing; one thinks of it as at least the absolute void, as something purely formal, and so on. One might think that the idea of things in themselves was a similar notion. But the idea of nothing can, after all, still be made palpable through the schema of empty space. Things in themselves, however, are expressly excluded from space and time. . . . So nothing is left but an idea that floats midway between something and nothing, i.e., which does not even have the virtue of being absolutely nothing (2:33).

This system, the interaction of conditioned sensation and things in themselves, is so nonsensical that the barest statement of it amounts to a refutation. Schelling has thus far avoided criticizing Kant directly, and even here in a footnote he exonerates Kant and blames the "tradition"[19] for the utter misunderstanding of the doctrine of the thing in itself, which culminated in the absurd claim that there are things that exist outside us, independent of our representations of them.

He then launches into a reconsideration of Hume's skepticism. Schelling summarizes Hume's argument as follows: Hume attributed the appearance of a succession of causes and effects to habit, or to the imagination's expectation that what has previously appeared in a certain order will do so again. Though Hume leaves it undecided (as he must, in order to remain faithful to his skeptical principles) whether or not our representations correspond to things, and declares the successions which do appear to us to be illusions born of habit, his system is still superior to that of Kant, because it is internally consistent. However, Hume's argument is circular:

> For that is after all precisely what is to be explained, namely *why the things have thus far followed one another in this order.* Is this succession somehow in the things outside us? But outside of our representations there is no succession. Or if it is merely a succession of our representations, then a reason must be capable of being given for the persistence of this succession. . . . Hume can say it *is* so, and that suffices for me. However, this is not philosophizing. (2:35)

There is a lesson to be learned from a consistent skepticism such as Hume's. Schelling takes this lesson to be that the *only* remaining alternative is to seek an explanation in the nature of the self for the necessity of the succession of representations. Schelling appears to be indicating here that it is to be found in the finite self; in the *System of Transcendental Idealism* it will be in the nature of the absolute.

Whether it is conceived of on the level of the individual self or the absolute, an all-important claim has been made that it is possible to understand necessity in the succession of representations only as at some level self-imposed, created by the self. The principle that we know only what we have made after a plan of our own is here taken to its logical limits: we know our own nature best (2:37), for the self produces itself. As was argued in the

"Treatises," all representation is construction, and the original representation is of the self's construction of itself in activity (1:414). It is the most basic premise of the philosophy of nature that if all of the self's construction could be philosophically reproduced, the complete system of nature would be the result. Since the self's essence is activity, it follows that the essence of nature is in process and the activity of coming into being:

> We observe the system of our ideas not in its *being*, but in its *becoming*. Philosophy becomes genetic, that is, it allows the entire necessary system of our ideas to arise and run its course before our eyes. From now on there is no more separation between experience and speculation. The system of nature is at the same time the system of our spirit . . . (2:39)

No more separation between nature and spirit also spells the end of the delusion of objectivity. The neutral scientific observer has no place outside the world left to stand, and the model for science is in the most literal possible sense self-knowledge.

In chapter 1 Herder was referred to as the likeliest source for Schelling's concept of genetic method; and when it is recalled that Herder laid an unprecedentedly strong emphasis on the significance of language, it will not seem too far-fetched to read Schelling as beginning in the *naturphilosophischen* works to advocate a hermeneutics of nature. By 1802, in the "Lectures on the Method of Academic Study," Schelling goes so far as to call the study of languages one of the necessary prerequisites for would-be scientists:

> All scientific education [all talent for discovery] consists in the ability to recognize possibilities, whereas ordinary knowledge grasps only realities. When a physicist has recognized that under certain conditions a phenomenon is actually possible, he has also recognized it as real. Study of language as an art of in-

terpretation, encouraging conjectural improvements on the reading of a text, cultivates this ability to recognize possibilities. . . . For us nature is a primordially ancient author . . . (5:246)

V. *On the World Soul*

Schelling's reflections in the "Treatises" and his introduction to the *Ideas* had both taken the problem of knowledge of the world as their starting point. The world of nature is clearly not the dead mechanically determined thing the dogmatist claims it is; for, Schelling argues, even if it were, we could never come to know it, since consciousness is not itself mechanical and thus would be incapable of grasping such a world of nature. More importantly, the picture offered by the dogmatist simply is not true to our experience of nature. Schelling explored the implications of the former objection in the "Treatises" and the *Ideas*; in *On the World Soul* [*Von der Weltseele*] of 1798 he considers the latter. In this work Schelling returns to his earlier interest in the problems raised by teleological causality in Kant's *Critique of Judgment* and attempts to give an account of organic structure and life in nature as well as their relation to a supersensible ground of unity (the world soul), by means of which he hopes to expose the glaring deficiencies of the dogmatic theories of nature.

The underlying unity which rules all of nature, inorganic and organic alike, is the key which will enable Schelling to reconcile these two apparently opposed realms:

> As soon as our observation has elevated itself to the idea of nature as a whole, the contradiction between mechanism and organism disappears, which has held up the progress of natural science long enough. . . . It is an old misconception, that organization and life are inexplicable by means of natural principles (2:348).

However, he scornfully rejects the shortcut of abstraction as employed by the dogmatist ("I hate nothing more than that unimaginative striving to get rid of the multiplicity of natural causes through use of invented identities" (2:347–48)). This dogmatic (science) typically consists of the selection of certain abstract principles and understands nature only insofar as it conforms to them.

The introduction to the *Ideas* had argued that the inability of the dogmatist to explain the organic is linked to the unavoidable necessity for dogmatic systems to assume a world creator in order to explain purposiveness in nature as well as the unity of nature. Schelling employs the same criticisms of this theory as Kant did in the third *Critique* (2:44–45) and concludes: "Since organization is only imaginable in connection with a mind, the human spirit was led early to the idea of a self-organizing matter [and] an original unity of spirit and matter in these things" (2:47). The claim that "the human spirit was led early" to these realizations has been explored by Joseph Lawrence, who has illustrated a number of parallels between Schelling's philosophy of nature and Aristotle's ideas, particularly his dynamic concept of matter and unwillingness to reduce qualitative phenomena to quantifiable structures. Lawrence's comparison between Aristotle's concept of prime matter as the ultimate undifferentiable which resists all attempts of reason to grasp it and Schelling's growing awareness that all his speculative explorations of matter keep leading him back to an indeterminate final ground of being is especially suggestive.[20]

The detached observation peculiar to reflective philosophy, in contrast, separates man from nature, with the predictable result that "as soon as I separate myself, and with me, all ideality from nature, nothing remains save a dead object and I cease to understand how life outside me could be possible" (2:47–48). This was the most telling indictment of both contemporary science and contemporary philosophy, that they "destroy from the ground up all ideas of life" (2:49). The problem of life forces us to seek a system in which spirit and matter are in relation in such a manner that nature is visible spirit and spirit invisible nature. Thus here, in the absolute identity of spirit in us and nature outside of us, the problem must be resolved of how a nature outside us is possible. The final goal of our further research is therefore this idea of nature (2:56). Schelling's arguments in *On the World Soul* are intended as answers to these objections. Using a method he calls *Induktion*, he will demonstrate which principles must ultimately be governing nature in order for us to experience it as we do.

When Schelling declares in the preface that "one and the same principle connects organic and inorganic nature" (2:350), he is already moving beyond Kant, who argued repeatedly that human cognition will never fully comprehend organic nature. In the third *Critique* Kant insists that although the living organism is composed of matter, its growth and organization shows such originality in the separation and composition of raw matter, that all art must remain infinitely far from copying the process. Indeed, "strictly speaking, the organization of nature has nothing analogous to any causality known to us."[21] This is why human science will wait in vain for a "Newton of a blade of grass,"[22] in Kant's view.

Schelling proposes that instead of continuing to struggle fruitlessly to explain the organic in terms of the mechanical, we ought to realize that mechanism taken by itself is not really anything self-sufficient or positive. Is it not, then, the mere negation of organism? In that case, organism must be more basic than mechanism, for the positive always precedes its negation. Furthermore, an unlimited mechanism would self-destruct; therefore the very existence of mechanism must depend upon its being enclosed and limited by a greater and nonmechanical whole. This line of argument, here so baldly stated, is unconvincing and puzzling, but it is an early example of a kind of reasoning Schelling applies frequently in the philosophy of nature: higher levels of development in nature, such as life, are inadequately understood if they are conceptualized as being a less complex level of nature (such as matter) plus a *qualitas occulta*, such as vitality.

Obviously the proper method would be to understand the lower levels in terms of the higher ones.

This also explains in part Schelling's fascination with the idea of the world whole or unity (as well as his repeated insistence that the world cannot be conceived on analogy with an immense machine). This world principle must be capable of encompassing and giving rise to life as well as every other level of being. He refers to it as "an eternal and infinite willing-of-itself . . . in all forms, grades, and potencies of reality" (2:362). This great chain of being is variously described as "a constant chain of life [*Lebenskette*] returning into itself" (2:373), and a "god-like unity . . . of all life" (2:362).

The influence of Spinoza is evident in more than just the last expression cited. What, Schelling asks, can the goal of the sublimest science be, if not to portray "reality, reality in the strictest sense, the present, the living existence [*Da-Seyn*] of God in the whole of things and in the individuals. . . . Can one question the existence of existence? It is the totality of things" (2:376). Schelling reminds us that there is no room for empty abstractions in his philosophy of nature: what is to be grasped is existence itself. Nature is not the product of an ultimately incomprehensible creation—it is itself the creation; as it was for Spinoza, Schelling's nature is not the appearance of eternal reality, but is eternal reality itself.

It is also Spinoza who pointed the way toward the detailed examination of nature which forms the bulk of *On the World Soul*, for it was he who enunciated the principle that the more we know individual things, the more we know God. Therefore it is with ever renewed conviction that Schelling "now calls to those who seek the science of the eternal: Come to physics and recognize the eternal!" (2:373). This is an anticipation of another theme central to the philosophy of nature: individuality. Yet every individual receives its identity from its relation to the whole, the life of all.

It may appear as though Schelling has attempted to replace Spinoza's *Deus sive Natura* with an immanent living absolute which would serve as an ultimate highest ground from which all other levels of being could be explained. If this is the case, wouldn't his first principle be vulnerable to the same sorts of objections as Spinoza's was? Schelling seems to speak directly to this objection:

> Everything, which . . . has been objected against a philosophy which deals with the divine is entirely vain with respect to us; and when will it finally be understood that with respect to this science we teach . . . immanence and transcendence are equally empty words, for it invalidates this opposition, and in it everything flows together to a god-filled world? (2:377)

Despite the fact that this is a statement and not an argument, Schelling does not further consider the issue, but proceeds directly to the first section, called, "On the Power of Nature," where he reasons about nature much as he did about the self in the "Treatises": everything in nature strives continuously to go forward—were this positive force unchecked, it would lose itself in infinity. An opposed negative force must therefore so affect the first one that all appearances in nature are guided "in an eternal circulation" (2:381) back to their original source. "These two conflicting forces, presented at once in unity and in conflict, lead to the idea of an organizing principle developing the world as a system. Perhaps the ancients wished to indicate [such a principle] with the world soul" (2:381). This early reference to the ebb and flow of a circulatory system seems a clear anticipation of the doctrine of the *Bruno* that the universe "is such a well-organized animal that it can never die" (3:278).

VI. Dynamism, Polarity, and the Philosophy of Organism

Schelling had objected in the "Treatises" to the dogmatic concept of matter as dead, lifeless "stuff," for, he claimed, it was impossible in principle to explain how consciousness could ever come to know it. The implications of the idea that the knower and the known must be related are here further developed: the common element in both will prove to be force, or, more specifically, the conflict of opposed forces, their temporary equilibrium, their renewed conflict. Therefore the first part of *On the World Soul* is devoted to the development of a dynamic concept of matter and all of inorganic nature as composed of increasingly complex polarities; the second part is devoted to the philosophy of the organic and its implications.

The goal of natural science is to understand every force in nature, not as absolute, but as in conflict with its opposite. The general dualism of nature cannot be empirically proved,

> but such a dualism must be assumed, because without opposed forces no living movement is possible. Real opposition is, however, only possible where that which is opposed is posited in one and the same subject. The original forces (to which all explanation finally returns) would not be opposed if they were not original activities of one and the same nature, which acted in opposed directions. (2:390)

In other words, nature as we know it cannot be explained other than by analogy with a subject; there is no other comparison adequate to reflect the essence of any living movement.

The conflict of forces at every level is the life of the world, and the temporary equilibrium reached between any set of opposed forces is an individual product of nature. Therefore as many individual things are possible in experience as there are levels of forces. At the most basic level, the gravitational pull of the earth is negatively opposed to the positive force of light: "In this original antithesis lies the seed of the general world organization" (2:396). Schelling admits that this is a postulate which is not empirically but transcendentally derived, but defends its necessity by heaping scorn on experimental physicists. These scientists are correct to cling to the immediately intuited—but this is merely the positive force of nature, which the philosopher of nature knows is not absolute in itself, but dependent on a negative force. The method of induction is to seek that conflict of forces which would make the individual intuited object possible; and the only acceptable proof of its superiority will emerge when the system it produces is compared with that of the experimenters, whose Achilles heel will prove to be their inability to explain life. It will be seen that "their one-sided kind of explanation, without inner opposition (the source of all vitality) . . . leads to nothing and does not make even the construction of the first appearances of nature possible" (2:397). This 'first appearance' is matter; all material things must be understood as polarities, based upon an ultimate duality of unequal forces continually seeking equilibrium, for only such a dynamic concept of matter can ever explain the existence of life.

The largest part of *On the World Soul* is devoted to inorganic nature and the identification of the polarities which govern it at every level. It is clear that since one of Schelling's earliest definitions of the essence of organized products is that it is one in which form and matter are inseparable, a definition repeated here (2:498), it was of the utmost importance to develop a concept of matter which would not be incompatible with organization. In the second part ("On the Origin of the General Organism") we see Schelling struggling to combine his various theories into a harmonious world picture, a task not accomplished even in outline until the *System of Transcendental Idealism*. Therefore only three of the most important ideas will be discussed here.

Schelling's interest in life led him to reject as failures those theories which regarded life as a mysterious something added to matter, or as a property of matter. Here he draws two conclusions from his previously mentioned theory that the lower levels of nature must be derived from the higher: as the higher levels are the more individualized, it follows that nature is best understood as an infinite series of decreasingly individual products of the most general organism (or the world soul). Organism is not a property of certain things; rather the things are "just so many limitations or individual ways of intuition of the general organism" (2:500). This reverses the relation between organic and inorganic nature: "The essence of all things (which are not mere appearances, but approach individuality in an infinite graduated sequence) is life; what is accidental is the kind of life it is, and also that which is dead in nature is not really dead—it is the absence of life" (2:500).

Schelling then embarks on a description of life as a process of continuous interruption and restoration of equilibrium. That which distinguishes the living from every other product of nature is its individuality. The nonliving may be distinguished from one another by their positions in time and/or space; the living are distinguished by the degree to which they successfully instantiate a concept. Schelling also tries to trace the source of individuality to the unique relationship every living being has to the whole of which it is a part, coming to the conclusion that the organism is that which is cause of itself (2:519) and organized according to a concept.

These conclusions lead Schelling to the realization that most thinkers have misunderstood the nature of the problem of the origin of organism (2:526). The problem lies in the reconciliation of freedom (implied by the stress on individuality) and obedience to law necessary for every natural product to be part of a larger whole. Its individuality is an expression of autonomy; yet it exists, grows, reproduces, and dies according to laws. "Instead, therefore, of saying that nature is both free and law-governed in its development, we could say that in organic matter an original impulse to development is active, by virtue of which it assumes, sustains, and continually reproduces a certain determinate content" (2:527). Here Schelling has found a temporary solution to the problem of reconciling free causality with a law-governed nature. That he immediately cautions against taking this impulse to development as an ultimate "final cause" or "absolute ground" (2:529) shows the precariousness and transitional role of these early speculations on the philosophy of organism.

Even at this early stage, Schelling has encountered limits to the empiricist's mode of explanation in science and attempts to substitute a more idealistic model of explanation. His "principles of science as *Wissenschaft*" suggest what is at stake: science must be systematic, involve both product and process, illustrate the relation of identity between product and process, and understand the activity of nature as constituted by hierarchically related opposing forces (3:288–91). Every natural phenomenon is to be understood in terms of the larger life of which it is a part; indeed, "in every product lies the germ of the universe" (3:291), yet the ultimate ground itself remains shadowy at best.

Schelling's theory of matter is a case in point: it remains vulnerable to the same criticisms as Kant's, namely, that the assumption of primordial or original attractive and repulsive forces as constitutive of matter *is* an appeal to a *qualitas occulta*, albeit a theoretically somewhat richer one than the absolute impenetrability of the atomistic theorists such as Newton (see discussion of Kant's theory above in section III). One fairly glaring problem with the dynamic concept of matter can be seen by comparing the detailed construction of Kant's argument, in which the repulsive and attractive forces are asymmetrical, and Schelling's, in which they are, and indeed must be, symmetrical. On Kant's view, "impenetrability is given immediately with the concept of matter, while attraction is not thought in the concept [of matter] but only attributed to it by inference."[23] The dynamic concept of matter is dangerously elastic when the two theories differ so substantially on such an important point as the nature of matter's constitutive forces.

Original forces, unsatisfactory though they proved to be in the understanding of any of the actual phenemena of nature, are at the heart of Schelling's understanding of nature as dynamic and living. In the *Ages of the World* of

1811, where he was no longer closely concerned with the details of the construction of the natural world, he declared more freely that the fundamental condition of life itself is contradiction, the paradox which underlies his views on both physics and metaphysics: "Without contradiction there would be no life, no movement, no progress, a deathly slumber of all powers. Only contradiction drives, yes even forces to action" (WA I:123). Schelling recognized that his understanding of nature as containing a power far beyond the grasp of human concepts was at once in disharmony with much of the science of his time and yet had elements of similarity to ancient views of nature. At the end of volume 4 of his works he remarks that all of the speculation on the philosophy of nature may still have left some readers unsatisfied, and for those he thought it might be edifying to approach what he emphasizes is the same subject matter from a very different angle; he then reproduces a short section of one of his more notorious youthful poetic efforts, the "Epicurean Confession of Faith of Heinz Widerporsten" (4:546–48), a fragment written in a curious style which Josiah Royce describes as a sort of "glorified doggerel."[24] Perhaps it will again serve to draw to a close a discussion of the philosophy of nature by indicating how much in nature escapes our narrow grasp. I present a selection from here in Royce's translation:

> His power, that fills the veins with ore,
> And renews in the spring the buds once more
> Labors unceasing in darkness and night,
> In all nature's nooks and crannies for light,
> Fears no pang in its fierce desire
> To live and conquer and win its way higher.
> Organs and members it fashions anew,
> Lengthens or shortens, makes many or few,
> And wrestles and writhes in its search till it find
> The form that is worthiest of its mind.
> Struggling thus on life intent,
> Against a cruel environment,

It triumphs at last, in one narrow space,
And comes to itself in a dwarfish race,
That, fair of form, of stature erect,
Stands on the earth as the giant's elect,
Is called in our speech the son of man,
Outcome and crown of the spirit's plan.
From iron slumber, from dreaming set free,
Now marvels the spirit who he may be.
Looks on himself with wondering gaze,
Measures his limbs in dim amaze,
Longs in terror once more to be hid,
In nature's slumber, of sentience rid.
But nay, his freedom is won for aye,
No more in nature's peace may he lie;
In the vast dark world that is all his own,
He wanders life's narrow path alone . . .
Yet he could say, the giant's peer,
I am the God who nature's bosom fills,
I am the life that in her heart's blood thrills.[25]

4

Metaphors for Nature

I. From the Philosophy of Nature to the *System*

The widespread tendency to see Schelling's pre-1800 work as virtually indistinguishable from Fichte's is not merely mistaken, it blinds us to the essential continuity of Schelling's thought as a whole. The affinity, and at the same time the distance, between Fichte and Schelling can be illustrated in a single brief passage from the "Treatises," which begins in impeccably Fichtean fashion and concludes with a sweeping claim which could serve as the motto for all of Schelling's *naturphilosophischen* efforts:

> What the soul intuits is always its own progressive nature. Yet its nature is nothing other than that evident conflict which it presents in the form of particular objects. In this way it defines, through its own products, the way, invisible to common eyes [though] to the philosopher clear and distinct, in which it gradually comes to self-consciousness. The external world lies spread out before us in order that we may rediscover within it the history of our spirit. (1:383)

Fichte and Schelling both see in the world of experience the workings of the spirit. But whereas Fichte sees only the self's thumbprint, as it were, on nature as an object which exists only to be acted upon by a subject, Schelling understands that the knowledge of nature is an avenue to knowledge of the self *only if* nature is taken seriously as an independent realm through which the absolute or unconditioned ground of being manifests itself just as it does through the activities of spirit. Hence the necessity of elevating the status of the philosophy of nature from a mere adjunct to philosophy to a necessary, indeed essential, part of it: it is the agenda of the *System* to demonstrate how this may be done.

However, the crucial transition to the view that the philosophy of nature is a necessary part of philosophy in its own right is undertaken in the *Introduction to the Sketch of a System of the Philosophy of Nature or on the Concept of Speculative Physics and the Inner Organization of a System of This Science* [*Einleitung zu dem Entwurf eines System der Naturphilosophie oder über den Begriff der spekulativen Physik und die innere Organization eines Systems dieser Wissenschaft*] of 1799 (hereafter "Introduction to the Sketch"). Schelling distinguished his ideas from the currently accepted concepts of physics by calling his philosophy of nature "the opposite of transcendental philosophy," because it posits nature (insofar as it is both product and productive simultaneously) "as self-sufficient" (3:273). The reader who persists in regarding the philosophy of nature as subordinate to theoretical philosophy instead of recognizing it as a unique and independent science, Schelling warns, will fail to understand it. The new, independent philosophy of nature described in the "Introduction to the Sketch" depends heavily on a distinction which is of growing importance for Schelling: the distinction between consciousness and the unconscious. The laws of nature are to be understood as unconscious forms of the laws of spirit: "Intelligence is productive in two ways, [as] either blind and unconscious or free and conscious" (3:371). That which is produced with consciousness is ideal (*ideelle*); through the unconscious, real (*reelle*). Philosophy denies their opposition insofar as it strives to understand them as originally identical; however, since philosophy is itself a work of consciousness, there is, so to speak, a temptation in the nature of things to try to grasp the real in terms of the ideal. This is transcendental philosophy. The task of a true philosophy of nature, on the other hand, is to provide an equally adequate explanation of the ideal in terms of the real; that is, it must explain how consciousness arises from matter.

If we take our actual experience of nature seriously, that is, as complete and existent in its own right, there is no other possible explanation, Schelling argues, taking his familiar approach of reflecting on experience in order to find the presuppositions without which the experience would not be possible or be what it in fact is. The argumentation of "Introduction to the Sketch" is permeated with an attitude not unlike Kant's in his moral philosophy: because human freedom and responsibility are ultimate and undeniable experiences, an adequate moral theory must explain their necessity, and explain it as essential to human nature. Similarly, Schelling finds the experience of regularity in nature (on the inorganic level) and the recognition of purposiveness (on the organic level) to be undeniable, immediate, and necessary. The affinity of inorganic to organic nature, and of both to consciousness, "can only be explained [if nature is] an unconscious productivity originally related to the conscious one" (3:272). Therefore if both nature and spirit are, properly understood, different kinds of productivity which have sprung from the same root, the choice of which to view as primary is arbitrary.

> If it is the task of transcendental philosophy to subordinate the real to the ideal, then it is on the other hand the task of the philosophy of nature to explain the ideal out of the real: both sciences are thus one science, distinguished from one another only by the opposed direction of their tasks; since furthermore both directions are not only equally possible, but equally necessary, they have the same necessity in the system of knowledge. (3:272–73)

Though Schelling does not mention Fichte by name, he is clearly taking aim at his "idealistic kind of explanation" when he declares that to claim that "everything in nature is only necessary because it is through nature that self-consciousness can arise . . . [is] senseless" (3:273). Walter Schulz has observed that the end result of Schelling's study of the philosophy of nature is the realization that if nature is genuinely ordered in its own right, then it is no longer possible to make the mistake of placing the conscious self squarely in the center of being. What in Fichte is presented as the history of human subjectivity has been transformed by Schelling into a new concept of history:

> For the Schelling of the philosophy of nature . . . nature and spirit are not to be understood as two separated static realms; rather they are the two intertwined stages and epochs of one single world development. The world is in its essence history, and in the first instance *natural history* and then *history of spirit.*[1]

Schelling knows that it is not possible to prove the superiority of his philosophy of nature by engaging in a battle of dueling abstractions: it will have to prove itself by being a better, that is, a more systematic and complete account. The most revealing test, Schelling thinks, will be whether or not his view is able to provide an adequate understanding of organic nature, something neither science nor philosophy has yet achieved. It is revealing that most of his studies (beginning in Leipzig in 1796 when he was still a private tutor) were in biology and medicine. These interests culminated in his becoming coeditor from 1805–8 of the journal *Jahrbücher der Medicin als Wissenschaft.*[2]

Since medicine stands at that point where nature and spirit, body and mind, most closely intertwine with each other, it is clear why Schelling may have hoped that the perspective of *Naturphilosophie* might be especially fruitful. In his initial attempt to find a publisher for the *Jahrbücher der Medicin*, Schelling wrote a letter outlining his plans for the new journal to an unidentified publisher, explaining that the circumstances of initial confusion as a science begins to establish itself are inevitable, even laudable, since such confusion invites a strict critique of all theoretical pretensions; it would be just such a critique that the *Jahrbücher* would provide.[3] Schelling showed by his lively interest in both the theories of John Brown and Andreas Röschlaub and their practical medical applications just how serious he was about the intimate connection between theory and practice.[4] The value of these speculations earned sufficient recognition that the medical faculty of the University of Landshut nominated Schelling in 1802 for an honorary doctorate as "the man who had rendered the greatest service to the study of medical science";[5] he was also elected an honorary member of the "Physikalisch-medicinischen Societät" of Erlangen in 1808.[6]

The Kantian inspiration for this view is explicit in Schelling's discussion of the concept of knowledge. Nature must be understood on its own terms, and as productive through its own forms, or we are simply observing it from outside, chroniclers without insight. Following Kant, Schelling declares that one can be truly said to know

> ... only such objects as one can understand the principles of the possibility of, because without this insight my entire knowledge of an object, for example, a machine, whose construction is unknown to me, is a mere seeing, that is, the mere conviction of its existence, while the inventor of the machine has the most complete knowledge of it, because he is as it were the soul of this product. (3:275–76)

If it can be shown that it is possible to have this kind of knowledge of nature, then the philosophy of nature will be recognized as "an entirely unique science, independent and distinguished from every other" (3:280).

II. Metaphors of Dominance and Control

Karl Marx was fond of quoting Montesquieu's observation that one can best judge the level of civilization achieved by a culture by considering the status of women in that culture. Perhaps not altogether surprisingly, it is in the vast differences in their answers to one form of the 'woman question' that Schelling distances himself most strikingly from Kant, Fichte, and Hegel. The form of the question I find it illuminating to consider does not in the first instance involve living, breathing, actual women, but rather the first figurative female—mother nature. Let us not be guilty of the error Elizabeth Spelman warns against:

> After all, it might be thought, how could one's views about something as unimportant as women have anything to do with one's views about something as important as the nature of knowledge, truth, reality, freedom?.... When one recalls that the Western philosophical tradition has not been noted for its celebration of the body, and that women's nature and women's lives have long been associated with the body and bodily functions, then a question is suggested. What connection might there be between attitudes toward the body and attitudes toward women?[7]

Kant, Fichte, and Hegel are remarkable for the low esteem, even for their day, in which they held women; Schelling does not seem to have shared this view.[8] It must be acknowledged that there are some difficulties in discussing the views of these thinkers that arise out of the much more common use of the neutral terms *Mensch* and *Menschheit* in German than the corresponding "member of the human race" and "humanity," which tend to sound stilted in English. The English "man," even if intended inclusively, retains its origins; the German writer may appear neutral and egalitarian, especially one like Kant, who argues that his principles apply to all finite rational beings, even nonhuman ones. He may, that is, until the tension between his generic language and theory is compared with his actual views on women. The easily discovered disparities present the contemporary reader of these historical figures with some important questions, Pauline Kleingeld has argued:

> The question for philosophical commentators, historians of philosophy, and theorists today is how to approach such cases. Should one, in discussing the work of such philosophers, go on using such terms as "humanity" and "human being" when it is clear that the philosopher in question did not mean to include women? Is it legitimate to introduce explicitly inclusive language ("she or he") in presenting this philosopher's views? Or should one replace terms like "the human race" with "males"?[9]

As Kleingeld goes on to conclude, it is high time to stop trivializing or ignoring the sexism of historical figures and to begin to learn from it. In the context of German idealism, it is significant for understanding Schelling to appreciate that despite the very great dependence of his thought on the foundations provided by his great predecessors and contemporaries, he shares neither their explicit sexism nor their metaphors of a feminine natural world which the (masculine) philosopher and/or scientist controls through reason. It suggests to me that we may gain otherwise inaccessible insights into the metaphysics of nature of each of these thinkers by considering their respective views of *female* nature.

III. Kant

Kant's[10] view of women is most unambiguously stated in his "Observations on the Feeling of the Beautiful and the Sublime" and arises in the context of his argument that all efforts to advance the moral perfection of either sex must take their peculiar characteristics into account. To be female is to be naturally sympathetic, goodhearted, and sensitive; woman has an understanding that is beautiful (in Kant's sense, this is the opposite of being deep or profound), that is, one "which takes for its objects everything related to feeling, and has no appreciation of abstract speculation."[11] Kant's identification of the female with feeling and sensation and of the male with reason and abstract speculation goes beyond the simple assignment of mental types. As Susan Mendus has shown, Kant appeals to this dichotomy to justify excluding women from full citizenship (they can achieve only the status of passive citizen) as well as limiting their freedom even within marriage.[12] Thus his most general definition of the proper sphere of woman's activity: "The content of a woman's great science ... is humankind, and among humanity, men. Her philosophy is not to reason, but to sense."[13]

The other details of this dichotomy of sense and reason, male and female, may be easily enough imagined if we remember Rousseau, whom Kant greatly admired, in particular the sex-segregated educational theories of *Emile*. Yet one might well feel that all this sort of thing is quite understandable in an untraveled older gentleman of the eighteenth century, and neither remarkable nor significant. It is indeed not remarkable in the sense of being original with Kant, or even an unusual point of view on the relationship of the sexes. Its true significance emerges only when it is seen against the background of the central assumptions of Kant's critical philosophy.

It was the admixture of the empirical (which has its origin in sensation) with the principles of pure reason that Kant deplored in his predecessors. For him, the very possibility of philosophical knowledge depended on the strictest separation of the two:

> The critique of pure reason will therefore contain all that is essential in transcendental philosophy. . . . What has chiefly to be kept in view in the establishment of such a science, is that no concepts be allowed to enter which contain in themselves anything empirical, or in other words, that they consist in knowl-

edge wholly a priori. . . . Transcendental philosophy is therefore a philosophy of pure and merely speculative reason. All that is practical, so far as it contains motives, relates to feelings, and these belong to the empirical sources of knowledge. (A14/B28 = A15/B29)

Reason must shake off the domination of nature and the senses and trust only to its own powers and conclusions: reason "must not allow itself to be kept in nature's leading-strings, but must itself show the way with principles of judgment based upon fixed laws, constraining nature to give answers to questions of reason's own determining" (Bxiii). Reason, in the form of pure speculative knowledge, must be supreme, and the empirical sources of knowledge devalued. Kant readily admits that this drastically narrows the scope of proper philosophical inquiry, but he does not find this to be too high a price to pay in order to insure that "the study of nature has entered on the secure path of a science" (Bxiv).

This insistence that "metaphysics is a completely isolated speculative science of reason, which soars far above the teachings of experience, and in which reason is meant to be its own pupil" (Bxiv), shows us that for Kant, only reason and its activity can be properly transcendental. Indeed, it is the whole of the empirical which is to be transcended. Kant solves one set of problems; unfortunately, his solution renders it mysterious what possible relationship reason might have to nature if they are utterly heterogenous. Here the incoherence behind the superficial appeal of the philosopher-as-judge model stands revealed, for what possible criteria can be employed in judgment of that which has been strictly defined as wholly other?

Kant's *Metaphysical Foundations of the Natural Sciences* (by which Schelling had been greatly influenced) illustrates the implications of this view most revealingly. Kant is highly critical of the Newtonian theory of matter, which understands matter as solid, inert stuff, characterized by a capacity for resistance, because it assumes what it purports to prove by claiming that matter is *by its nature* impenetrable [*undurchdringlich*], a word which can mean either physically impermeable or intellectually unfathomable. That Kant intends to invoke both meanings is clear: "Absolute impenetrability is in fact nothing more or less than [a] *qualitas occulta*."[14] Yet Kant too finds a point at which he must admit that the basic forces of matter [*Grundkräfte der Materie*], even in his improved dynamic understanding of them, are utterly inexplicable.[15] In other words, matter, which stands at the opposite pole from reason insofar as it can be grasped at all, is known merely through sensation (which for Kant is not truly knowledge). It seemingly has no formal aspects for the mind to grasp. Thus Kant's description of matter as somehow eluding full rational comprehension is oddly reminiscent of his observation in the *Anthropology* that "Man is easy to understand; woman does not reveal her secret" [*Geheimnis*].[16] At bottom the heterogeneity of mind and matter cannot be overcome, posing insuperable limits to the progress of science.

IV. Fichte

A careful reading of the "Critique of Teleological Judgment" section of the third *Critique* shows that Kant was very well aware of the insufficiencies of the critical philosophy with respect to the understanding of nature or the integration of the powers of reason into a harmonious whole. Fichte did not take the hint offered in the *Critique of Judgment* concerning the supersensible substrate, but that does not mean that he was not vitally interested in remedying what he saw as the incompleteness of the critical philosophy. He transformed the need to unify the powers of reason almost unrecognizably by locating the source of all reality in the absolute self. Nature and the nonconscious became for him projections of the self's own activity, ultimately no more than the moral theater in which the drama of the self coming to know itself is enacted. So Fichte repeats Kant's dichotomies with still more vehemence and force. Indeed, on Fichte's view the self cannot even achieve consciousness without awareness of something opposed to it; were it to lose this awareness, it would lose itself.

It might at first seem that if nature is understood to be originally a part of the self, rather than a mysterious, inaccessible thing-in-itself, then Fichte might not be as inclined to view nature as the incomprehensible entity that it is for Kant. All reality arises through the self-positing of the self (Fichte 1:97–98), which is an act of unmediated intellectual intuition (Fichte 1:463). Philosophy, as the science which discovers and explains the grounds of experience, has as its task the discovery of the laws of intelligence behind the presentations (Fichte 1:441).

However, the moral vision informing Fichte's philosophy takes its inspiration from Kant's moral philosophy, which predicates membership in the intelligible world on the ability to recognize the moral law. What is this ability? In the second *Critique* Kant admits:

> The consciousness of this fundamental law may be called a fact of reason [*Faktum der Vernunft*], since one cannot ferret it out from any antecedent data of reason.... In order to regard this law without any misinterpretation as given, one must note that it is not an empirical fact but the sole fact of pure reason, by which it proclaims itself as originating law.[17]

This "fact of reason" enables a man to make the judgment that because he *ought* to do something, he also *can* do it; the categorical imperative is the unconditional principle of self-legislation.

For Fichte, the moral realm is founded on the categorical imperative (Fichte 1:260 n). Kant had argued that we must act *as if* our moral causality is effective in the empirical world, although we will never know how it could be. Fichte takes this a step further: because objects *ought* to conform to the self, the world of objects must be seen as something which is the direct expression of the self.

Should the implications of this view not be clear to anyone, Fichte spelled them out in his lecture "On the Dignity of Man," with which he concluded his 1794 lectures on the *Science of Knowledge*. We have taken the measure of the human spirit, Fichte claims, and philosophy has taught us to seek everything in the self. "It is only through the self that order and harmony enters the formless mass. Only through man does *regularity* extend, radiating from him to the limit of his observation" (Fichte 1:412). The self is thus responsible for the whole of the great chain of being:

> It is through the self that the whole fabulous progression from the flea to the seraph arises; . . . man expects that the law of the self which he gives to himself and to her [i.e., nature] will be obeyed. It is the self which holds the guarantee that it will spread infinite order and harmony where at present there is none. . . . Everything, which is now still unformed and disorderly will, through humanity, arrange itself into the most beautiful harmony . . . (Fichte 1:413)

In short, where man treads, nature awakens in pleased expectancy, that man might command the raw material to organize itself according to his ideal. It is difficult to imagine a view of nature more spectacularly at odds with Newton's claim that nature was a book written by God in the language of mathematics; for Fichte, nature is a book written by and for man.

The central role of the other is the key to Fichte's metaphysics. It is in keeping with his belief that the self constitutes itself through opposition to the other that his moral or practical philosophy relies so heavily on will and resolution, so much so that we can well understand why the very meaning of humanity is identified with the pursuit of goals, the moral and practical overcoming of obstacles, and the dominance of nature.[18] Notable throughout this account is the strong emphasis on law, control of nature, and dominance; the similarities in his account of *female* nature are all the more striking.

Apparently blissfully unaware that there seems to be at least some contradiction between the vision of the human being as so powerful that he is the cocreator of nature and the idea that that human being is nevertheless limited by having a predetermined male or female nature, Fichte explains in *The Science of Right* that "although it cannot be maintained that women are *less* intelligent than men," still the sexes have completely different mental talents: "woman is, by virtue of her femininity, above all practical, but not in the least speculative. To mentally go beyond the limits of her emotion[s] is neither possible nor desirable for her" (Fichte, 3:351–52). A woman's morality and reasoning power are most appropriately expressed in her ability to be subservient, to her father if she is single, or to her husband if she is married:

> It ought to be duly noted, and indeed this is implied by my whole theory, and has repeatedly been explicitly expressed therein, although it is perhaps not superfluous to emphasize it yet again: Woman is not subjugated in the sense that her husband exerts *force* over her, she is subjugated through her own enduring and necessary wish, which conditions her morality, to be subjugated. She could take her freedom back, if she *wanted to*; but here is the crucial point: she cannot rationally *will* to be free (Fichte 3:345).

This view does represent a step beyond Kant, in that women are rational beings, according to Fichte; yet female rationality seems curiously circumscribed. In some respects Fichte's view seems to resemble Aristotle's claim that women's rationality is like that of men, save that it exists in an ineffective form: "the woman has [a deliberative faculty] but it is without authority."[19] What support this difference in intellectual function provides for Aristotle's conclusion that therefore "the male is by nature superior and the female inferior, the one rules and the other is ruled, this principle of necessity extends to all mankind,"[20] is a topic that cannot be pursued here. However, Fichte does seem to go further than Aristotle, in that he assigns women a distinct nature.[21]

Still a part of nature herself, woman is not her own mistress for Fichte, and can never become fully rational in the same sense that a man can.[22] The a priori basis of Fichte's view emerges unmistakably in his discussion of why it is impossible in principle for a woman to take on public responsibilities such as elected office, for she lacks the autonomy necessary to the conscientious discharge of public duties. It is the most basic foundation of her nature to be "fated to love, and love . . . does not depend on her free will" (Fichte 3:349). Woman's openness to emotion and her inability to go beyond it to the speculative flights of which man is capable also explain why there have been so many female novelists and "scribblers," yet no great female philosophers or mathematicians (Fichte 3:352).

V. Hegel

Since Hegel promises an ultimate reconciliation of reason and nature—indeed, he says that the real is rational and the rational real—one might hope to see a more nuanced theory of nature, and of female nature in particular, than those passive entities in need of judgment and domination described by Kant and Fichte. In a certain sense this might be considered to be true, and the liberatory potential of Hegel's insights into the dialectic of the transcendence of oppression have recently been investigated by Heidi M. Ravven and Susan Easton. This is not to deny that the widely accepted feminist view of Hegel as a biological determinist with an ahistorical concept of female virtue which confines women to the sphere of the family has considerable textual support. Still, I will argue that the relationship between Hegel's concept of nature and female nature is a complex one.

At first blush Hegel does not seem startlingly different from Fichte: woman indeed possesses rationality, but inasmuch as her life unfolds within, and is dedicated to, the family, she does not develop this rationality in such a manner as to enable her to function in the public sphere; thus she requires domination by, and completion through, the more highly developed rationality of the male.

> Women are capable of education, but they are not made for activities which demand a universal faculty such as the more advanced sciences, philosophy, and certain forms of scientific production. Women may have happy ideas, taste and elegance, but they cannot attain to the ideal. The difference between men and women is like the difference between animals and plants. Men correspond to animals, while women correspond to plants because their development is more placid and the principle that underlies it is the rather vague unity of feeling. Women are educated—who knows how—as it were by breathing in ideas, by living rather than acquiring knowledge.[23]

Another way to make the same point is the claim in the *Philosophy of Nature* that "the male is the active principle, and the female is the receptive, because she remains in her undeveloped unity."[24]

Ravven has observed that Hegel's insistence that the differences between men and women are based on physiology does not square with the fact that "women fare so much better in comparison with men in the *Phenomenology* than in the *Philosophy of Right*, [and] better in Greek society than in the modern European state."[25] That is, Antigone's ethical heroism in upholding the divine law of the family can be directly compared to the heroism of Oedipus, as it is in section 469 of the *Phenomenology*, because the Greek woman and the Greek man live in a historical moment in which the full unfolding of individuality has not yet taken place. Bourgeois man, by contrast, has undergone "self-diremption into explicit personal self-subsistence."[26]

In other words, it appears that only men have evolved culturally, socially, politically, or historically. In ancient Greece, woman was identified with the unique ethical sphere of the family, in which she lived and moved and had her being (this is the import of the tragedy of Antigone). Unlike man, she remains so identified at present:

> ... thus one sex is mind in its self-diremption into explicit personal self-subsistence and the knowledge and volition of free universality.... The other sex is mind maintaining itself in unity as knowledge and volition of the substantive.... It follows that man has his actual substantive life in the state, in learning, and so forth, as well as in labor and struggle with the external world.... Woman on the other hand, has her substantive destiny in the family.[27]

What, then, is the relation of woman to man? As Patricia Mills sarcastically puts it: "Fortunately, the man can come home from a hard day of 'self-diremption' to the woman who offers him 'a tranquil intuition of... unity'; in this way man achieves a wholeness, a connection to first nature, through woman."[28] One of the most important aspects of nature, on this view, is that it serves the purpose of reminding men what it is they have overcome.

Given the necessary dialectical structure of family, civil society, and state in which the family is maintained but superseded by the later stages of historical development, we can see two consequences for those doomed to remain under the aegis of the family: they remain outside history, and thus are excluded from even the possibility of achieving true freedom. Hegel can even be read as claiming that women are not individuals:

> Natural and at the same time religious morality, is the piety of the family. In this social relation, morality consists of the members behaving toward each other not as individuals—possessing an independent will; not as persons. The family therefore, is excluded from the process of development in which history

takes its rise.... Freedom is nothing but the recognition and adoption of such universal and substantial objects as right and law, and the production of a reality that is in accord with them—the state.[29]

This exclusion from the public sphere leaves women outside of history and cut off from all possibility of change, apparently in order to provide man with some contact to all that he has left behind in his efforts at self-development and individuality. Ironically, too, since woman has power only within and through the family, her efforts to increase this power are doomed to produce the reverse effect: woman becomes the enemy of all that man has achieved, as Hegel explains in the *Phenomenology*:

> Since the community only gets an existence through its interference with the happiness of the Family, and by dissolving (individual) self-consciousness in the universal, it creates for itself in what it suppresses and what is at the same time essential to it an internal enemy—womankind in general. Womankind—the everlasting irony [in the life] of the community—changes by intrigue the universal end of the government into a private end; transforms its universal activity into a work of some particular individual and perverts the universal property of the state into a possession and ornament of the family.[30]

This conclusion seems essentially indistinguishable, despite its dialectical trappings, from the Kantian view:

> It is astounding how indifferent the female sex is to what constitutes the common good ... the idea of the whole has absolutely no power to move them.... They were not made to take a general view of things, and find it foolishness to worry about more than one's own affairs. That is very good. Men can refresh themselves from their public affairs with them.[31]

Thus "a phenomenology of *woman's* consciousness would, for Hegel, stop with Antigone, i.e., with woman as the quintessential spirit of the ever selfsame family."[32] One of the many implications of this reading of Hegel is that like the Hellenic ideal itself, she is destined to be and exists in being transcended. Women are not just less transcendent than men, they (and the family) serve as the necessary basis of that which men must transcend to become men and citizens of the world.

VI. Schelling

The *System of Transcendental Idealism* of 1800, despite the title, contains Schelling's most detailed attempt to show the relationship of the unconscious world of nature to the conscious self, wherein it was understood that nature must have just such a structure as to be capable, at its highest level of development, of giving rise to the conscious self. The self has been returned to, and reintegrated with, nature; it has been explained as a product of natural forces. Thus it is unsurprising that there is no counterpart in Schelling to Kant, Fichte, and Hegel's comments on female nature in particular, since a symbolic representation of what is to be transcended is no longer necessary. This is all the more striking since it is evident from a passage in his early work *On Myths* (1794) that the young Schelling knew and employed the same metaphors of man's relationship to nature used by his contemporaries:

> As man grows toward higher activity, he forgets the images and dreams of his youth, and seeks to make nature comprehensible to his understanding. Previously he was a friend or son of nature, now he is its lawgiver; previously he wanted to experience himself in all of nature, now he wishes to explain all of nature in himself; previously he sought his image in the mirror of nature, now he seeks the archetype of nature in his understanding which is the mirror of everything. (1:74)

After 1797 and the first publications on the philosophy of nature, we can see how Schelling increasingly tends to reject the false objectivity of Kant's "judge" asking stern questions that nature must be compelled to answer, as well as the sort of legislating activity attributed to Fichte's moral "commander." Both of these systems clearly err in placing the philosopher (and in Kant's case, scientist as well) somehow "outside" nature.

Since Hegel was closely associated with Schelling during much of the time that he was developing the philosophy of nature, it may seem strange that their views ended up diverging as much as they did. The relationship of Hegel's philosophy of nature to Schelling's is complex.[33] Both nature and the "ever selfsame" female nature achieve significance only in being transcended; thus they remain outside history in a way that is unacceptable for Schelling. There are many similarities between Hegel's and Schelling's views of nature, but in the end, where Hegel stresses a dialectic that would collapse into incoherence without its hierarchical structure, Schelling emphasizes a dynamic view of both nature and spirit which does not subordinate one to the other but rather sees both as instantiating the same truth.

Sometimes the real direction of a long process of development becomes clear only at the end: looking ahead to the later Schelling may illuminate the differences between Schelling and Hegel only beginning to emerge here. Edward Beach has claimed that at the root of the differences between Hegel's and Schelling's philosophical systems is a significantly different understanding of dialectic. For Hegel, the dialectical process is one of sublation (*Aufhebung*), eliciting in contradiction and then making explicit the conceptual logic of any determination. Beach calls this a "dialectic of sublation" [*Sublationsdialektik*] and contrasts it with Schelling's "dialectic of production" [*Erzeugungsdialektik*]:

> Schellingian dialectic, by contrast, seeks to infuse the process of reasoning with a strong volitional component, so as to be capable of recovering the willing

> that allegedly precedes rational thought itself. . . . The emphasis on volition is directly coupled with a call for experience; for willing and experiencing alone can *produce* a truth that goes beyond the abstract demonstrations of logic. Schelling's treatment of dialectic obtains its successive forms not as though implicitly contained in the foregoing ones, but rather as produced or reproduced [*erzeugt*] by a kind of procreative causality . . . [34]

Although Beach is primarily concerned with the later Schelling, especially the positive philosophy in which the turn to experience is of vital importance, even the Schelling of the *Naturphilosophie* works shows in his choice of problems (How is nature as a whole to be conceived? What is the true nature of causality? What is the relation between inorganic matter and organic life?) his concern with reconciling the underlying unity of all being with the possibility of a genuinely fruitful polarity—a concern which will later lead to the development of a dialectic of procreation.

Clearly, the metaphor of procreation does not subordinate or transcend one element in favor of the other, even as it preserves the emphasis on volition and desire as the most original forces in the cosmos and the individual. Procreation also partakes of the spontaneity of creation, in that a genuinely unique individual is its result. This is a dialectic preserving the wonder of the beginning of life, with all its potential and possibilities; yet whether it represents a progression is certainly open to question. Schelling will later argue that Hegel's orchestrated parade of concepts is abstract and lifeless, and his claim to absolute knowledge necessarily false: here in the philosophy of nature and its metaphors we can see the roots of those objections.

As early as the "Introduction to the Sketch," Schelling had pointed out that even success beyond the wildest dreams of experimental science could never, even in principle, lead to absolute knowledge, because "experiment... can never get beyond the natural forces which it itself uses as its means... the last causes of the phenomena of nature no longer appear themselves" (3:276–77). Yet the fundamental *naturphilosophischen* assumptions of an underlying unity and genuine polarities constituting nature seem to have been immensely fruitful as heuristic experimental principles for those scientists influenced by *Naturphilosophie*: for example, H. C. Oersted attributed his discovery of electromagnetism in 1820 to his metaphysical belief in the unity of all natural forces.[35] Similarly, the physicist J. W. Ritter, upon hearing the news of Herschel's discovery of infrared rays beyond the spectrum of visible light, felt that a basic polar symmetry of the spectrum had been violated and that there must thus exist a complement to infrared. Walter Wetzels observes that "the question was never whether it could be found, but only how to detect these new, invisible rays beyond violet which the doctrine of polarity simply demanded.... Ritter proved on 22 February 1801 the existence of ultraviolet rays. Clearly the philosophical concept of polarity had preceded and guided his experiment."[36]

These examples of the practical application of *naturphilosophischen* principles may help to illuminate the way Schelling and those influenced by him came to understand the scientific enterprise: it is increasingly interpretive and respectful of nature's otherness rather than entirely focused on controlling and transforming. In the first book of the *Ideas* the shift of emphasis from metaphors of control and a view of man as an independent actor exerting force on nature to the recognition that all force and strength are in nature to begin with is clear:

> The purest exercise of man's rightful dominion over dead matter, which was bestowed upon him together with reason and freedom, is that he spontaneously operates upon nature, determines her according to purpose and intention, lets her act before his eyes, and as it were spies on her at work. But that the exercise of this dominion is possible, he owes again to

nature, whom he would strive in vain to dominate, if he could not put her in conflict with herself and set her own forces in motion against her. (2:74)

Everything in nature, including ourselves as scientists, is part of an organic totality; therefore knowledge is and always must be partial, because we cannot, as Marx was later to observe in a different context, squat outside the world. This exposes the common mistake behind all metaphors of domination, legislation, or transcendence of nature: lack of awareness of the absolute identity of nature and spirit.

I return to some of the difficulties with the philosophy of identity later; yet it must be briefly acknowledged that the assumption of an ultimate identity of nature and spirit enables Schelling to elevate science to the status of genuine, and not merely instrumental, knowledge. Moreover, it made possible the insight into consciousness as itself a product of opposed forces at every level, and thus paved the way to a concept of the unconscious in which irrational forces were not a conceptual embarrassment or something to be overcome but a necessary and important part of the psychic economy.

The *System* was intended to demonstrate how the opposed unconscious and conscious forces interacted and were related forms of one another. The unconscious is a welter of undetermined forces; consciousness is achieved through inhibition and repression of these forces or activities. The history of the human spirit is a genetic construction which consists of the efforts of spirit to make conscious to itself the levels of activity it has already transcended, rising at last to the creative process and product of the artist, which Schelling is unafraid to stress can never be fully understood.

Thus we see that in Schelling's hands, the concept of the transcendental has come to mean almost the opposite of Kant's definition of it as that which is concerned exclusively with the operations of reason. For Schelling it is the means of coming to know the unconscious depths out of which the conscious self has risen (precisely that which is not immediately accessible to reason):

> The nature of the transcendental mode of apprehension must therefore consist essentially in this, *that even that which in all other thinking, knowing, or acting escapes consciousness and is absolutely non-objective, is therein brought to consciousness and becomes objective; it consists, in short, of a constant objectifying-to-itself of the subjective.* (3:345)

For the Schelling of the *System*, the otherness of nature is neither preordained nor unchanging. The emphasis on unity, especially the unity of man and nature, which will be the focus of the philosophy of identity is already in evidence.

Yet I do not wish to leave the impression that Schelling's approach is better (or, God forbid, more politically correct) only because he does not employ the metaphor of male/female to illustrate the opposition of the ideal to the real, as Kant, Fichte and Hegel, in their different ways, have; or that he is somehow more laudable because he can at least be read as implying that the status of the female (nature) may be raised to equality with the male (reason). These would certainly be significant differences worth taking note of, if that were all that could be said for his views, but what is genuinely revolutionary in Schelling's uses of the metaphor of male/female occurs after the *System*. I want to claim that the logic of the development of his later thought away from idealism and toward, for lack of a more precise term, a more existential focus is reflected in Schelling's recognition of the limits of the previous employment of sexual metaphor, and that he transformed the very terms male and female themselves in ways we now recognize the power and significance of from Schopenhauer, Nietzsche, and Freud.

The essential element of antagonism, or at least opposition, between both real and symbolic males and females so evident in Kant, Fichte, and Hegel gives way in

Schelling's post-*System* works to a stress on both danger and desire. The danger in an inappropriate (it is tempting to say, an unnatural) relation of male and female is evoked in memorable terms in a startling passage from *Of Human Freedom*:

> Modern European philosophy as a whole, from its beginning (in Descartes), has this common flaw: for it, nature does not exist, it lacks a living ground. Spinoza's realism is in this regard as abstract as Leibniz's idealism. Idealism is the soul of philosophy, realism its body. Never can the latter [realism] provide the principle, but it must be the ground and the means in which the former actualizes itself, assumes flesh and blood. . . . Yet wherever the ideal principle actually works its effects to a high degree, while unable to find the reconciling and mediating basis, it generates a turbid, wild enthusiasm that erupts in self-mutilation or—as with the priests of the Phrygian goddess—self-emasculation [*Selbstentmannung*]. (7:356–57)

The danger in containing no real philosophy of nature, in having no genuine relation with the female, is the danger of losing one's own essential nature through self-castration. Thus for Schelling the stakes are incomparably higher than for his contemporaries: he sees masculine identity itself as constituted by the proper relationship to nature (the feminine); moreover, it is an identity that can be lost.[37] Neither the actual female nor her symbolic counterpart has such significance for Kant or Fichte, for whom I would suggest women are not so much the "other" as the "lesser." Hegel does assign femaleness a more important role, at least in the family and the creation of ethical consciousness, yet her power is still clearly inferior to, and circumscribed by, his.

I will discuss only one suggestive passage from the *Stuttgart Lectures* in order to indicate the direction Schelling is now beginning to take. It starts from a distinction reminiscent of Hegel's infamous comment in the

Philosophy of Right about women being analogous to plants whereas men are analogous to animals, yet comes to a vastly different conclusion. Schelling also begins by saying "the indifference of plant and animal . . . is the crowning instance of creation = man. Yet once again the same opposition reappears in the discreteness of gender (woman = plant, man = animal)" (7:453). However, he continues in a way that emphasizes the equal importance of both members of the opposition:

> The mystery of the division of the sexes is nothing other than the presentation of the primordial relation between two principles of which each is real *for itself* and to that extent independent from the other, although it does not and cannot exist without the other. Both this duality which does not exclude identity and this identity which does not exclude duality, are reconciled by *love*. God Himself is reconciled to nature by virtue of a spontaneous love, that is, He is not dependent *on nature* and yet he does not want to exist without her. . . . Of such a kind, then, is also God's *true* relation to nature, that is, not a *unilateral* relation. (7:453)

Nature, and man as a part of nature, are necessary beings: because Schelling so strongly insists on nature's reality in its own right, not as a means to or a primitive stage of something else, he transforms the meaning of the male/female metaphors of both the Enlightenment and of the Romantics. Neither domination and control nor pursuit and capture, but an authentic unity in duality, one which makes the mystery of love possible, is the emerging focus in the later Schelling.

Of Human Freedom and *The Ages of the World* contain startling images of castration, birth, pregnancy, birth, and the longing to give birth that indicate how fundamentally Schelling's view of man's relation to nature has changed. These texts are discussed in detail in the next two chapters; here I wish only to reflect upon how the separation between man and nature has narrowed, and how nature has steadily gained in power, even danger, and significance in Schelling's thought, to the point that many of the idealistic assumptions with which Schelling began his investigations in the philosophy of nature have been seriously undermined from within.

5

The Emergence of the Unconscious

I. The Purpose of the *System*

In the *Differenzschrift* of 1801 Hegel declares himself to be in agreement with Schelling that the most fundamental task of philosophy is to overcome (*aufheben*) the traditional oppositions such as subjectivity and objectivity, reason and sensuality, mind and nature. It has been claimed that Hegel's *Phenomenology of Spirit* of 1807 and Schelling's *System of Transcendental Idealism*[1] (1800) can be fruitfully interpreted as parallel attempts to overcome these oppositions, identified by Hegel as ultimately deriving from the dichotomy between absolute subjectivity and absolute objectivity. Since Schelling claims to present a history of consciousness (retracing the genesis of reason's original self-construction), whereas Hegel intends to demonstrate the history of spirit in its alienation and progress toward knowledge of itself as spirit (the attainment of absolute knowledge), it has often been supposed that the *System* was a preliminary, abortive attempt at the all-inclusive vision the *Phenomenology* claims to provide. Hegel himself seems to have held such a view, yet Schelling vigorously disputes this assessment of the *System* in his "Lectures on the History of Modern Philosophy," delivered in the 1830s (10:95ff.).[2]

Werner Marx has offered a valuable suggestion which facilitates a more nuanced appreciation of Schelling's thought by helping to free him from the long shadow of Hegel. Although he agrees that it is tempting indeed to regard the *Phenomenology* and the *System* as rival attempts to present "the genesis of the same principle, the subject-object identity,"[3] he finds the methods in each work to be dictated by their respective goals. One might say that the ends illuminate the means.

In this chapter I discuss an application of Marx's insight concerning the influence of the goal of the *System* on Schelling's method. Schelling claimed that the aim of the *System* is "setting forth idealism in its full extent" (3:330) by enlarging transcendental idealism into a system of all knowledge. Not only will this effort resolve problems heretofore considered by philosophers to be insoluble (it is not clear which problems Schelling has in mind here), it will, Schelling claims prophetically, generate "entirely new problems, never before considered, and by a general shattering of received opinion give rise to a new sort of truth" (3:329–30). Schelling would accomplish this by presenting every part of philosophy as belonging on a continuum, thereby forming "a progressive history of self-consciousness" (3:331), which would culminate in the proof of the identity of the subject and object in aesthetic consciousness.

Why was Schelling's goal the sort of identity of subject and object which occurs in aesthetic consciousness? The *System* can be described simply as an elaborate proof of the proposition that only aesthetic intuition can provide, in the production of a work of art, the reconciliation *in consciousness* of finite and infinite, conscious and unconscious activities, without assimilating the unconscious to the conscious. Schelling accomplished this in much the same fashion as he overcame the difficulty of accounting for the organic in a mechanistic universe: the higher form is assumed as the most basic; thus the unconscious is a form of consciousness.

I argue that Schelling's method of drawing analogies to the artist and artistic production are best understood in the context of his struggle to do justice to the power of the unconscious. Despite the difficulties it gives rise to, I find that the most enduringly valuable achievement of the *System* is the use it makes of the concept of the unconscious, which expanded the limits of the idealistic understanding of consciousness.[4]

Like Kant and Fichte before him, Schelling wrestled with the paradox that in order for reason to be free and self-determining, it must be its own highest law; yet in order to account for the constraint and irrationality of the world of experience, the workings of the law of reason must be at least partly hidden from us. Therefore the chief task of the *System* was to reconstruct the genesis of the lawlike activities which lie behind the apparently nonrational, to bring the unconscious to consciousness, to demonstrate the ultimate harmony of thought and object. In other words, Schelling thought he was completing the project begun by Kant. In the *System*, Schelling failed to fully accomplish this, which is hardly surprising, as Alan White has noted:

> Writing the 1800 *System*, Schelling believed he had discovered true land beyond Kant's "land of pure understanding"; he was convinced he had found the land Spinoza had sought in vain. Confident of his success, Schelling moves through that land with the eagerness and haste of the conqueror, not with the patience or care of the explorer. It is not surprising, considering both the immensity of Schelling's subject matter and the relative brevity of his treatment of it, that the *System of Transcendental Idealism* does not solve—or even clearly recognize—all the problems that arise within it.[5]

Yet it is the very structure and nature of the failure of this glorious and extravagant attempt at building a system of idealism which was to prove so significant for his later development, as well as for the emergence of that concept of the unconscious with which Freud has been most closely associated.[6]

It might still be said that establishing that the *System* is not a failed *Phenomenology* does not indicate what is of value in it; therefore a brief illustration of the extent and nature of this difference with respect to the treatment of philosophy as a historical process in each may prove instructive. The *Phenomenology* recounts the history of the experience that consciousness has with itself by beginning with the most immediate form of consciousness, namely, sense certainty, and culminating in "the form of spirit that knows itself as spirit."[7] For Hegel, history is the increasingly rational elaboration of the unfolding of absolute spirit as it comes to know itself completely. The process of striving for total self-transparency reaches a resolution only in Hegel's own system of science, which can be seen as the goal and end of that striving, rendering the end of history conceivable, if not actual.

Regardless of one's stance on the meaning of the concept of the end of history in Hegel, it is illuminating to reflect that Schelling's understanding of history (and thus of philosophy) in the *System* is quite different. Hegel's entire philosophical endeavor takes place within the framework of the advance of reason toward complete rationality. However, Schelling presents freedom as a drama uniting freedom and necessity, subjective and objective elements, in a way which is and must remain less than transparent, even to the author of the drama. Thus even history is in a sense a work of art, for in order for freedom to be possible, it must contain more than its author could ever have consciously intended:

> ... if the playwright *were to exist* independently of his drama, we should be merely the actors who speak the lines he has written. If he *does* not exist independently of us, but reveals and discloses himself successively only, through the very play of our own freedom, so that without this freedom even he himself *would not be*, then we are collaborators of the whole and have ourselves invented the particular roles that we play. (3:602)

Thus in order for freedom to be preserved, its ultimate ground can never be wholly revealed. History, as the "self-disclosing revelation of the Absolute" (3:603) can never come to an end or be completed. Without wishing to seem to endorse this transitional concept of history as Schelling's last word on the topic, which it certainly was not, I would like to point to the evidence in even an early work such as the *System* that Schelling's thought on history, art, and philosophy demonstrated an unusual ability to do more than simply acknowledge or accommodate human irrationality—Leibniz had already accomplished as much. The irrational becomes a source of movement and life within the system, yet does not become entirely subsumed into the rational. This is of particular interest in our own time, when the interrelationship of freedom and irrationality can be argued to be an even more central focus for philosophy than it was in Schelling's time.

II. A Clash of Paradigms

Edward G. Ballard has argued that Kant's struggle to make sense of and retain the dignity of human moral experience in a rigorously determined world can best be understood as a gargantuan clash between a body of knowledge (natural science) built upon a mechanistic analogy and the classic tradition of Plato, which has understood the human being as "not reducible to nonhuman elements and in which, on the contrary, nature itself is explained by analogy to the artist."[8] Kant's effort to understand how human values are attainable and possible in a determined physical universe therefore leads him "to hold that the doctrines in philosophy derived from both the mechanistic analogy and the artist analogy are coherent and possible within the same intellectual framework."[9] One way to understand Schelling's complex relation to Kant is to see him as having taken what Ballard calls the "artist analogy" more seriously than Kant could or would.

In his early works, before his interest in the philosophy of nature had been aroused, Schelling did little more than act on Kantian hints, such as the suggestion in section II of the introduction to the *Critique of Judgment*, in which Kant speaks cautiously of the *possibility* of a supersensible basis of unity of the laws of nature and of human nature (i.e., freedom):

> ... it must be possible to think of nature as being such that the lawfulness in its form will harmonize with at least the possibility of [achieving] the purposes that we are to achieve in nature according to the laws of freedom. So there must after all be a basis *uniting* the supersensible that underlies nature and the supersensible that the concept of freedom contains practically, even though the concept of this basis does not reach cognition of it whether theoretically or practically and hence does not have a domain of its own, though it does make possible the transition from our way of thinking in terms of principles of nature to our way of thinking in terms of principles of freedom.[10]

Although Kant allows only for the possibility of an intuitive understanding which would be able to overcome the discursiveness of reason (as if, as George di Giovanni has observed, "the metaphysics not possible for man were still possible for God"),[11] Schelling found this basis to be a *necessary* one and known to intellectual intuition, as he argues at length in the "Letters" (1795).

The second Kantian hint is to be found in Kant's views on the significance of organic nature. Like Kant in the "Critique of Teleological Judgment," Schelling realizes that the evidence of order in nature at every level, but especially the organic, cannot be attributed solely to the self who is perceiving nature. Kant admits that the study of organisms, which "ought to be studied according to the principles of the mere mechanism of nature," compels our reason "to conceive of a different principle from that of natural mechanism as the ground of possibility of certain forms in nature."[12] This principle will prove to be "the works of art of man";[13] Schelling rescues this observation from the footnote Kant has hidden it in and makes it a central principle of his transcendental idealism.[14] More radical than Kant, Schelling is willing to see nature itself as somehow rational and orderly and possessed, in Walter Schulz's words, of *analoga* to spirit.[15] The *kind* of rationality exhibited by natural phenomena puzzled Schelling for many years. As I argued above, his willingness to see nature as an "author" and his comparisons of the scientist and the poet, illuminating as they are, also point to the ultimate unknowability of nature. Even the most fruitful analogy implies a remainder of irreducible difference.[16]

When Schelling describes the period of the composition of the *System* in the "Lectures on the History of Modern Philosophy," he stresses the fundamentally different intent of his philosophy from that of Fichte. It was indeed Fichte, he admits, who demonstrated the importance of the self for philosophy, but Fichte had not found it either necessary or possible to show how the representation of nature as an external, independent realm is *necessary* to consciousness. Without such a proof, consciousness and its structure must remain of primary importance, as indeed they did for Fichte. Schelling, in contrast, saw himself as revealing the true significance of the philosophy of nature in the *System* by means of a transcendental history of the self:

> I sought, therefore, in a word, to explain the inseparable connection of the self with the external world represented by it as necessary by means of a transcendental past of this self, preceding *real* or empirical consciousness [with] an explanation which then led to a transcendental history of the self. And thereby the tendency toward the historical already betrayed itself in my first steps in philosophy . . . (10:93f.)

This transcendental history of the self coming to consciousness of itself (*der zu sich gekommenen Ich*) through unconscious nature and thereby becoming its own object led to Schelling's discovery that the self, properly understood, must contain both subject and object, both the conscious and unconscious. The *System*, in Schelling's mature reading of it at least, presents the process as "a fully immanent one, in which the self is occupied only with itself, with its own self-posited contradiction [of being] at once subject and object, finite and infinite"[17] (10:97).

It will be recalled that the connection between representation and object was ultimately explained in the "Treatises" by showing nature to be "the history of our spirit" (1:383), although perhaps prehistory would be more accurate. In search of a principle of identity to ground knowledge, the Schelling of the "Treatises" found that "the only example of an absolute identity of representation and object is found *within ourselves*" (1:366), in self-intuition. However, speculation about problems in the philosophy of nature produced changes in Schelling's understanding of the way in which we come to be aware of this principle of identity. In the early works it is still an awareness of almost Cartesian clarity and distinctness, an inner sight or *Tiefsinn* which owed much to Jacobi and Spinoza. However, in the speculation of *On the World Soul* about an ultimate ground of unity for all of nature, the bounds of the individual finite consciousness have already been exceeded. This tendency is still more pronounced in hints in the "Introduction to the Sketch" about the necessity of a substrate for nature. "The first postulate of the science of nature is an opposition in the pure identity of nature. This opposition must be completely purely thought, [and] not as having some substrate other than activity; for it is the condition of all substrates" (3:308). This substrate is also called the indifference of the original duality of nature's activities—an indifference never achieved but constantly striven for. Similarly, since self-consciousness requires an awareness of a not-self, that state prior to self-consciousness is a kind of psychic indifference point—a stage of spirit's

The Emergence of the Unconscious

activity of which the philosopher can become only retroactively aware.

It was, therefore, only the preceding years of intense study of the philosophy of nature which made it possible for Schelling to arrive at the point of view with which the *System* begins:

> ... the problem [of the concurrence of subject and object] only requires an explanation of the concurrence as such, and leaves it completely open as to where explanation starts from, as to which it should make primary and which secondary.—Yet since the two opposites are mutually necessary to one another, the result of the operation is bound to be the same, whichever point we set out from. (3:342)

Our certainty that our presentations coincide with objects outside them is the most fundamental of what Schelling calls the primordial prejudices; indeed, this presupposition underlies all experience and science. On the other hand, we are equally certain that our representations (thought) can be efficacious in the real world, and that certain modifications of reality are our doing. "In a word, for certainty in theory, we lose it in practice, and for certainty in practice we lose it in theory; it is impossible that both our knowledge should contain truth and our volition reality" (3:347). This problem demands a solution neither theoretical nor practical philosophy can provide. Our ability to know nature and yet dictate to nature points toward an ultimate identity of thinking and willing; therefore there must be "an identity of the non-conscious activity that has brought forth nature, and the conscious activity expressed in willing, without its being decided where the principle of this activity belongs, whether in nature or in ourselves" (3:348).

The ultimate identity from the point of view of transcendental philosophy in the *System* is in "an absolute that is both cause and effect of itself—in the absolute identity of the subjective and the objective, which we call nature, and which in its highest potentiality is again nothing but self-consciousness" (3:356). The assumption that self-consciousness must be the basis of all knowledge is claimed both to require no proof and to prove itself, because results are obtained with it as first principle which no other principle can produce. At this point the reasoning takes a curious turn. Schelling has been arguing that we seek to ground the system of our knowledge on that which is most certain to us; and he continues:

> undoubtedly that which determines everything in my knowledge is the knowledge of *myself*—Since I seek to ground my knowledge only *in itself*, I do not ask further as to the ultimate ground of this primary knowledge (self-consciousness), which, if it exists, must necessarily lie *outside* knowledge. Self-consciousness is the lamp of the whole system of knowledge, but it casts its light ahead only, not behind. (3:357)[18]

This passage is significant for its indication that self-consciousness is a kind of one-way street that we cannot turn back on or retrace our steps on. As will be seen in what follows, Schelling finds there to be an element of irreducible facticity in the not-self, or unconscious, which will prove to be a key element contributing to the instability of the *System* as a whole. Even more significantly, it signals the emergence of an emphasis on the nonrationality of the unconscious; whereas nonconscious nature had been assumed, in the *naturphilosophischen* works, to be ruled by a rationality we do not yet understand, here in the *System* Schelling is beginning to explore the possibility that the nonconscious may be *intrinsically* nonrational. Even some of the reflections on "speculative physics" had featured claims about ultimate or primordial givens in nature, points beyond which the scientist could not hope to go: for example, the argument in the "Introduction to the Sketch" that all knowledge of nature depends upon prior acceptance of a "primordial sundering [*Entzweiung*] in nature itself" led to the conclusion that all scientific explanations finally only reduce every natural entity "to that primordial antithesis of innermost nature, *which does not itself appear*" (3:288).

This realization is reflected in the changes in the concept of intellectual intuition in the *System*; it is *not* defined as a means of access to an undefined absolute, as it was in the earlier works, but as *constitutive* of the self, which is a "permanent intellectual intuition" (3:370), and therefore the only form of insight into the self's activity. Intellectual intuition is constitutive of the self in two ways. It comes into being for itself as producing itself, and it is also that which is produced. That is why there is an original and ineradicable duality in the identity of the self: it "is at once cause and effect of itself, producer and product, subject and object" (3:373). Schelling finds it significant that nature, too, is simultaneously productive and produced, "and the fundamental duality in nature is itself ultimately explicable only inasmuch as nature is taken to be an intelligence" (3:373). Intellectual intuition is the only avenue of access to the unconscious activities of the self; and the self only knows itself as active—as productive of a world. This, as Freud was to make a life's work of discovering, means that we must become skilled at finding traces of the unconscious in the conscious production to which we have access.

Schelling considers himself to have proven that all reality which can be reality for the self must arise in and through self-consciousness, but this alone does not complete the system of transcendental idealism. It

> ... continues to leave unanswered the question: how, then, is the entire system of knowledge (e.g., the objective world, with all its determinations, history, etc.) posited through the self? It can be demonstrated, indeed to the most obstinate dogmatists, that the world consists only in representations; but full conviction only comes upon completion of the

mechanism of its emergence from the inner principle of mental activity. (3:378)

The nature of the self is thus both the first and the last concern of transcendental philosophy, and as we shall see, the relation of this self to its absolute ground. Schelling had already struggled in the philosophy of nature with the dogmatic concept of nature as an inert, static stuff, impenetrable to mind and utterly heterogenous to it. The *System* can be viewed as an elaborate proof of the proposition that the only being accessible to spirit, the only being knowable to us (because constructed by us), must be the self's free activity. Freedom is therefore the ground of being: "The beginning and end of this philosophy is *freedom*, the absolute indemonstrable, authenticated only through itself.—Being, in our system, is merely *freedom suspended*" (3:376).

III. Paradoxes in the *System*

As was discussed in the preceding section, Schelling's focus on the unconscious reflected his awareness that irrationality and incompleteness were the unavoidable results of the self's struggle to know itself. Rather than a smooth progression from ignorance to enlightenment, knots of actuality and unresolved puzzles were found. A brief survey of Schelling's method will illustrate some of the difficulties he encountered in his detailed exposition of the relation of self and world.

At the most basic level, the principle of an ultimate dualism of principles is expressed as a permanent conflict in the self as subject = object. The opposition of subject and object in the self must be an *absolute* one, or the activity of unification would not be continuous, necessary, and involuntary. Using a kind of argument first employed in the discussion of organic construction as a model (*Sinnbild*) of the original construction of nature in "Introduction to the Sketch" (3:306–12), Schelling claims:

The Emergence of the Unconscious 131

> If we conceive the objective self (the thesis) as absolute *reality*, its opposite will have to be absolute *negation*. But absolute reality, just because it is absolute, is not reality, and both opposites are thus in their opposition merely ideal. If the self is to be real, that is, to become an object to itself, reality must be blotted out in it, that is, it must cease to be absolute reality . . . if the opposite is to become real, it must cease to be absolute negation. If both are to become real they must, as it were, share out the reality between them. (3:394)

It is the history of this "sharing out of reality," its laws and structure, which philosophy deals with.

The general idea is clear enough: the philosopher charts the progression which is the infinite and necessary producing of the self. However, a rationally inexplicable paradox insinuates itself into the argument at this point when the question of the *original* act which sets the process in motion is considered. This act is truly one of origination, indeed of creation ex nihilo, if we are to take Schelling at his word: "Why the self should have originally become aware of itself, is not further explicable, for it *is* nothing else but self-consciousness" (3:392). The self has its being in its unending effort to resolve the opposition of subject and object in it, which is only mediated by the self of self-consciousness, the subject = object.

A related puzzle concerns the temporality of the self. The subject = object, which is beyond limitation, is eternal (3:369); how, then, does it break into the time series as a particular finite self? Schelling's revealing answer is that it must be *arbitrary*:

> Anyone who perceives at all that the self arises only through its own acting, will also perceive that, through the arbitrary action in the midst of the time series, by which alone the self arises, nothing else can arise for me save what comes about for me originally and beyond all time. (3:396)

It will be recalled that Schelling holds that the self both limits itself and comes into being for itself through self-intuition; therefore to be intuited and to have being are one and the same (3:389–90). As he argued in the "Treatises," if the role of intuition as the highest (because most immediate) element in knowledge is acknowledged, philosophy will become more than a mere play of abstractions. The essence of self-intuition is that it is productive (of the self as an object for itself); and all productive intuition is still based on an *immediate* cognition.

What is the source of the immediacy so unmistakably peculiar to sensation? The discussion of this issue in the "Treatises" seemed to be moving in the direction of a hybrid of Kant's view of the self as capable of at least regulative teleological judgments and Jacobi's naive realism: "'The principle of the sensible cannot itself lie in the supersensible' according to Kant, as have all the philosophers before him and of his time Jacobi best and most clearly expressed" (1:406). Schelling held Kant's concept of the thing in itself to be a symbol for the supersensible substrate. Any other interpretation would be an "improper idealism, a system, that is, which turns all knowledge into illusion . . . one which eliminates all immediacy in our cognition, e.g., by positing external originals independent of our presentations" (3:427). Rather than this empiricism of shadows, Schelling characterizes the best knowledge, indeed the most perfect realism, as that which

> cognizes things in themselves and immediately[;] it is possible only in an order which perceives in things its own reality merely, confined by its own activity. For such an order, as the indwelling soul of things, would permeate them as its own immediate organism and—just as the master has the most perfect knowledge of his work—would fathom the inner mechanism from the first. (3:428)

Here again, if Schelling may be forgiven the rare lapse into praise of 'mechanism' which he so frequently rails against in other writers, the broad outline of the system can be grasped. It is interesting to see how themes are employed which were first developed in the philosophy of nature, such as the idea of the soul of things as an organism, the view of all realities as in essence activities, and particularly the notion of a law-governed spirit fathoming the world by means of laws which mirror its own organization. Yet the detailed deductions yield surprisingly nonrational results. There appears to be a certain stubbornness in the world's organization: Schelling finds that the self limits the thing, and the thing limits the self, but that their common limit cannot lie any more in one than in the other. He concludes: "Since the ground of the limit lies neither in self nor thing, it lies nowhere; it exists absolutely because it exists, and it is as it is because that is how it is" (3:425).

It is not clear how disturbing Schelling finds such conclusions, since his notion of the self is repeatedly stated to be that of an identity in constant contradiction with itself, an oscillation of the subject = object between the self and the thing in itself (3:392; 3:346). It is the self's nature to be constantly producing, and to the degree that there is reality in the self, the thing is negated, and vice versa. Limitations, and hence production, are the inevitable consequences of the original (and arbitrary) emergence of the self into the time series, and the tendency of the self to become an object for itself. But the *manner* of this limitation "*is the one thing that philosophy can neither conceive nor explain*" (3:410). We as philosophers can only employ intellectual intuition to reconstruct the original series of the self-constituting acts of the self of self-consciousness, and we accept the results when we find that the self which produces itself in self-intuition is not accessible to consciousness, and that therefore in producing itself the self limits itself by transferring reality to the object preconsciously. The conscious self is capable only of recognizing an immediacy in cognition, which is the source of both reality and its own activity, transformed into the object.

Schelling's test of any system is its ability to explain experience; and an obvious strength of the arguments of the *System* is their acknowledgement that a consciousness which consists of nothing but self-transparency cannot explain the reality of the external world, for it can never make plausible the connection of mind with a thoroughly nonmental reality. (This is the import of Schelling's claim in the "Treatises" that Hume is more consistent than Kant, for Hume at least honestly admits that it is a mystery how objects affect either one another or us.) The distinction, common to all philosophy, between inner and outer experience, cannot be explained other than by postulating an ultimate ground of unity, which has turned out to imply the positing of a "region of consciousness where this separation *does not yet exist*" (3:428). What Schelling means here by "a region of consciousness" is mental activity which is not conscious—the paradox central to the *System* as a whole. Schelling feels that this unconscious consciousness will be accepted by all those who realize they already recognize and acknowledge its workings in another kind of production in which freedom and necessity are in harmony, that is, artistic production.

> Anyone, e.g., for whom in all the activity of the mind there is nowhere anything unconscious, and no region outside of that of consciousness, will no more understand how the intelligence can forget itself in its products, than how the artist can be lost in his work. (3:430)

Yet Schelling had earlier argued that the "beginning and end" of his philosophy was freedom, and that the only being accessible to spirit is the self's free activity (3:376); now it gradually emerges that the self's activity includes an unconscious element—to which there is some kind of not entirely conscious access, at least in the case of the artist and his production. Just as daunting is the discovery that the "lamp of self-consciousness casts its light ahead only, not behind" (3:357); thus it is *in principle* impossible to know the self or why it originally became aware of itself (3:392). Some of these tensions are addressed in the aesthetic idealism (discussed below) developed at the end of the *System*. However, the appearance of these anomalies in the concept of the self, so central to the entire economy of the *System*, makes it difficult to see the *System* as simply one more ambitious attempt at what White calls Schelling's lifelong "single project," namely, "the development of a system of freedom."[19]

IV. Aesthetic Idealism

Schelling plunged into the philosophy of nature by way of attacks on the self-proclaimed Kantians and their mistaken doctrines of the thing in itself, their dogmatic concept of matter, and their mechanical model of the world. In opposition to dogmatism, he strove to show how it might be possible to render all levels of nature comprehensible by means of the same pattern Fichte had described in the *Science of Knowledge* as most fundamental to consciousness: the interaction and equilibrium of opposed activities. It then remained only for the parallelism of the philosophy of nature and transcendental philosophy to be demonstrated in the *System*. In other words, the presentation of the construction of the system of nature had been accomplished; all that was needed for a complete system of philosophy was the complementary deduction of the process of the emergence of the individual self. Some of the difficulties that deduction proved to be fraught with were discussed in the preceding section.

Intellectual intuition, or the philosopher's reconstruction of the history of self-consciousness, reveals to us that the only in-itself is that producing of the self which is not at the same time conscious of itself (3:390); but though the role once played by the thing in itself has been replaced by unconscious production, it does not appear that we are any closer to the absolute which is the ground and being of all than was the case in the *natur-*

philosophischen works. The main body of the *System*, encumbered as it is by internal inconsistency, does not succeed in presenting an intelligible theory of the relation of self and absolute, but the final sections on teleology and the philosophy of art do provide some provisional answers to these questions.

It is only now, at this decidedly late stage in his investigations, that Schelling concedes that the philosophy of nature cannot fully illuminate the nature of the absolute, for the identity of the nonconscious production of nature and conscious production has not yet been decisively proven. In direct contrast to the viewpoint of the philosophy of nature writings, Schelling no longer finds it possible even in principle to find such an identity in nature: "The objective world is simply the original, as yet unconscious poetry of the spirit; the universal organon of philosophy—and the keystone of its entire arch—*is the philosophy of art*" (3:349).

The philosophy of art will provide Schelling with both an instance of, and an insight into, the sought-after identity of conscious and nonconscious producing. Though nature can be presented as a system and understood as the product of the self's activity, the individual finite self does not produce nature. However, the lesson learned from the philosophy of nature was that nature's productivity can best be understood nonmechanically, as ultimately the product of intelligence.

> Nature, in its blind and mechanical purposiveness, admittedly represents to me an original identity of conscious and unconscious activities, but [for all that] it does not present this identity to me as one whose ultimate goal rests *in the self itself*. . . . Now the aim of *our whole science* was in fact *precisely* this, of explaining how the ultimate ground of the harmony between subjective and objective becomes an object to the *self itself*. (3:610)

The philosopher of nature can reveal that the identity of unconscious and conscious producing in the purposive product of nature is structurally similar to the original opposition out of which consciousness arises, but the individual self is not aware of this similarity. If an intuition could be found in which the self was simultaneously unconscious and conscious *for itself*, in which intelligence produced for itself, then "by such an intuition . . . we [could] also resolve the entire [the supreme] problem of transcendental philosophy (that of explaining the congruence between subjective and objective)" (3:347–48).

Part Six is entitled "Deduction of a Universal Organ of Philosophy, or: Essentials of the Philosophy of Art According to the Principle of Transcendental Idealism." Schelling remarks that a system is completed when it is led back to its starting point. Both the philosophy of nature and transcendental idealism depend upon intellectual intuition, which alone can reach the ground of all harmony between the subjective and the objective. The philosophy of nature at best deciphers the unconscious poetry of the spirit "lying pent in a mysterious and wonderful script" (3:628). Theoretical philosophy passes over at its highest point into practical philosophy in the absolute act of will, which is conscious; yet as directed to something external, it must presuppose something opposed to it, and hence not accessible to consciousness (3:633–34).

Yet philosophy must start from an absolute which is an identical principle. It therefore remains to be shown how intellectual intuition can reveal an identity to the self in consciousness, or make the unconscious conscious. Intellectual intuition is self-intuition: its essence is in the activity of objectifying itself to itself, a process which can only end in a complete self-intuition (which for Schelling is the aesthetic intuition of the genius). Art successfully captures what philosophy can never hope to show, namely the unconscious element in acting and producing, and its original identity with the conscious. Art is paramount to the philosopher, precisely because it opens to him, as it were, the holy of holies, as if in a single flame, that which in nature and history is rent asunder, and in life and action, no less than in thought, must forever fly apart (3:627–28).

All of transcendental philosophy is a depiction of the progress of self-intuition as it raises itself to increasingly higher powers, of which the highest is the aesthetic. It alone is capable of grasping, in an intuition unmediated by concepts, the identity of conscious and unconscious activity, the union of freedom and necessity, and the infinite contained in the finite which are the essence of art (and which have elsewhere been established as characterizations of the absolute). *How* this is possible cannot be grasped, but only symbolized; the union of freedom and necessity in a finite product can be explained only "by means of the obscure concept of *genius* . . . or, since genius is only possible in the arts, the *product of art*" (3:613).

Yet Schelling would go on to develop a concept of scientific genius in the "Lectures on the Method of University Studies" of 1802; although it is quite clear that he is speaking of an entirely conscious process, there nevertheless seems to be an intuitive element in all scientific insight as well:

> The ability to see everything, including the individual discipline, in connection with the original whole depends upon one's ability to work in the individual discipline with intelligence and that higher inspiration called scientific genius. Every thought that cannot be incorporated into this active, living whole is . . . dead matter to be eliminated sooner or later—such is the law of all living organisms, and certainly there are also too many sexless bees in the hive of science, who, since they cannot be productive, keep churning out as inorganic excretions the many expressions of their stupidity. (5:217)

The vivid comparison of sexual and scientific productivity might seem merely odd in this context, but it returns as a central theme in *Of Human Freedom*, where metaphors of birth and desire are prominent.

Art, like all other production, proceeds from a contradiction; but unlike all other production, it resolves the contradiction into an infinite harmony, producing a feeling of tranquillity.[20] It is already obvious from the "testimony of all artists" that "it can only be the contradiction between conscious and unconscious in the free act which sets the artistic urge in motion; just as conversely, it can be given to art alone to pacify our endless striving, and likewise to resolve the final and uttermost contradiction within us" (3:614).

Art is the result of activity which reproduces the essence of the absolute; therefore aesthetic intuition is the only means of unveiling the identity at the basis of being. The expression of the self in art reveals for a moment the kinship of the individual self with the infinite producing of the absolute; only genius can produce an infinity concentrated in a finite product.

This briefly describes the path by which Schelling's desire to unearth and reconstruct the transcendental past for a self whose existence is a conflict and a contradiction led him to an emphasis on the unconscious (and ultimately arbitrary and irrational aspects of the self). That such a self might ever come to know itself completely either theoretically or practically is finally seen to be impossible, and Schelling finds the highest self-knowledge and culmination of the *System* in the creativity of the artist. In the work of art—and only there—is the dichotomy between conscious and unconscious production overcome.

I am in firm agreement with Werner Marx in his claim that the common disparagement of Schelling's aesthetic idealism as a *Verlegenheitslösung* (solution for lack of any other) is unjustified and "measure[s] Schelling's basic notions according to the standard of Hegel's basic notion, that of 'the concept' of absolute reflection."[21] I have shown that Schelling's earliest attempts to develop an understanding of nature which did not fall into a Fichtean one-sidedness are informed by an originally Kant-inspired attempt to find *analoga* between conscious and unconscious production. Schelling began the *System* by stressing that he takes nature seriously as an independent reality: "it forms no part of the conception of nature that there should be something intelligent to represent it. Nature, it seems, would be, even if there were no one aware of it" (3:340). Similarly, he admits that just as nature's ultimate ground may not be accessible to intelligence beyond a certain point, our own self-consciousness is at bottom a prejudice—something beyond which human reason cannot go.

> There is nothing immediately certain except the affirmation that I am, which as it loses all meaning outside of immediate consciousness, is the most individual of all truths, and the absolute prejudice, which must be assumed if anything else is to be certain. (3:344)

The body of the *System* demonstrates the implications of these acknowledgments of the inability of reason to fully comprehend the ground of the being either of nature *or* of the self. Only in the work of art are the oppositions between intelligence and nature, subjective and objective, conscious and unconscious even temporarily overcome. The logic of Schelling's analogies with artistic production have allowed him to preserve at least an element of freedom in reason, history, and the self, if the power and irreducible mystery of the ground out of which they arise is respected.

Here also we begin to appreciate the magnitude of the task Schelling has set for himself as he begins to grow away from his idealistic origins after 1800 and struggle increasingly directly with the implications of his discovery of the unconscious. The significance of the nonrational for the entire project of metaphysical system building and idealism itself would become a *Verhängnis* for Schelling, as Karl Jaspers expressed it: that this nonrationality is present even within the self is nowhere more clear than in *Of Human Freedom*.

6

Of Human Freedom

I. The Idealism of Freedom

Since Schelling lived—and worked—for another forty-five years after the publication of *Of Human Freedom* (*Philosophische Untersuchungen über das Wesen der menschlichen Freiheit und die damit zusammenhängenden Gegenstände*) in 1809, it may seem peculiar that it was his last major published work save for the polemical essay directed against Jacobi in 1811. Frederick de Wolfe Bolman speculates that the negative public reception of the freedom essay as well as a growing sense of isolation from the philosophical world of his day may have combined to make Schelling reluctant to expose his next work, *The Ages of the World*, which he called his "favorite child," to the same hostility.[1] There are a number of ways in which *Of Human Freedom* is only a beginning, a first step toward those concerns which were to occupy Schelling for the rest of his life, and it is as a first step away from idealism that it is often read. However, the many valuable insights and anticipations of contemporary philosophical concerns contained in *Of Human Freedom* remain rootless, isolated flashes of brilliance without an appreciation of the sense in which this treatise is also an end, a final reckoning with some of the central preoccupations of Schelling's youth, and an abdication from idealism itself. This is the perspective from which I regard *Of Human Freedom*: a perspective that brings together the concerns of the earlier chapters and shows how, if not always why, Schelling pushed beyond the constraints of idealism. What was he working toward?

We may be spared some confusion if we briefly consider Hegel's well-known dismissal of the significance of *Of Human Freedom*: "Schelling has made known a single treatise on Freedom. It is of a deep speculative nature, but it stands alone. In philosophy a single piece cannot be developed." And we will also consider Heidegger's reply to it: "These words of Hegel show . . . the limitation of his judgment. Hegel didn't see that just this single thing, freedom, was not single for Schelling, but was thought and developed as the essential foundation of the whole, as a new foundation for a whole philosophy."[2] That is, whatever Schelling was after, the understanding of human freedom was indisputably central to it: and this way of looking at his task already suffices to show his profound dissatisfaction with the theories of freedom of both Kant and Fichte. Among recent writers, Alan White is the most willing to take Schelling at his word when he declares as early as 1795 and as late as 1827 that his goal was to construct "a system of freedom" which would be "the complete antithesis to Spinoza."[3] Is *Of Human Freedom* an attempt at a *system* of freedom, as White and others contend?[4] I will argue that it is not, for its most central and profound arguments cast a deeply ambiguous light on the very desire to construct systems; however, these same arguments do reveal unprecedented insights into the utterly fundamental importance of human freedom, as Heidegger promises.

More successful as a characterization of the focus of *Of Human Freedom*, in my view, is Heidegger's phrase "the idealism of freedom." This expression at least has the merit of reminding the reader of Schelling's own assessment of the goal of the treatise: to discredit the Cartesian dichotomy of nature and spirit (with its relegation of freedom to the realm of spirit alone) and replace it with the opposition of necessity and freedom. Schelling's dynamic philosophy of nature has prepared us to recognize the kinship of the preconscious forces in nature with the consciousness of man (itself the product of unconscious forces); thus there are degrees of necessity and freedom in both nature and spirit, and we begin to see how an idealism of freedom may be possible. That there is no freedom in nature is seen to be as false an oversimplification as the claim that man is always free.

There are four main themes or ideas, all touched upon in earlier chapters, which emerge again in *Of Human Freedom*. From a chronological point of view the first, or oldest, is Schelling's critique of the Enlightenment and his antagonism to Jacobi; indeed, in its best-known form this set of problems continues beyond the scope of *Of Human Freedom*, finally erupting into the Schelling-Jacobi controversy of 1811-12, which was the occasion of Schelling's last publication, the vituperative *Memorial on the Divine Things (Denkmal der Schrift von den Göttlichen Dingen)*.[5] There are many aspects of Schelling's critique of the Enlightenment, and certainly his suspicion of the false clarity of its pseudo-scientific style is one of the most evident; it stands alone as a brilliant anticipation of Nietzsche's attack on the religion of science. However, the relative lack of sustained argumentation, especially in the early essays, makes it difficult to know exactly how to weight the importance of his various criticisms: on balance, I find that his attacks on the Enlightenment view of reason are the most fruitful. Still, what is decried and cast aside must also be replaced, and Schelling's own view of reason is often anything but clear. It could be argued, although Schelling does not do so explicitly, that reasoning about the limits of reason is bound to produce paradoxes; but it is not that alone. It is pressing against the limitations of systematic philosophy itself which affects Schelling's style as well as every other aspect of *Of Human Freedom*.

The second theme that Schelling repeatedly returns to, that of the proper understanding of nature, also grows out of his quarrel with the Enlightenment: in particular, with the mechanistic worldview of its scientists. Indeed, Schelling goes so far as to claim in the introduction that *Of Human Freedom* is intended as a complement to the philosophy of nature (7:334). If, in his view, idealism is not grounded in "a vital realism" (7:356), it will be as empty and abstract as any dogmatic system. In a direct reference to Fichte, Schelling remarks pointedly that "God is more of a reality than a mere moral world-order, and he has in him quite other and more vital activating powers than the barren subtlety abstract idealists ascribe to him" (7:356). A philosophy of nature worthy of the name would provide the indispensable insights into these powers that a mechanistic science must forever remain incapable of generating.

The third important complex of problems has to do with the puzzles of individuality which were discussed in connection with the Sunday's child paradox (chapter 2) and Schelling's concept of genius (chapter 4). Schelling had always been drawn to the concept of the self as the most perspicuous means of symbolizing the connection and balance of forces which constitute reality, and the evolution of his views on the self and the intellectual intuition which he for a time claimed to be its most essential activity is as complicated as it is fascinating. Here in *Of Human Freedom* he reaps the benefit of those earlier studies and produces a nuanced and profound answer to this question in its most poignant form: what is it to be human? Here Schelling completes the evolution of his thought on this central question, moving from a concept of the self to the idea of personality, and this advance, together with his views on the relation between divine and human personality, provide some of the most difficult and thought-provoking passages in the treatise.

The mention of personality, which is usually associated with consciousness, brings to mind the fourth and final theme discussed in earlier chapters, that of the unconscious and the philosophy of identity. It is more than open to question whether any real progress beyond the *System of Transcendental Idealism* has been made; indeed the changes have been so great that to speak of continuity is perhaps more misleading than helpful. Still, it may be very generally observed that the catchall of slumbering forces which was the hazily characterized unconscious of the *System* has been replaced by something much more definite—almost *too* definite—but at least as puzzling: the concept of will as primordial being. I am here speaking of a structural similarity. What Michael Vater has called "the opaque knot of actuality"[6] of sheer givenness, insofar as it applied to the self, was eventually given a name in the *System*: the "unconscious." That we never come to know with any precision what the unconscious consisted of was, explained albeit unsatisfactorily, by the transitional role of the *System*, and Schelling was too honest a thinker not to have recognized the problems the very notion of the unconscious created. It was his struggle with these problems that led to the formulation of a more fundamental problem—*the* fundamental problem: what is the nature of being?

I contend that Schelling does have an answer to this question in *Of Human Freedom*, and that it is best understood not as a rejection of what has gone before but as its culmination. This view is of course not original with me. It is perhaps Heidegger who has most often been quoted in refutation of those (beginning with Hegel) who claim Schelling conducted his philosophical education in public and was given to frequent changes of standpoint: "The truth is that there was seldom a thinker who fought so passionately ever since his earliest periods for his one and unique standpoint."[7] However, even those who quote this statement approvingly do not always agree on what Schelling's unique standpoint was. Heidegger himself is not entirely clear on this score: although he stresses Schelling's dedication to the metaphysics of being and credits him with the courage to face the implications of basing all reality on an *Ungrund*, or groundless, he also insists that Schelling was unable or unwilling to entirely free himself from the logic of the idealistic worldview.

I find that the contribution made by Schelling to the question of the enigma of being is most aptly captured in Joseph Lawrence's phrase "*die Unvordenklichkeit des*

Seins."[8] It is characteristic of German idealism to claim that the absolute is the proper object of the science of philosophy; the unsettling message of *Of Human Freedom* is that the Absolute is not completely accessible to reason. Moreover, this is not an obstacle which might conceivably be overcome by some future philosopher: the opacity and resistance to reason of being is part of its essence. Schelling had struggled with the implications of the nonrationality of being in his philosophy of nature and in the *System*, but these difficulties were not a central focus. In *Of Human Freedom*, the acknowledgment of the reality of evil presents the most radical challenge conceivable to systematic philosophy. Schelling's handling of that challenge is what sets him apart from every other thinker of his time, and it is what forces him ultimately to produce a devastating critique of what he later calls negative philosophy, that is, a philosophy which can grasp only what is understandable in terms of concepts.

II. Difficulties

The delicate and precarious position occupied by *Of Human Freedom* as a sort of farewell to idealism written by one who had entertained the highest hopes for the future of idealism in his youth has been noted. Many of the difficulties of understanding and appreciating this work arise from this internal tension. No less important are the difficulties engendered by Schelling's rejection of the Enlightenment norms of clarity and distinctness and his embrace of an intentionally obscure style, as well as his increasing use of allusive and metaphorical arguments, some taken from the theosophical tradition in which he had become interested several years before. The question of the significance for Schelling of Jakob Böhme in particular is a vexed one, to say the least; I agree with Wilhelm Wieland, who in 1956 noted tartly that the "appalling custom" of explaining Schelling with reference with the supposed influence of Böhme "has made a thoughtful appreciation of these matters much more difficult, if not impossible."[9] There is the additional difficulty of explaining a little-known thinker in terms of one still less well known, particularly in the English-speaking world. However, Robert F. Brown has provided a careful comparison of the evolution of the thought of Böhme and Schelling which addresses these questions without making exaggerated claims on the issue of direct influence.[10]

It is clear, given Schelling's rather grumpy remarks in the preface, that he feels himself to have been widely misunderstood, both by his opponents and by "so-called self-constituted followers" (7:334). He admits that these misapprehensions may be due to the incompleteness and fragmentary nature of his system and hopes that this treatise will "serve to overcome many a prejudice" (7:335). However, the opponents and self-appointed followers are put on notice (in a footnote) that he is practicing what Alan White calls "conscious esotericism."[11] "Many things could have been defined more precisely and kept less informal; many things could more expressly have been saved from misinterpretation. The author failed to do so in part purposely. Whoever cannot accept it from him in this way, or does not wish to, had better take nothing from him at all . . . " (7:410 n).

Another kind of deliberate obscurity is introduced by the use of theosophical language, in particular the frequent use of anthropomorphic language with respect to the absolute, most frequently referred to as God. Given Schelling's repeated assertion that an adequate philosophy of nature is vital to the understanding of the true meaning of human evil—indeed, that the characteristic insufficiency of rationalism is the short shrift it gives to nature—his defense in *The Ages of the World* of his preference for theosophical terms takes on new significance:

> [Theosophy] has just as much advantage in depth, fullness and vitality of content over . . . philosophy as the real object has over its image, nature over its representation; and of course the two become incomparably disparate if a dead philosophy seeking

the essence of things in forms and concepts is taken for comparison. Therefore the preference of the inwardly disposed for theosophy, is just as easily explained as a preference for nature in contrast to art. (8:204)

A third source of potential difficulty is tied to Schelling's heavy reliance on metaphor and analogical argument. It is misleading, not to mention prosaic, to speak of Schelling's three central metaphors—of birth (and the longing to give birth), of disease, and of personality as if they were regrettable departures from a properly abstract and rigorous standard of argument. In a work in which primordial being is declared to be will, a great change in style is only to be expected, a shift from a language of concepts adequate to reason to a language that embodies the movements of willing. The rhetorical beauty and richness that the metaphors bring to the treatise is undeniable, and in that sense they strengthen, not weaken, the argument. Yet it is the very complexity of such powerful images that makes us uneasy when we encounter them in philosophical writing. Schelling, in his discussion of the difference between the "reasonable" and the "creative" author, carefully explains that the former employs "sheer, pure reason," but the latter's work has "personality and spirit in it" (7:395). *Of Human Freedom* comes out of a tradition which respects reason above all, but it is no accident that it displays too much "personality and spirit" to remain wholly within that tradition.

Although it did not appear in print until 1813, Schelling's correspondence with K. A. Eschenmayer about *Of Human Freedom*[12] allows us to see how Schelling responds to the charge that he illegitimately applies human concepts and superlatives to God (8:147) and that even to speak of God as living, let alone as animated by desire (*Sehnsucht*) is "inappropriate to God's dignity" (8:148). Yes, indeed, replies Schelling a little wearily, this is the view of "all Kantians, Fichteans and Jacobians, in general the whole of the philosophy of subjectivity, which dominates our time" (8:167). His further explanation is worth quoting at length, since it shows so clearly that in his view, his approach is properly understood as neither pre-Kantian nor post-Kantian, indeed that this way of looking at things involves what later will be called a category mistake:

> As I have already said, I do not want to get involved with this controversy. The main reason is that I can find no validity whatsoever in this way of arguing. There can be absolutely no question about what right we have to apply our concepts to God; we would first have to know what God is. . . . If, as you say, my reason has set itself above God, then so would you have done the same in what you deny to God, indeed far more so, in that you have allowed yourself to judge a priori, without any investigation, purely subjectively of God[.] I on the contrary have maintained nothing on my own account about God, but have sought only to follow his path. On which side lies the audacity, then[?] (8:167–68)

We would do well to keep these observations in mind as we try to discover what the true significance is of this work, which, in Heidegger's view, "shatters Hegel's *Logic* before it was even published."[13] I have mentioned the critique of the Enlightenment and the disagreement with Jacobi, the renaissance of the philosophy of nature, the evolution of the concept of the self, and the development of the idea of the unconscious; and these are all important elements of *Of Human Freedom*. Still, at most they are aspects of the larger concern animating the treatise, and this concern is an unfamiliar one: acknowledgment of the reality of evil, and the necessity of rethinking both the nature of being and human freedom such that evil's reality is genuinely acknowledged. Authentic openness to being means no foreclosure of possibilities, as is practiced by the philosophers of subjectivity, with their deceptive modesty.

One measure of Schelling's radical openness to new ways of seeing questions that have been staples of philosophical discussion for centuries—and the problem of evil is just such a perennial question—is to look carefully at the way he phrases the problem. Instead of assuming the truth of the Christian view of God and creation, he inquires: "What is God's relation as a moral being to evil, or, in the common expression, how is God to be justified in view of evil?" (7:394). The orthodox Christian asks how evil is possible, given God's goodness, thus taking the divine reality as primary. Schelling takes the human experience of the reality of evil as primary, and asks what sort of God could possibly coexist with our knowledge of evil. This is a distinctly postidealistic stance which assumes the validity of the human experience first. The bridge between the worst in human beings and the best in God, and the struggle to do justice to both as comprehensible aspects of a larger whole, are the tasks of *Of Human Freedom*. Heidegger calls the book an attempt to construct a metaphysics of evil, a suggestive way of indicating both the scope and the audacity of Schelling's struggle to incorporate the reality of evil in his theory of being.

This is the last great metaphysical effort of German idealism, according to Walter Schulz, and as such it is not surprising that in this heroic attempt to present God and man as honestly as possible, Schelling is confronted, and confronts the reader, with an urgent sense of the unavoidability of his central concern: the connection between freedom and evil. William Desmond has suggested that the persistent way in which the existence of evil challenges and even seems to mock philosophy's attempt to come to terms with it produces a "speculative insomnia" and "a kind of metaphysical migraine."[14] Yet he adds that "one of the supreme nobilities of speculative metaphysics is its willingness to mindfully return again and again to such ineradicable yet essential perplexities."[15] By this measure *Of Human Freedom* is a noble undertaking indeed.

III. The Introduction: A Redefinition of Freedom

There is a passage near the end of *Of Human Freedom* which serves both as an epitaph for the pretensions of the Enlightenment view of reason and as an indication of the new directions to be explored in *The Ages of the World*:

> ... however highly we place reason, we still do not believe, for example, that anyone can through pure reason become virtuous or a hero or any kind of great man, nor even—in the well-known phrase—that the human race can be propagated by it. Only in personality is there life; and all personality rests on a dark foundation which must, to be sure, also be the foundation of knowledge. (7:413)

Schelling does not see himself as devaluing reason but rather as paying it proper respect by acknowledging its history, its context. This context, speaking very generally, is its growth out of the irrationality of primordial being; nature is transfigured in intelligence, but there is no mystical crossover to another order of being entirely, as with Descartes. Schelling insists that both nature and intelligence must be present in those who would truly know either. Thus, reason and its limits are no longer the central focus, for Schelling is concerned in this treatise with a more vital matter: what is the essence of human freedom?

The lengthy introduction, which aims at nothing less than a new definition of freedom, arrives at it by presenting the genesis of this problem in Germany after the impact of the pantheism controversy. I will keep my discussion of Schelling's rather cryptic remarks brief, since many of these issues have already been treated in chapter 1. What is of greatest significance for Schelling's view of freedom is his sketch of his understanding of pantheism: I will call this the pantheism of a living God. The problem, as Schelling sees it, is to identify God and nature without sinking into either blasphemy or absurdity. This requires a radical rethinking of what is meant by the concept of nature, and it is here that Schelling's years of labor over the philosophy of nature, a dynamic and organic vision of nature as animated by a world soul, come to fruition in his claim that the "highest expression of philosophy is: Will is primordial Being" (7:350).

The primacy of will: this is a radical departure for the former student of Kant, and yet the ground had been prepared for it years ago in the philosophy of nature. This passage from the *Ideas for a Philosophy of Nature*, for example, reads as if it had been written by Schopenhauer:

> Nature has admitted nothing, in her entire economy, which could exist on its own and independently of the whole interconnection of things, no force which is not limited by an opposing one, and finds its continuance only in this conflict. . . . The beginning of Nature is everywhere and nowhere, and whether in retrospect or prospect, the investigating mind finds the same endlessness of her phenomena. (2:111)[16]

The reader will look in vain for sustained argumentation for this fundamental shift, but inasmuch as we are uncomfortably close to paradox in asking for a rational justification for the claim that the world is at the most basic level nonrational, I feel that the best test of this claim is to thoughtfully consider what Schelling accomplishes with it. Ultimately I will be asking whether Schelling has succeeded in constructing a metaphysics of evil.

Schelling begins his discussion of pantheism by reminding us that although "the feeling of freedom is ingrained in every individual, the fact itself is by no means so near to the surface that merely to express it in words would not require more than common clarity and depth of perception" (7:336). *Of Human Freedom* discusses eight concepts of freedom; however, Schelling's first concern in the introduction is to persuade his readers that there is no essential antagonism between the idea of freedom and the idea of system. The form in which pantheism became most widely known in Germany, which according to

Schelling rests upon the crassest of misunderstandings, is based on the idea that there *must be* such a fundamental antagonism, as was expressed in this formula: "Pantheism is the only possible system of reason but it is inevitably fatalism" (7:338).[17] Jacobi wanted to claim that reason (which creates systems) and true human freedom are mutually exclusive. Either the mind rigorously insists that all things are embedded in a seamless system of causes and effects, or we admit the reality of the "feeling of freedom" of which Schelling speaks in the opening lines of the treatise. That such a false dichotomy was ever taken seriously "will always remain a striking circumstance in the history of German intellectual development," Schelling says, but now that "the higher light of Idealism shines for us, this same declaration would neither be comprehensible to a like extent nor promise the same results" (7:348).

Jacobi was able in part to create the contrast between "ruinous philosophy" and his own view of the centrality of "the Heart, inwardness of feeling and faith" (7:348) by misrepresenting Spinoza's pantheism as both a system of blind, irrational necessity and at the same time, the only possible system of reason. Schelling refers to this elsewhere in a footnote as "unmanly pantheistic bunkum" (7:410 n). He goes on to demonstrate that the fatalism of Spinoza's system is not logically tied to, or the result of, his pantheism. The acceptance or denial of freedom does not depend on the acceptance of pantheism, the immanence of things in God, for Schelling argues that the world is related to God as consequences are to their ground. On analogy with the causality of organic life, he points out that every organism is, strictly speaking, dependent on another organism for its genesis; this does not mean that it remains in the thrall of that which gave rise to it. "A single organ, like the eye, is possible only in the organism as a whole; nevertheless it has life of its own, indeed a kind of freedom, as is manifestly proved through those diseases to which it is subject" (7:346). The source of fatalism in Spinoza's system is not his pantheism but his abstract and mechanistic conception of God and the world; nothing has a life of its own, indeed, nothing is alive. It is Spinoza's determinism which, consistently applied, must become fatalism: "He treats the will, too, as a thing, and then proves, very naturally, that in every case of its operation it must be determined by some other thing, which in turn is determined by another, and so forth endlessly. Hence the lifelessness of his system . . . " (7:349).

Difficult as it may be to put into words, the conviction of freedom is common to all. Since only "he who has tasted freedom can feel the desire to make over everything in its image" (7:351), Schelling wants to illuminate the connection between life and freedom; he does not deny that his system could be called pantheism, but he insists that in contrast to Spinoza's, his is a pantheism of a living God.

> God is not a god of the dead but of the living. It is incomprehensible that an all-perfect being could rejoice in even the most perfect mechanism possible. No matter how one pictures to oneself the procession of creatures from God, it can never be a mechanical production. . . . God can only reveal himself in creatures who resemble him, in free, self-activating beings for whose existence there is no reason save God, but who are as God is. (7:346–47)

There is a great deal compressed into these few lines. Schelling is rethinking what it means to be made in God's image, and he appeals to our intuitions about autonomy and individuality in a direct and effective way. If man is created by God, and God is in the highest degree autonomous, how could that to which he most directly gives rise utterly fail to possess that which characterizes God so unmistakably? I have already referred to Schelling's distinction between the reasonable and the creative author (and can we doubt that God is a creative author?); Schelling also mentions one of the most puzzling and delightful experiences of every thinker and writer when he says, "thoughts are doubtlessly born in the soul; but a thought once born is an independent power which works on in its own way, and which indeed grows so great in the human soul that it masters its own mother and prevails over her" (7:347). This conjures up an almost irresistible picture of God as an unspeakably prolific author who is gazing in amazement at the antics of the characters with whom he has peopled the vast fiction of the world. The German expression *für sich fortwirkend*, which is translated by Gutmann as "works on in its own way," might more felicitously and idiomatically be rendered as "takes on a life of its own"; this seems to me to better capture the sense of the burgeoning autonomy of both ideas and human individuals to which Schelling is referring, and which forms an important basis for his concept of personality.

The pantheism of a living God contains all the other finite and limited lives, which are grounded in God, as are all things, but still governed by their own inner laws. Yet Schelling has rejected the model of mathematical and logical necessity of Enlightenment science and reminds us that there is more than one kind of logic, more than one kind of necessity. This is as true of the natural realm as it is of the human individual: "All nature tells us that it is in no wise the product of mere geometric necessity; not sheer pure reason but personality and spirit are in it" (7:395). In the case of man, Schelling develops a theory of character which will be discussed at greater length in connection with his changed conception of the self; still the Kantian inspiration of his claim that "only that is free which acts according to the laws of its own inner being and is not determined by anything else either within it or outside it" (7:384) remains evident.

An entity must have a life of its own and act according to the laws of its own nature to be free, according to Schelling. With this in mind, the full import of Schelling's criticism of the lifelessness of Spinoza's system can be appreciated.

> Spinozism in its rigidity could be regarded like Pygmalion's statue, needing to be given a soul through the warm breath of love: but this comparison is imperfect, as Spinozism more closely resembles a work of art which has been sketched in its most general outlines and in which, if it were endowed with a soul, one would still notice how many features were lacking or incompleted. (7:350)

A blueprint cannot come alive. Schelling declares that this is not the place to further amplify the details of the criticisms he has given in earlier works of Spinoza, for they all sprang from the same objection; he says only that his earlier efforts aimed at a mutual interpenetration of realism and idealism. Spinoza's realism needed to be complemented by the insights of idealism: that nature is not inert, but dynamic; recognition of the unity of the dynamic and the spiritual; and incorporation of freedom into the system as a whole.

As was demonstrated in previous chapters, the *naturphilosophische* complement was no mere external addition but rather effected a radical transformation: radical in the original sense of going to the root of it all, for Schelling saw that the concept of being itself had to be rethought until it could be understood as compatible with the reality of freedom. He does not shy away from the consequences: "In the final and highest instance there is no other being than Will. Will is primordial Being, and all predicates apply to it alone—groundlessness, eternity, independence of time, self-affirmation! All philosophy strives only to find this highest expression" (7:350). And he does strive, for the remainder of the treatise, to articulate the meaning and implications of this concept of being.

It is an enterprise fraught with pitfalls, as Schopenhauer was later to discover, and one demanding an often painful intellectual honesty: if freedom and therefore Being itself are not themselves ultimately rational, how far can philosophical reason be expected to go toward fathoming them? If the philosopher is not passively reading a book written by God in the language of mathematics, as Newton would have it, what *is* he doing and what is the measure of his success at doing it? We are still in the introduction to the treatise and see at this point that the certainties and pieties of Enlightenment rationalism have dropped away as if through a trapdoor.

It is at this point that Schelling performs a rhetorical masterstroke. It ought to be noted that the quality and above all the clarity of Schelling's writing had been astonishingly variable in the fifteen years since his first publication, "On the Possibility of a Form of All Philosophy" (1794), which was remarkable chiefly for its abstractness. The philosophy of identity writings produced before *Of Human Freedom* have been described by even such a sympathetic critic as Xavier Tilliette as "labored, boring . . . [characterized by] a monotony discouraging to even the most motivated reader."[18] Yet here the movement of his thought is almost too swift: there is no wasted motion and little elaboration, a confirmation of his description in the preface of this treatise as the completion of a sketch, not the fully developed system itself. The reader is not just invited to return to the earlier writings; he is almost compelled to do so in order to put flesh on the bare bones of the argument.

Having shown the impact of idealism, the metamorphosis that taking freedom seriously has brought about in the concept of being, he moves directly to the insufficiencies of idealism, which he means to redress here. It will not do "to declare that 'Activity, life and freedom are alone true reality.' For even Fichte's idealism, subjective idealism (which does not understand itself) can go this far. Rather it is required that the reverse be proved too—that all reality (nature, the world of things) is based upon activity, life and freedom . . . " (7:351). Idealism provides a concept of freedom which remains too formal and abstract. In other words, it is a concept of freedom which still does not reflect the ambiguous essence of human experience: "the real and vital concept of freedom is that it is a possibility of good and evil" (7:352).

After the dismantling of the Enlightenment view of reason and its powers, after the redefinition of primordial Being as will, we are challenged to reconsider what kind of freedom is constitutive of being human. How is the possibility of a freedom which is capable of choosing evil to be explained? This possibility changes everything, as Heidegger recognizes when he says: "The system is split open by the reality of evil."[19] The unity of reality, whether it is called God or the Absolute or any other name, is essential to the possibility of system; the reality of evil threatens this unity in several ways, and Schelling devotes the remainder of the introduction to the discussion of other theories of evil, which all ultimately err in denying the reality of evil. This would be a serious enough error on the grounds that it is untrue to our experience; however, Schelling stresses that the chief difficulty with denying the reality of evil is that the possibility of human freedom disappears with the denial of its reality. Schelling argues his point with skill and passion, but I leave his discussion at this point in order to turn to the ideas behind "the real and vital conception of freedom" presented in the main body of the treatise.

IV. The "Real and Vital Conception of Freedom"

If human freedom consists in the possibility of choosing either good or evil, and if evil is not just a form of deficiency or ignorance but has its own positive reality, then there is an apparently insurmountable problem in accounting for the origin of evil. Schelling sets up the problem as a dilemma: either God's goodness and omnipotence must be denied (roughly the Manichean position), or evil's reality must be reinterpreted as mere lack of perfection (Augustine's view). He avoids the choice between the two by offering an alternative: "if freedom is a power for evil it must have a root independent of God" (7:354). The metaphysics of this alternative are complex but repay careful attention, not least because these arguments are the underpinning for Schelling's claim, in the final pages of *Of Human Freedom,* to "have established the first distinct conception of [the divine] personality in this treatise" (7:412).

Because Schelling has so frequently referred to the inadequacies of the philosophy of nature of his predecessors in his introduction, it comes as no surprise that he brings the introduction to a close with a final broadside: "The whole of modern European philosophy since its inception (through Descartes) has this common deficiency—that nature does not exist for it and that it lacks a living basis" (7:356). However, at last it is fully explained *why* the lack of an adequate philosophy of nature is a fatal flaw. It is because Schelling credits "the philosophy of nature of our time" (7:357), that is, his own philosophy of nature, with first establishing the all-important distinction between Being as existence and Being as the basis of existence. This distinction between Being and the ground of Being is explained first in terms of God and his relationship to nature:

> As there is nothing before or outside of God he must contain within himself the ground of his existence. All philosophies say this, but they speak of this ground as a mere concept without making it something real and actual. This ground of his existence . . . is *nature*—in God, inseparable from him, to be sure, but nevertheless distinguishable from him. (7:357–58)

An additional analogical argument is provided in which gravitation is called the "eternally dark basis" of light, "which truly exists" (7:358). What are we to make of this? Is Schelling weaseling back into a tacit dualism in anticipation of the difficulties entailed by his concept of human freedom? Which of these two concepts of being is to be understood as ontologically prior?

Schelling's answer to these questions is straightforward, but puzzling nonetheless. As if expecting the accusation of dualism, he observes in a footnote: "This is the only correct dualism, namely a dualism which at the same time admits [of] a unity" (7:359f.). What kind of unity can encompass such a distinction as that between Being and the ground of Being? Is the ground of Being ontologically prior to Being, and doesn't this lead to difficulties such as that of the ground of God's existence preexisting God? A direct answer is not provided; however, in connection with the question of whether or not gravity can be said to precede light, Schelling completely denies the applicability of causal models of thought to this kind of question:

> [It] is to be thought of neither as precedence in time nor as priority of essence. In the cycle whence all things come, it is no contradiction to say that that which gives birth to the one is, in its turn, produced by it. There is here no first and no last, since everything mutually implies everything else, nothing being the 'other' and yet no being without the other." (7:358)

Thus, in answer to the question concerning the causal relation between ground (gravity) and being (light), Schelling rejects causality; a slightly more subtle way of getting at the same point is to attempt to establish hierarchical relations, but this is also rejected as inappropriate. It seems to me that Schelling has remembered why he originally decided he had to eliminate mechanism and efficient causality from his philosophy of nature: they do not accurately describe the organic and the living. Since God is a living God, he cannot be placed in a causal nexus. The rejection of a hierarchical ordering of Being and the ground of Being is thus closely tied to the rejection of the nature/spirit dichotomy, of which Schelling had long been critical. As the passage quoted above shows, the very meaningfulness of the idea of 'otherness' is called into question; the possibility that philosophical thinking need not be exclusively concerned with a dialectic which turns on the knowledge, the subsumption, or the comprehension of the other is almost too radical a possibility to be heard.

To be willing to turn away from familiar models of thought when they no longer serve a purpose is courageous in itself, but what does Schelling put in their place? We are now clear that the ground of Being does not produce Being as a chicken produces an egg; it is not an earlier link in the chain but rather a nonground (*Ungrund*). What, then, is their relationship? Schelling suggests that if "we wish to bring this being nearer to us from a human standpoint," we ought to bring to mind "the longing [*Sehnsucht*] which the eternal One feels to give birth to itself" (7:359).

This is a truly revolutionary statement: the clarity of reason and even the immediacy of intuition have yielded to the recognition of longing or desire as the most basic experience—moreover, as the experience the divine Being and the human being have in common. This is also the limit of reason, for as Kant and Fichte have shown, and as Schelling had earlier agreed, reason requires an 'other'. (One has, for example, only to think of Schelling's insistence in the *System* that other minds, those "indestructible mirrors" (3:555), are necessary for the possibility of objectivity itself). That other in Kant and Fichte was often implicitly, and occasionally explicitly, female, as was discussed in chapter 4; surely it is highly suggestive that Schelling argues here that prior to awareness of the other in any form, there is only the essence of longing, and it is primary and irreducible. Schelling admits that the idea that reason is based on the nonrational is hard on human vanity (7:360), but just as the rationalist systems did not shy away from reducing all the splendid variety of reality to components in an unimaginably vast world machine, so he is willing to reconceive all that is in terms of the central mystery of organic life: birth itself. "All birth is a birth out of darkness into light. . . . Man is formed in his mother's womb; and only out of the darkness of unreason (out of feeling, out of longing, the sublime mother of understanding) grow clear thoughts" (7:360). This, of course, is another of the evocations of the view of reason with which *Of Human Freedom* ends: say what you will of reason, it is not the force which ensures the propagation of the human race.

As alluded to in chapter 4, a full exploration of the metaphors of gender in the German idealists would be a massively complex undertaking, and I do not undertake it here, even in outline. Still it is revealing that whereas a clear continuous thread of development can be traced from the female 'other' who required control and domination for Kant and Fichte, or to be transcended (Hegel) on the path to full human and historical development, here in *Of Human Freedom* the female principle is evoked in terms of a much older image, that of the "sublime mother of understanding." Certainly the feminine remains opposed to rationality; yet the limitless fecundity of the source and origin could hardly be further removed from the image of the properly domesticated subordinate.

The importance for Schelling of the central metaphors of desire and life have been noted by other commentators; among the most intriguing are the parallels between Schelling's thought and Freud's.[20] Here it will suffice to ask whether Schelling has not already given the best answer to the question of what the cause of birth is, namely, longing and desire. Longing by its nature is not susceptible to rational explanation. Werner Marx maintains that "the meaning that the notion of 'life' had for Schelling . . . was the decisive factor here [in *Of Human Freedom*]."[21] Schelling has greatly enriched what it means to be *causa sui*, but he has also taken a fateful step away from the Kantian ideal that we know only what we have fashioned according to a plan of our own. A living being, as Kant implied in the third *Critique*, has its own structure, purposes, and destiny; we can never comprehend it fully. Schelling has accepted the inevitability of a dark origin if life is to be able to emerge, but the consequences on the divine, cosmic, and human levels will never cease to occupy him.

This question of origins is one of the contexts in which Schelling's unusual intellectual honesty is most clearly visible. Like Hegel, he had begun his philosophical journey expecting to be able to say that what is rational is real, and what is real is rational. It remains true even in *Of Human Freedom* that Schelling affirms that reason both can and must go to work on existing reality and bring order to it. Yet Schelling found himself unable to deny his sense that:

> ... the unruly lies ever in the depths as though it might again break through, and order and form nowhere appear to have been original, but it seems as though what had initially been unruly had been brought to order. This is the incomprehensible basis of reality in things, the irreducible remainder which cannot be resolved into reason by the greatest exertion but always remains in the depths. (7:359-60)

Such an unapologetic acknowledgment of the ineradicability of the nonrational is a large step away from one of the cardinal assumptions of idealism. A still more significant step, though easier to overlook, is recognizing that the nonrational cannot be equated with the natural or nonhuman; rather it is at the very core of reality itself. There is God, the ultimate reality, and the ground of God's existence, and in Schelling's attempt to deduce "the concept and the possibility of evil from first principles" he finds it to "lie in the distinction between existence and the ground of existence" (7:373). Although it may be misleading to use the term "progress," which seems to imply the unfolding of a rational plan, Schelling does present us with a kind of growth or progressive development from inchoate longing to the emergence of God as fully existent. He is clear that this is a progression only possible for God: "He alone is self-born" [*er allein ist von sich selbst*]" (7:360). Indeed, the progressive "tension of longing" can be expressed only "in a graded evolution" (7:362) of increasingly differentiated beings: it is the task of the philosophy of nature to describe and recreate the profusion of beings generated by this tension. At the apex of this progression is man—Schelling assumes rather than argues for the proposition that man is the crown of creation—who, like every other existent, contains what Schelling calls "a double principle" (7:362); however, in man alone is there an awareness of this doubleness and inner division.

Well, not quite; God too has an awareness of the distinction between his Being and the ground of his Being, but the gulf between God and man is nowhere more compellingly evident than in Schelling's claim that in God the unity of the two principles is indissoluble; not so for man. This is the key to Schelling's view of evil: man is a created being (or takes his rise from the depths, in Schelling's idiom) and thus "contains a principle relatively independent of God" (7:363). Alone among creatures man is capable of self-will *and* self-awareness (and awareness of God), which endows him with choice: "that unity which is indissoluble in God must be dissoluble in man—and this constitutes the possibility of good and evil" (7:364). This way of looking at the difference between the divine and the human is reminiscent of Kant's distinction between the holy will and the good will. The being possessed of a holy will is not unaware of the existence of evil, but it is not a possibility for him; men, who have at best a good will, are always alive to the possibility of not acting in accordance with the good will.

"That unity indissoluble in God" refers to the ordering of the ground of Being and Being itself. God cannot act other than to transform the longing to give birth to himself into the light of all creation; the progression of being is unbroken, now and forever. In contrast, the balance between the dark principle in man (self-will) and the striving toward the light is constantly in jeopardy. Schelling expresses this poignantly in what is probably *Of Human Freedom*'s best-known passage:

> Man has been placed on that summit where he contains within him the source of self-impulsion towards good and evil in equal measure; the nexus of the principles within him is not a bond of necessity but of freedom. He stands at the dividing line; whatever he chooses will be his act, but he cannot remain in indecision . . . (7:374)

As Sartre would put it, to not decide is also to decide. This certainly has a contemporary ring to it; but again we must remind ourselves of Schelling's context, that of attempting to construct a metaphysics of evil. To attempt to explain the basis of human action in terms of first principles—this is idealistic through and through. The admission that at least one of these principles (self-will) is opaque to rational understanding—this is a step beyond idealism. Yet even the process leading to the discovery of the intractability of the unfathomable takes place in the context of an ongoing struggle to put the unfathomable in its place. A truly systematic thinker who is relentless in his desire to include everything in some way in the system cannot avoid coming up against the limits of systematic thought. It is what Schelling does in the face of these limits that distinguishes him from other idealists and contemporary thinkers as well.

V. "Man's Being Is Essentially His Own Deed"

Since Schelling has made human choice central in the way that he has, his theory of evil is in direct conflict with all those theories which claim either that evil does not truly exist, but is rather an imperfection or deficiency of some kind, or that apparent evil ought to be understood from a Hegelian perspective, as a manifestation of the cunning of reason, a necessary episode in a universal world history. He even goes as far as to identify the human capacity for evil with what is best in him; indeed, "the mere consideration of the fact that man, the most perfect of all visible creatures, is alone capable of evil, shows that this basis can by no means consist of insufficiency or deprivation" (7:368). This agrees well with our sense that evil is a reality, that it has a gestalt and even a life of its own (certainly it is parasitic on the good, but even a parasite has an existence, albeit a dependent one). What is highest and best in man is that by virtue of which he resembles God: his selfhood. The primordial Being is will, and this is no different for man, who is self-will. Evil arises out of exaltation of self-will (7:365); that is, man's will steps out of its proper relation to the universe and strives to live for itself, disregarding its place in the whole.

Thus evil is a willful disorder, a false life. Schelling's central metaphor of disease conveys both the parasitism and secondary nature of evil, as well as recognizing the reality of evil: "The most appropriate comparison is here offered by disease, which is the counterpart of evil and sin, as it constitutes that disorder which entered nature through a misuse of freedom" (7:366). Disease is the paradigm case of an entity inappropriately subsuming everything to itself at the expense of the whole of which it is a part. This also explains, in Schelling's view, why we are horrified by evil in a way that we are not horrified by mere weakness or impotence, which at most inspires pity; sin is compared to fever, a lack of inner harmony which affects the whole being (7:391). Another way of expressing the contrast can be seen in the choice of metaphors: traditional neo-Platonic theories of evil explain evil as a lack or deficiency, like anemia; it is understood that this shadowy sort of evil in no way detracts from the reality of the good. Schelling's imagery is closer to that of cancer, with its overtones of transforming what had originally been orderly into a fearsome and self-destructive disorder, and thereby at least potentially threatening the integrity of the whole.

Thus evil is "a positive perversion or reversal of principles" (7:366), which is in itself nothing essential yet is felt to be real. Here Schelling is appealing to the experience of being ill, of having, as we say in English, a disorder: an expression which implies a larger order with respect to which this temporary state is an interruption, and if sufficiently prolonged, a threat. (The subtlety and power of this view is if anything more evident in the twentieth century, in contrast with a medical culture most comfortable with crude military metaphors of declaring war on and conquering mysterious "bugs" which are invasive foreign entities to be zeroed in on or eliminated with magic bullets.)[22] On Schelling's view, all life-forms are characterized by having successfully reached an equilibrium, and an equilibrium temporarily lost may be restored by strengthening the organism's own powers—hence his medical ideal was of a science in service to natural processes, not one which tried to improve upon or even supplant them. Yet the analogy between evil and disease also throws their common question into sharper relief: What causes the disorder that we call disease on the physical level and evil on the human level?

The human being has a role to play in the creation of which he is a part. It is, to be sure, a unique role, for man has consciousness and thus, although he is himself a part, he also contains the whole in a sense. But this does not mean that man should put himself in God's place and see the universe as the object of his will. This would be the ultimate perversity, a complete reversal of principles, what Gutmann translates as "the reverse of God" [*der umgekehrten Gott*] (7:390). Schelling also employs the image of the relation of the center to the periphery, taken from Baader, to illustrate this point (7:367, 7:367 n, 7:381); to make the periphery central is to destroy the whole. "The general possibility of evil . . . consists in the fact that, instead of accepting his selfhood as the basis or the instrument, man can strive to elevate it to the ruling or universal will, and, on the contrary, try to make what is spiritual in him into a means" (7:389). Werner Marx, in his thoughtful discussion of the implications of Schelling's view of evil for contemporary ethical questions in *Is There a Measure on Earth?* especially stresses Schelling's understanding of selfhood and its connection to evil.[23]

Just as Schelling was careful to avoid old dichotomies by insisting that the non-rational was not identified with nature as such, but located in reality itself, he is equally careful to distinguish the source of evil from the passions. Evil is a reversal or perversion of what is highest or best in us, that is, of the self, which is the basis of the spirit. This explains the intentionality of evil, our undeniable sense that there is will and desire, not just ignorance or misunderstanding, behind truly evil acts. Evil is not merely the absence of goodness: "just as there is an ardor for the good, there is also an enthusiasm for evil" (7:372). The human essence is will; but will in and of itself is just intensity. It is the direction of the will, its relation to the whole, which is all-important. This accounts for what might otherwise seem paradoxical, that "whoever has no material or force for evil is also impotent for good" (7:400).

In a sense the temptation to assert one's own will over against the whole instead of becoming subsumed in it is unavoidable, a part of the meaning of what it is to be an individual will, so the temptation to evil is a defining characteristic of the human condition. Since the course of a disease is itself a kind of false life, it is not surprising that the career of evil is also described as a life. Schelling recalls the mythological figure of Archaos, who was "provoked to desert his quiet residence at the center of things and step forth into the surroundings" (7:366), and goes on to describe the initial hiddenness and subsequent manifestation of evil in history, religion, and salvation (7:379–80).

The human being is a part of a larger whole, yet everyone is an individual; one's being is one's own deed, and yet one does not act in a vacuum. Schelling's theory of freedom has to acknowledge the peculiarity of what it is to be human, neither independent nor wholly dependent, and he first decries earlier ideas, such as the view of freedom as arbitrary unfounded action or action without reason; these are as mistaken in their own ways as the deterministic denial of freedom. They both fail to incorporate "that higher necessity which is equally far removed from accident and from compulsion or external determination but which is, rather, an inner necessity which springs from the essence of the active agent itself" (7:383). This is the essential contribution of idealism; it for the first time made it clear that "only that is free which acts according to the laws of its own inner being and is not determined by anything else either within it or outside it" (7:314). Now this sounds unimpeachably Kantian, yet I observed earlier that a part of Schelling's motivation in writing *Of Human Freedom* was his profound dissatisfaction with the theories of freedom of both Kant and Fichte. Therefore it might be fairer to say that he arrives at his view of freedom by way of idealism, but there are several respects in which it is no longer an idealistic theory. In the introduction, where the redefinition of primordial Being as will is first discussed, Schelling adds that "all predicates apply to it alone—groundlessness, eternity, independence of time, self-affirmation!" (7:350). One way to delimit Schelling's task in defining human freedom is to ask how these predicates apply to human being.

The predicate of *self-affirmation* seems the most straightforwardly idealistic: unlike all other created beings, the human being is grounded in itself; to be *self-positing* is another way of saying that man's being is essentially his own deed. Kant would have no objection to Schelling's claim that "free actions immediately result out of that which is intelligible in man" (7:384). However, as will be seen in greater detail in the discussion of Schelling's theory of character below, Schelling insists upon a much more complex understanding of human action than Kant is willing to entertain. For Kant, there is only the intelligible world and the moral law, or the realm of external determinations (physical, psychological, and social causes of action are all equally 'external' in Kant's sense); and to be guided by these is to be unfree. One is, then, either acting freely and rationally, or one is not.

Schelling's understanding of self-affirmation is also an advance beyond Fichte, for although Fichte said that the Ego is its own deed, Schelling points out that such positing is not "primary" but mere self-apprehension; for "like all mere knowledge it presupposes the actual 'Being'" (7:385). It has remained for Schelling to demonstrate that the being assumed prior to knowledge is not a being at all, but a willing.

Eternity and independence of time are the predicates of primordial Being best recognized by Kant, in Schelling's view, although it "will always remain strange" that Kant, who in the *Critique of Practical Reason* "treated independence-of-time and freedom as correlative concepts" (7:351–52), did not realize the implications of his view. Schelling feels strongly that he is adhering to Kant's spirit, if not his letter, in his view of the intelligible nature of man. In order to be truly free, man's essence must be outside all causal connections and thus independent of time: nothing determines it but itself. It is a classic conundrum of Kantian moral theory that the good will is described as resisting all influence from inclinations, whether benign or malign, and determining itself by means of the moral law alone. Students of Kant have long been confessing themselves stymied by the notion of determination to action by reason alone; in fact we may speculate that enough of the original students of Kant found this a stumbling block that Kant attempted to clarify his meaning by invoking the feeling of respect for the moral law. This is not an inclination, Kant reminds us, but a pure feeling. A pure feeling—this expression, verging as it does on the oxymoronic, reflects Kant's struggles to capture the sense of self which we undeniably do have especially strongly at moments of moral choice.

I propose that if in place of Kant's concept of the self (as constituted by its own capacity for rational self-determination) Schelling's concept of the self as determining itself through its own deeds—which it is painfully aware may be either good or evil—is introduced, much of the air of paradox may be dispelled. The awareness of a harmony of the self with the larger law-governed order of which it forms a part *is* both a cognizance of rational structure and a sense of place—of respect—for both oneself and the larger whole; this is why it seems to take place outside time. Transgression against this order always involves both a distorted view of the self and a rationality employed in defense of this distortion.

It is the remaining predicate of being, *groundlessness*, which demarcates the gulf between Kant's and Schelling's concept of the self. Although it is true that Schelling's view originates with Kant, the logic of his questioning of freedom ultimately steers him toward what I call a theory of intelligible character which is much closer to Aristotle than Kant. Selfhood is a beginning, and yet it is also the sign of a separation from the whole: "The principle which rises from the depths and by which man is divided from God, is selfhood" (7:364). True freedom is self-determination, action in accordance with one's essence. What, then, determines this essence? Whatever it is, it cannot occur in time, for then it would have a determinate relation to all other beings and events and would not be self- but other-determined. Convinced that this determination of man's own nature cannot occur in time, Schelling boldly declares that it must happen outside time:

> hence it coincides with the first creation even though as an act differentiated from it. . . . Moreover it does not precede life in time but occurs throughout time (untouched by it) as an act eternal by its own nature. Through it man's life extends to the beginning of creation, since by means of it he is also more than creature, free and himself eternal beginning. (7:385–86)

Human freedom means that man's being is grounded in his own act; he is grounded in himself.

This is the sense in which the primordial being of man, which is will, is ungrounded: man's being is his own deed. In the beginning is a "free act which becomes necessity": it is outside time and, Schelling admits, consciousness, "since the act precedes it as it precedes being and indeed produces it" (7:386). All free activity "is necessarily an activity of determinate character; for instance—to refer to what is nearest at hand—it must be a good or bad activity" (7:384). Though Schelling understands that these ideas "may seem beyond the grasp of common ways of thought" (7:386), he insists that the notion of intelligible character having been determined freely, yet outside time, does account for two universal but otherwise inexplicable feelings. The first is the sense he claims we all have of the persistence of personal identity through time: that one has always been basically the same through all change, that the young girl and the woman and the old woman who is near death are all the same person, a person who regards alterations wrought by age and time as external to her true being. One does not need a very extensive knowledge of the history of philosophy to recall theories of personal identity far odder than Schelling's.

However, it is with the second phenomenon that he claims to be able to explain that the idea of intelligible character has the profoundest impact; and that phenomenon is the lived experience of human action and choice. Schelling reminds us that we are as little able to believe of our own free acts that we have acted for no reason (or purely arbitrarily) as we are able to really believe that we have been compelled to act. Rather, every thoughtful person "must admit, if he observes himself, that he is in no wise good or bad by accident or choice, yet a bad person, for instance, seems to himself anything but compelled, but performs his acts willfully, not against his will" (7:386). We are not what we are by accident, says Schelling, nor by choice, if what is meant is that a wholly unconditioned freedom presents itself at every juncture (which is what Schelling takes Kant to be arguing for). The choice, that is, the sum of choices which have crystallized into a particular character, were made long ago, and everything a person does or can do flows from that; still we retain an awareness of the freedom we had when making those original choices. Echoing Aristotle, Schelling explains, "Thus someone, who perhaps to excuse a wrong act, says: 'Well, that's the way I am'—is himself well aware that he is so because of his own fault, however correct he may be in thinking that it would have been impossible for him [at the present moment] to act differently" (7:386).[24]

One might say, stretching the evidence of the text a bit, that the process of character-formation which in Aristotle's view has its decisive moments early in life and continues until death, for Schelling is more fancifully located altogether outside time (or "is untouched by time": 7:386). And yet both thinkers are pointing, in very different language, to the same experience: the sense that we are what we have made ourselves, and that crucial choices took place, if not without consciousness, still in a situation as different from our present state of consciousness as it is unrecoverable. Schelling illustrates his view beautifully with the story of Judas, who could not help but betray Christ, yet did so freely. A theory of evil as ignorance or imperfection makes Judas's actions unintelligible, and Judas himself a pawn or buffoon rather than a tragic figure. Similarly, the explanation that Judas was overcome by greed for the thirty pieces of silver denies the full horror of what he has done, "for it is not the passions which are in themselves evil, nor are we battling merely with flesh and blood, but with an evil within us and outside us, which is spirit" (7:388). A theodicy that requires Christ to be betrayed that mankind might be redeemed is still less satisfying, for the logic of that view inadvertently makes Judas into a martyr. Evil is real, as Schelling has emphasized throughout: ultimately it is betrayal, a reversal of principles. There seems also to be tacit acknowledgment of a parallel between love and evil: just as the ability to love is closely tied to self-love, the first betrayal in an evil act is always the betrayal of oneself which has preceded it.

A corollary is presented in the story of Cato, illustrating the reality of good (and Schelling's rejection of Kant's formalism). Arbitrary goodness is just as incoherent and unthinkable as arbitrarily evil action (7:391); both good and evil are the result of man's action and ultimately, of his character.

> Thus it was in the soul of Cato, to whom an ancient writer ascribes such an inward and almost divine necessity of action, in saying that he was most like virtue, in that he never did what was right in order to do so (out of respect for the commandment of duty) but because he simply could not have done otherwise. (7:393)

Respect (however pure a feeling it might be) has here given way to character, the result of the self-affirmation which is the expression of human freedom. Self-affirmation in time becomes the ground of being we call character. We have acted, and those actions have formed our being.

Attentive consideration of who Judas and Cato were reveals Schelling's meaning. Just as the will, in and of itself, is nothing but intensity and must be formed and directed before it can act for either good or evil, so too was each man once free. Each one acted, and by these actions created the laws of his being, which he was then bound to obey, the good Cato just as much as the evil Judas. Thus an evil act, even the most evil act, is *not* a horrid surd in the fabric of reality; it too can be explained in terms of the laws governing the being of the person who committed the act. To speak of it using a disease metaphor that a twentieth century Schelling might favor: an oncologist evaluates malignancies in terms of their TNF, tumor necrosis factor. This measures something undeniably real, even though the life of the tumor is in every way dependent on the host. The reality of evil is in the degree and kind of disorder it represents, the magnitude of the threat it poses to that reality out of which it arose.

VI. An End of Idealism?

The argument of *Of Human Freedom* has reached a point where, far from the real being the rational, the most real is the least rational. And this is the case in several important respects. The previous section showed what it means for Schelling to say that man's being is essentially his own deed, and how distant this conception is from its Kantian origins: in a free act, which, since it produces being, in some sense precedes it (although it is outside time, as a "free and eternal beginning" [7:386], that man invents himself). To ask for reasons in this connection is to misunderstand what kind of entity man is—one that is its own beginning and origin. All existence has to be conditioned or limited in order to be personal existence; to set aside these conditions is to no longer be human. In evil actions man attempts to transcend the limitations of finitude, but this is not possible:

> Man never gains control over the condition even though in evil he strives to do so; it is only loaned to him independent of him; hence his personality and selfhood can never be raised to complete actuality. This is the sadness which adheres to all finite life. . . . Thence the veil of sadness which is spread over all nature, the deep, unappeasable melancholy of all life. (7:399)

In section IV I discussed God as the indivisible unity of the two principles of Being: as existence and the ground of existence; and here, too, a certain recalcitrance to rationality was noted in the very nature of things. God is not a god of the dead, but of the living; thus God is "the living unity of forces," indeed, "the highest personality" (7:395). It is therefore not surprising to learn near the end of the treatise that "God is not a system but a life" (7:399); a system can be completely grasped in terms of rational concepts, but a life is a becoming, a process, and thus defies confinement in any static, universal, and unchanging concepts, with respect both to its origins and its destiny.

Schelling's discussion of *das Regellose*, the unruly which is "the incomprehensible basis of reality in things, the irreducible remainder which cannot be resolved into reason by the greatest exertion but always remains in the depths" (7:360), indicates clearly that this is not the sort of difficulty which might eventually be overcome. In order for creation to have reality, it must arise out of darkness—darkness is its "necessary heritage" (7:360). To go on asking *why* this is so is futile: what Schelling learned from the successes of *Naturphilosophie* and the failures of idealism is that all existence must have both a real and an ideal aspect. The real by its nature can never become fully transparent to thought, for then it would be ideal and not real.

Schelling expresses what I have called the recalcitrance of reality with the images of darkness, of will, and of birth. Darkness yields, at least partially, to light, will is illuminated by understanding, and birth is the beginning of life. At the end of the treatise, Schelling again raises the question I referred to at the beginning of the chapter as postidealistic: what is God's relation to the world as a moral being? (7:394). An appreciation of the reality of evil has to lead us to the question, "does evil end, and how?" (7:394). "Has creation a final purpose at all, and if so, why is it not attained immediately, why does perfection not exist from the very beginning?" (7:403). In other words, why is there something, rather than nothing (1:310), as Schelling had put the question in his earliest writings.

Has Schelling suceeded in constructing a metaphysics of evil? In a sense, and at a fatefully high price. Evil has been put in its place as a false life, a disorder, a disruption of being. The enormity of evil can be understood in terms of the good it destroys—this captures both its parasitism and its reality. However, the high price, the metaphysical gamble, on which Schelling has staked the very intelligibility of *Of Human Freedom*, is the idea of an ultimate reality which can encompass these oppositions, the groundless. This "being before all basis and before all existence, that is, before any duality at all" (7:406) must now somehow contain all oppositions; "reality and ideality, darkness and light, or however else we wish to designate the two principles" (7:407), threatens to explain too much. As was the case in the identity philosophy, Schelling must account for how this groundless identity utterly spontaneously divides into two equally eternal beginnings, "in order that the two which could not be in it as groundless at the same time . . . should become one through love; that is, it divides itself only that there may be life and love and personal existence" (7:408). How is this to be understood? The emergence of difference out of primordial unity is *the* defining question for the rest of Schelling's philosophical life, and especially for *The Ages of the World*, which will be discussed in the next chapter.

The metaphysical conundrum Schelling circles around in *Of Human Freedom* has been likened to the conceptual difficulties encountered by physicists attempting to explain the Big Bang. As Andrew Bowie puts it: "The attention in contemporary theoretical physics to the very emergence of a differentiated universe of space and time from that which involved neither increasingly reveals the limitations of the causal model of physics that served so well until the rise of quantum mechanics and the questioning of existing modes of causality."[25] The use of terms like identity and indifference is perhaps more misleading than helpful in the effort to characterize the groundless, yet White's claim that Schelling has conflated the logical and the psychological meaning of indifference, and that "his account of the *Ungrund* as indifference is either unclear, incomplete, or incoherent,"[26] fails to recognize the difficulties that necessarily attend the attempt to move beyond existing models of thought.

Much as he disagrees with Leibniz's suggestions that evil is either a means or a sine qua non of the perfection of the world, for this would make evil inevitable and necessary, not the result of the perversion of human freedom, Schelling does agree with the spirit of this idea at least in part. Love and life are supremely valuable precisely because they are not states of static perfection but burgeoning and progressing. Perfection does not exist from the very beginning, because "God is a life, not a mere being. All life has a destiny and is subject to suffering and development" (7:403). It might be objected that God could surely have foreseen the suffering and evil attendant on life. Schelling acknowledges this, yet finds such a suggestion tantamount to the triumph of the absurd (and as such truly evil): "For this would be as much as saying that love itself should not be, so that there could be no contrast to love; that is, the absolutely positive should be sacrificed to that which has its existence only as a contrast; the eternal should be sacrificed to the merely temporal" (7:402).

Speculation about why there is something rather than nothing always seems at least vaguely tainted by bad faith, for there so manifestly *is* something. A similar difficulty afflicts speculation about the purpose of evil, since it always involves the tacit (and sometimes quite explicit) assumption that evil is the problem, the exception, the deficiency: it is manifestly not the norm. An awareness of this may be what brings Schelling, with characteristic bluntness, to dismiss the complex of difficulties which absorbed Leibniz's energies for years by saying: "in order that evil should not be, God himself would have not to be" (7:403). Reflection upon the relation of health to disease is here particularly useful in illustrating the primacy of God's existence and the derivativeness of evil: health must exist for disease to occur, but health does not *cause* disease. Nor are disease and health opposites which form a duality: a duality requires two beings in opposition to one another. "Evil, however, is no being but a counterfeit of being, which is real only by contrast, not in itself" (7:409). What *is* real, sometimes shockingly so, is evil's threat: but the very possibility of a threat presupposes the existence of something of value to be threatened.

Schelling began with the kinds of questions which forced him to struggle to find new concepts to express adequately the nature of the beings which chiefly interested him: the self and the Absolute. Here in *Of Human Freedom* being has been supplanted by becoming, and concepts by metaphors. A living reality cries out for a living language to reflect it, and it is clearly difficult for Schelling—a failed poet in his youth—to rise to the demands of his subject. The questions raised by the acknowledgment of the reality of evil have posed a particular challenge, which Schelling attempted to meet with the images of perversion and inversion; this allowed him to keep the all-important stress on the law-governed nature of all human action intact, while giving full weight to evil's destructive and nonrational nature. As successful a strategy as this is (and I have tried to make clear its superiority to other theories of evil), it ultimately explains only the structure of the evil act itself and leaves unanswered the most important question: what is the origin of evil?

Schelling does indicate in passing that our very existence as individuals in a sense predisposes us to evil, but he does not develop this insight. Thus the "aroused selfhood" (7:399) or "activated selfhood" (7:400), which constitutes the awakening of man's will can, as Schelling had to recognize, given his view of freedom as a real choice between good and evil, be manifested with equal vigor in both directions: "in the good the reaction of the depths works towards goodness, in the bad it works toward evil, as Scripture says: in the pious thou art pious; in the perverse, perverse" (7:400).[27] Because human choice and human being are the ultimate mystery, because genuine freedom cannot be wholly separated from its ground, Schelling has arrived at a coincidence of opposites at the center of human reality, and of reality itself.

The suspicion that the human being is the exception, the anomaly, *the* problem for philosophy, beginning to emerge in *Of Human Freedom*, only intensifies in the later Schelling, to the point where he says, in a tone both exasperated and resigned:

> Far from it being true that man and his activity makes the world comprehensible, he is himself the most incomprehensible of all, and drives me relentlessly to

the view of the accursedness [*Unseligkeit*] of all being, a view manifested in so many painful signs in ancient and modern times. It is precisely man who drives me to the final despairing question: Why is there something? Why not nothing? (13:7)

7

BEYOND IDEALISM? *THE AGES OF THE WORLD*

> Kant calls the necessity of being—the necessity which is unconditioned, preceding all thought—the true abyss (*Abgrund*) of human reason (14:163).

I. Schelling's Later Philosophy

In *Of Human Freedom*, Schelling shattered the assumptions that had provided the framework for his earlier thought. He had conclusively demonstrated, at least to himself, that it was as impossible to return to a preidealistic metaphysics as it was to remain within the worldview of idealism; the need and desire to go beyond idealism gave rise to what he later came to call the positive philosophy. This put him in a remarkable position, as Emil Fackenheim pointed out more than forty years ago:

> Schelling is not only the first in a long line of post-idealistic metaphysicians, but he also possesses unique qualifications. For having himself been the founder of absolute idealism, he is the critic who can be trusted most to understand what he is criticizing. This fact alone should make us suspect that the *Philosophie der Mythologie und Offenbarung* is of first-rate importance not only for historical scholarship but also for contemporary philosophy.[1]

It is surely significant that Fackenheim speaks of the philosophy of mythology and revelation as if they formed a single whole. In a sense this is true, for both belong unequivocally to Schelling's later philosophy and represent a permanent break with the concerns of Schelling the idealist. However, Schelling himself seems to have regarded the two as distinct and at least in principle separable, as he indicates in the structure of the 1841 Berlin Lectures, in which lectures 28–33 are devoted to the philosophy of mythology and the movement toward monotheism as a preparation for the philosophy of revelation. Schelling later expressed the difference in terms of his favorite opposition, that between necessity and freedom: the philosophy of mythology elucidates the forms the divine necessarily passes through in all religions; the philosophy of revelation is the philosophy of God's development through freedom. Indeed, "without an antecedent philosophy of mythology, no philosophy of revelation is conceivable" (13:197).

One of the first and most dedicated and extensive commentators on the later Schelling, Horst Fuhrmans, has made a herculean attempt to understand Schelling's writing after 1809 as religious writing, what he calls "Schelling's explicative theism."[2] Yet it would be a serious, if understandable, mistake to see the concentration on Christianity as a covert return to the faith of his fathers on the part of an aging and embittered thinker. Even in very late writings, Schelling makes no attempt to hide the fact that his first allegiance is to philosophy, not religion:

> The more difficult or incomprehensible something is (with the understanding that it must first be authentically grounded), the more the explanation calls for thinking. For me it is not a matter of agreeing with any one church doctrine. I have no interest in being orthodox, as it is called, just as I would have no difficulty in being the opposite. For me, Christianity is merely a phenomenon that I seek to *explain*. (14:201)

As Brown has stressed, Schelling's focus remains on the importance of *thinking*. "In carrying out the explanation,

Schelling does not especially seek to be either orthodox or heterodox in the confessional sense; instead he seeks to lay bare a philosophical foundation more basic than either alternative."[3]

Beginning in 1810, Schelling wrote the first of many versions of *The Ages of the World*, and his correspondence with his publisher, J. G. Cotta, shows that he was on the verge of publishing twice—in 1811 and in 1813. Yet despite years of work and the production of many versions and drafts, Schelling was never able to complete *The Ages of the World*. There is really no work by Schelling properly designated by that name, as Aldo Lanfranconi has pointed out.[4] K. F. A. Schelling selected what he took to be the most nearly complete manuscript, that of 1815, for inclusion in his edition of his father's works, and this is the only version for which an English translation exists.[5] Manfred Schröter has edited the printer's proofs for the versions from 1811 and 1813,[6] (hereafter referred to as WA I and WA II), and most scholarship on *The Ages of the World* draws upon both the 1815 version and Schröter's text. Lanfranconi has made the most extensive attempt to compare the three published versions with one another.[7] Although I agree with Brown that the texts of the *Ages of the World* period form "the prerequisite philosophical introduction to the philosophy of mythology and revelation,"[8] my main focus here is on examining the ways in which *The Ages of the World* reveals how Schelling has moved beyond idealism.

In assessing that aspect of the significance of Schelling's later philosophy, the most helpful, if provocative, guide I have found is in Walter Schulz's claim that it is in the later philosophy of Schelling that we see "the completion of German idealism,"[9] not because it is successful, but on the contrary, because the way in which it fails permanently closes that avenue of approach to metaphysics. As a result, Kierkegaard, Marx, Schopenhauer, and Nietzsche take a radically different view of the possibility and meaning of metaphysics. We have seen in the earlier chapters why Schelling felt he had to abandon the constraints of idealism: the evidence had become overwhelming that reality was not completely rational. In this chapter I address the question of how, in the *Ages of the World*, Schelling arrived at the view of the insuperable incompleteness of what he was later to call negative philosophy, and thus the impossibility of traditional metaphysics, which set the stage for the philosophies of mythology and revelation.

Although Schulz is widely acknowledged to have initiated this reconsideration of the later Schelling as an important, even decisive, influence on later thinkers, I do not wish to imply that his view should be taken as the last word. *The Ages of the World* has sparked considerable recent critical interest that in part goes well beyond what Schulz argued for or perhaps could even have imagined. I do not attempt to provide an exhaustive survey of Schelling commentary; excellent general summaries have been provided by H. J. Sandkühler,[10] Thomas O'Meara,[11] and more recently, Hermann Braun.[12] But the unusual flowering of scholarship on this transitional period of Schelling's thought deserves mention. I concentrate on significant areas of agreement and disagreement with recent commentators as well as noting fruitful alternative directions in which many of the questions Schelling raises might be pursued. In our contemporary situation of widespread doubt about the very possibility of philosophy by many and its outright rejection in favor of literature or even silence by others, it may prove unexpectedly instructive to evaluate another "end" of a philosophical era.

Why was *The Ages of the World* a failure? Because it amounts, in many ways, to a guided tour of the limits of philosophy. That this is itself a tremendous philosophical achievement seems never to have occurred to Schelling, whose later years were marred, if not precisely by the increasing melancholy some have attributed to him, at least by an increasingly acerbic and contentious tone in both his private and public controversies. Whereas Schelling's early works show evidence of a growing dissatisfaction and restlessness with "that real which is merely rational,"[13] as Frederick de Bolman has claimed, the later works are built upon the realization that the real is not so much opposed to the rational as it surpasses, exceeds, and bursts the bounds of the rational. There seems to be no language ready to hand to express this insight, and like many of his successors, Schelling appropriated idioms and modes of expression which caused great scorn among his detractors because of their obscurity and religious or theosophical overtones. What was the development of this new philosophical language a preparation for? Wolfram Hogrebe suggests that it is nothing less than the emergence of a new sensibility, a new attitude toward the reality the philosopher has sworn to unveil: "Schelling is certainly a thinker whom one can, in a sense, describe as an analytic idealist. But what he dissects analytically is finally idealism itself, and as a byproduct he produces something quite different: the presuppositions of the ideal, conceptual, rational, which are the prerequisites for a meditative sensibility."[14]

The Ages of the World shows Schelling wrestling with the limits of idealistic metaphysics in three crucially important respects: (1) the problem of the relation between the finite and the infinite receives a startling solution in a new emphasis on the radical incommensurability of the two and the claim that the distance between them can be bridged only by a radical leap or fall; (2) the recognition of the historical character of reality requires a metaphysics of becoming to replace the metaphysics of being, which in turn necessitates a fundamental rethinking of the concept of time; and (3) the enterprise of philosophical inquiry itself is reconceived as evolutionary when Schelling shows how the life of God can be adequately grasped only in this way.

II. The Doctrine of the Fall

Schelling's doctrine of the fall is part of a spectacular and dangerous effort to satisfactorily explain the maddeningly elusive relation between the Absolute (or infinite) and the finite which had been a central concern from the time of his earliest essays. Like Kant, Schelling recognized that the central paradox generated by the attempt to define limits for reason is that it brings with it the recognition (in some sense) of what lies beyond reason in the very effort to prove its inaccessibility. How can we claim to know what we can't know? Jacobi's provocative answer had been that the only bridge between the finite and the infinite was by means of faith (*Glaube*), and in earlier chapters I examined Schelling's interest first in intellectual intuition and later in aesthetic production as more philosophically respectable means of bridging the gap.

The culmination and at the same time acknowledgment of the limitations of these efforts can be seen in the Sunday's child problem: the insight of the philosopher is explicitly compared to the unique talent of the artist for the purpose of pointing out that just as not everyone is artistically creative or even capable of appreciating the meaning of art, so too the creative philosopher stands alone and is often misunderstood. The philosopher may claim to understand the connection between infinite and finite, but when he maintains that their relation is one of identity, as Schelling had been doing since 1800 in the excessively abstract and starkly counterintuitive identity philosophy, it may not be the mere lack of philosophical talent of the readers that causes widespread misunderstanding. Perhaps, as Schelling slowly came to recognize, Jacobi had had an insight into something of inestimable importance when he insisted that rational concepts, no matter how carefully systematized, were never capable of grasping reality. The philosophy of nature had enabled Schelling to move away from a static, logical metaphysics to a dynamic, vitalistic one when he recognized that the spontaneity at the basis of life cannot be contained in any concept but lies forever beyond rational grasp. From this conclusion sprang the corollary insight that an inexplicable basis or ground of being implies an inexplicable ground of human being as well.

The later philosophy takes a second step toward what might be called a metaphysics of becoming by acknowledging the dark basis of the real, from which the profusion of creation is endlessly unrolling; the paradoxes of *Of Human Freedom* are concentrated in the central notion of the groundless. This way of reconciling the infinite and the finite, by means of a unifying identity, is rife with pitfalls. To examine briefly just the most notorious example, it is all too frequently assumed that Hegel was taking aim at the Absolute of the identity philosophy when he disparagingly invoked the "night in which all cows are black" in his preface to his *Phenomenology of Spirit* of 1807.[15] It is not nearly so often noted that as early as 1802, in the *Bruno* and the "Further Presentations of the System of Philosophy," of the same year, as well as in *Philosophy and Religion* (1804), Schelling showed a clear awareness of the difficulties attendant upon claiming that only a superior philosophical insight could provide the basis for discerning the relationship between the finite and the absolute identity.

In an exhaustively detailed but happily witty exchange, H. S. Harris, Michael Vater, and George di Giovanni have recently applied themselves to the task of squinting through this dark night, and perhaps have laid the ghost of the old insult to rest at last. Harris begins the exchange by admitting that the editors of the new critical edition of Hegel "say categorically 'Hegel is here aiming at Schelling's Identity Philosophy.' But, for once, I think they are wrong."[16] Harris gives an entertaining genealogy of the figure of speech as it was used at the time and a close reading of the various targets in Hegel's preface, concluding that Hegel was sincere in his famous letter to Schelling of May 1, 1807, in which he claims to have only been criticizing some of the excesses of Schelling's followers, not Schelling himself.[17] Harris goes on to make a case for Reinhold and Bardili as the intended offenders, with honorable mention for Heinrich Steffens. Vater argues for Reinhold as the intended target, although in his view the controversy ultimately has interest only insofar as it sheds light on the limitations of arguing "for or against" in contexts where this is inappropriate (Harris and Vater take the *Phenomenology* to be such a context). I tend to agree with this conclusion; rather than milling around in the dark night, it would be more profitable to see how Schelling deals with the problems the assumption of an ultimate Identity has confronted him with.

The evidence clearly indicates that Schelling was well aware that none of his earlier formulations of the relationship of the infinite and the infinite had yet satisfactorily addressed the most fascinating question of all: How do the infinite and the finite, God and man, come to be separated? In *Philosophy and Religion* he proposes his first formulation of the doctrine of the fall, which he apparently thought would render otiose all claims that the finite is somehow swallowed up in the infinite. *Philosophy and Religion* is a peculiar work. Ostensibly written as an extended reply to K. A. Eschenmayer's *Die Philosophie in ihrem Uebergang zur Nichtphilosophie*,[18] it seems out of place among the other identity philosophy writings and in particular in contradiction with the views defended in the work published immediately before it, the dialogue *Bruno* (if we assume the realist Bruno to be taking Schelling's part against the idealist Lucian, who speaks for Fichte). Only many years later did Schelling comment on this apparent contradiction:

> This [work] was intended to express another perspective from that of the *Bruno* (1802). A third dialogue was to have reconciled the the contradiction between the two. *It never happened!* It was in fact the contradiction between the negative and the positive philosophy which had then just begun to come alive . . .[19]

The moment of the discovery of the "contradiction between the negative and the positive philosophy" is difficult to pin down.[20] As later formulated, it is the difference between philosophizing about what is accessible to reason and amenable to formulation in concepts, counterpoised to the struggle to adequately grasp what is known because it contingently happens to exist—positive knowledge of contingent being. At this point, casting about for a way to speak about that which in our actual particular experience cannot be grasped adequately in concepts, Schelling instead seemed to speak in riddles.

The bafflement, if not amazement, clearly felt by the readers of *Philosophy and Religion* when they encountered the initial formulation of the doctrine of the fall still rankled five years later, when Schelling remarked darkly in the preface to the freedom essay that "the beginning made in *Philosophy and Religion* . . . remained obscure" (7:334). It is here for the first time that we find an express repudiation of the sort of emanationism strongly suggested in the philosophy of nature works which stressed the doctrine of potencies and linked levels of development as encompassed by a single world soul. Schelling notes that of all the attempts to pass from the infinite to the finite,

> the oldest and most often repeated is known to be that of the doctrine of emanation, according to which the efflux of the divinity, in a gradual step-wise descent and separation from the source, loses the divine perfection, and so finally passes over into its opposite (matter, privation) just as light finally dissipates into darkness. (6:35)

He now abruptly rejects this approach and embraces what could be seen as its opposite: "there is no steady transition from the Absolute to the actual; the origin of the world of sense is to be conceived only as a complete break from the Absolute, as a leap" (6:38). The notion of a sudden and rationally inexplicable fall is of vital importance in the later Schelling and is interpreted by A. O. Lovejoy as the moment of breakthrough which made it possible to replace the pure, perfect, unchanging One of the Neoplatonists with an idea of God as expressed in the great chain of being which is the universe.[21]

The emphasis on freedom which will swell to occupy the whole of the freedom essay is explained only formally in *Philosophy and Religion*: the production of the finite world is a result of the freedom and self-knowledge of the Absolute as ideal. Schelling has two questions to address: How is the existence of the temporal world possible, and why is it necessary? He argues that the Absolute as ideal is not truly free, since mere essence or ideality still requires form or reality in order to exist. Thus the temporal world is *possible* because it is an exercise of the limitless freedom of the ideal; it is *necessary* in order for the ideal to have a counterpart in existence.

The infinite self-knowledge of the Absolute enables it to recreate its ideality as reality, thereby producing "a counter-image [*Gegenbild*] which is at the same time, by itself, truly another Absolute" (6:34). This is what it means to say that reality is historical. From this point forward Schelling will be concerned with the attempt of the human to reach the divine, or the return of reality to its point of origin, the Absolute:

> History is an epic composed in the mind of God; its major parts are: that which represents the going-forth of mankind from its center to its greatest distance from Him, the other which represents the return. The former is the Iliad, the latter the Odyssey, of history. . . . The great design of the entire appearance of the world expresses itself in this manner in history. The ideas, the spirits, had to fall away from their center and enter into nature, the general sphere of the Fall, into particularity, in order that afterwards they might, as particulars, return into the indifference, be reconciled to it . . . (6:57)

Schelling's insistence that since the essence of the Absolute is freedom, this essence must also be essential to the counterpart (reality) as well, is echoed in the freedom essay (as discussed in chapter 6). In describing the pageant of history he employs the language of necessity: "the spirits *had* to fall away"; so too the empirical individual is in a sense doomed to evil in order to achieve reconciliation:

> For if evil was already roused in the first creation and was finally developed into a general principle through the self-centered operation of the basis, then man's natural inclination to evil seems all at once explicable, because the disorder of forces once having entered creatures through the awakening of self-will is already communicated to man at birth. Indeed the dark ground operates incessantly in the individual man too, and rouses egotism and a particularized will. (7:381)

Thus the whole of human history is the story of the recovery from this fall and the struggle to regain the Absolute. This process will continue into "a distant future when God will be all in all," and explains "the final purpose of creation, that which could not be in itself, shall be in itself through being raised out of darkness as a depth independent of God, and elevated into existence" (7:404).

Yet all of this does not suffice to explain why God created the world, or as Schelling puts it in the freedom essay, the ultimate question of the whole inquiry remains: "what is to be gained by that initial distinction between being insofar as it is basis, and being insofar as it exists?" (7:406). *The Ages of the World* is an attempt to retrace God's steps, especially with respect to the fall or creation of the temporal world. Schelling had already hinted in *Philosophy and Religion* that the usual causal modes of explanation will be inapplicable here, for the fall is as eternal as the Absolute itself, and thus that the origin of things took place outside time (6:41). It is revealing that it is at this point that Schelling no longer speaks in terms of reasons or explanations for the fall or creation: "God's decision to reveal his highest self in epochs came from the purest freedom" (8:307). The radical incommensurability of the infinite and the finite has not only been admitted but has been made central to this new metaphysical stance.

III. The Historical Character of Reality: The Philosophy of Time

If the fall is taken as seriously as I have argued it ought to be taken, the content of reality is evident, at least in its broadest outlines: "the great design of the universe and of its history, is none other than the perfected reconciliation and resolution in Absoluteness" (6:43). *Of Human Freedom* provided a discussion of two characteristics of what makes the revelation of the Absolute possible: freedom and antithesis; but it was too brief to do much more than introduce these themes. The changing language reflects the growing realization that reality is essentially historical in character: metaphors of growth, development, and equilibrium from the philosophy of nature prefigure the language of life and evolution in the later works. It is the beginning of this history, "The Past," which all versions of *The Ages of the World* are concerned with.[22]

What does it mean to say that reason has a history? At a minimum it means to leave behind a static metaphysics of being for what Lovejoy called Schelling's "innovating idea" of "a radical evolutionism in metaphysics and theology."[23] Yet even this does not really capture the revolutionary nature of what Schelling is after in the *Ages of the World*, for an evolutionary development implies a unitary subject which evolves. Without fully agreeing with Andrew Bowie's suggestive claim that *The Ages of the World* "is perhaps best understood as a speculative theory of predication, a theory of why there is truth in the world at all,"[24] it must be admitted that Bowie focuses attention on the most puzzling aspect of these puzzling texts: how, given the fact that both cosmic and individual being precede any possibility of assigning meaning to them, do we come to be able to do so?[25]

Schelling shows that he is well aware of the magnitude of the change in the introduction to *The Ages of the World*, which sketches the chasm between "the conception of science [*Wissenschaft*] hitherto accepted" and the "true conception [of] the development of a living, actual essence" (8:199). He cautions us that this true science cannot be communicated in sterile formulas or universal concepts, it must be relived. As if intending to respond boldly to any suspicion that he has crossed some sort of invisible line from suggestive imagery to unblushing anthropomorphism with this profusion of references to the idea of life, Schelling openly acknowledges the connection between man and the world:

> It is certain that whoever could write of his own life from its very ground, would have thereby grasped in a brief conspectus the history of the universe. Most men turn from the obscurities of their own inner lives just as from the depths of that great life, and avoid a view into the abysses of that past which still is in man too much at present. (8:207–8)

Schelling had already looked into that abyss in the freedom essay in his discussion of our deepest presuppositions with respect to moral character: both Judas and Cato are determined to act as they do by the necessity of their characters, yet they are free. In one of the earlier versions of the *Ages of the World* he makes explicit what our insight into our moral freedom means for metaphysics, and yet how difficult it is to confront: "Common moral judgment therefore recognizes in every person—and to that extent in everything—a region in which there is no ground [*Grund*] at all, but rather absolute freedom.... The unground [*Ungrund*] of eternity lies this close in every person, and they are horrified by it if it is brought into consciousness" (WA I, 93).

The discussion in the freedom essay turns to how the original unity, or *Ungrund*, divided itself into two equally eternal beginnings (7:408). The relation between God (as essence) and the ground of his existence (Nature in God) is one of identity in separation: "inseparable from him, but nevertheless distinguishable from him" (7:358). I suggested in chapter 6 that the rejection of hierarchical or temporal ordering implies calling the meaningfulness of the very notion of "otherness" into question. The later works show more fully that Schelling is not assailing otherness per se but rather temporalizing the understanding of the other. For the later Schelling there is no concept of the other, if by that is meant a static and unchanging entity; the other comes to be known only in its process of becoming.

As is often the case, Schelling is most unambiguous in the heat of polemic, and in the effort to distinguish his view from what he thinks Jacobi has claimed that it is, he explains why God must be named differently at different points in his development:

> I posit God as first and as last, as Alpha and Omega, but as Alpha he is not what he is as Omega, and insofar as he is only God *sensu eminenti*, he cannot also be God in the actual sense of the word, nor even strictly be called God, unless one were to say explicitly, the undeveloped [*unentfaltete*] God, *Deus implicitus*, since as Omega he is *Deus explicitus*. (8:81)

In the later works, Schelling has taken to heart the insight that God is not a thing, and this insight has transformed his understanding of philosophy. No longer, he explains in the *Erlanger Lectures*, does he begin with "the so familiar question of what the principle of philosophy is" (9:215) and seek to deduce a chain of consequences from it. In just this fashion "had Descartes his first principle: *Cogito ergo sum*, Fichte: I am I, but in a living system which is a sequence, not of propositions, but of the movements of progress and evolution, we cannot speak of this sort of supreme proposition" (9:216). God appears only in time and through freedom. To act on the basis of freedom is to act in a way that by definition has no causal explanation. This way of answering the question raised in *Philosophy and Religion* might seem to be almost worse than no answer, since it seems to present the highest reality as in effect the most highly random principle of all.

There are enormous difficulties of exposition in any discussion of the philosophy of time, for narrative is linear and unidirectional, and much of what Schelling is trying to describe is not to be understood in terms of a progression: the inner workings of freedom (Schelling had encountered similar difficulties in his philosophy of nature, when he strove to replace the dominant language of mechanism with a language of organism). The difficulties are hardly lessened by his focus on that primordial instance of God's freedom, the creation of the world, especially since "God has taken pains to envelop in dark night the beginning of the past" (8:207). Schelling tries to explain the relation of God (who is not a being) to time allegorically and with reference to myth, but finds he must remain true to his own insight that God is a reality greater than any name or concept can grasp: "God is the oldest of beings. This judgment is said to be as ancient as Thales of Miletus. But the concept of God is of great, indeed, of the very greatest compass, and thus not to be expressed in one word" (8:209).

Schelling is clear that the root of the insufficiency of current Christian doctrine is that it does not understand God's relationship to time: "The current doctrine of God is that he is without any beginning. Scripture, on the other hand, says that God is the beginning and the end" (8:225). Schelling protests that this is a negative vision of a perfect passivity. On the contrary, the beginning in God is an eternal beginning, defined as a beginning that never began and never ceases to be beginning. To express it another way, God is not eternal, "but is himself his eternity" (8:238). Nothing "in God is potential; he is pure actuality" (8:238). Every finite thing has a relationship to time as that which expresses how its potentiality is related to its actuality; God alone stands outside this necessary relation.

Thus God is, or rather has, what man longs for: "Freedom, or will insofar as it does not really will, is the affirmative concept of unconditioned eternity, which we can imagine only outside of all time, only as eternal immobility. Everything aims at that, everything longs for it" (8:235). God alone is eternal freedom and rules over all things, being ruled over by none. God is "essentially a will at rest (pure freedom)" (8:259). The emphasis on will as primordial being stressed in the freedom essay in combination with Schelling's philosophy of time produces a transformed understanding of human being and striving:

> Every creature, and especially man, really only strives to return to the position of willing nothing. This is true not only of the man who abstains from all covetousness but also of the man who, though unwittingly, gives himself up to all desires, for even the latter longs only for the condition where he has nothing more to will, although such a situation flees before him, and the more eagerly it is followed, the farther it draws away from him.
>
> It is customary to say, man's will is his kingdom of heaven, and it is true, if the pure, naked will alone is understood by this. For only the man who would be transported into pure willing would be free of all nature. (8:236)

How are we to understand this? God has a relationship to time of which all but the most extraordinary men can only dream. Another way of expressing this is to say that God has a real past, whereas most people know the past only as an unreliable container of the enlarging series of remembered present moments. Schelling's philosophy of time and its eternal basis is an effort to bring alive the relation between the human and the divine. "True eternity is not that which excludes all time, but that which contains time (eternal time) subjected to itself" (8:260). As Brown explains it with reference to significant parallels in Böhme, it is God's eternal life process which forms the ontological relations of the archetype of time: "God's eternity is a life process and thus involves opposition and conquest, just as do all life processes."[26] Here too is what Brown calls "the germ of the later distinction between negative and positive philosophy."[27] Since God is free, we cannot know him through even the most exhaustive examination of the past or of the structure of thought (negative or purely conceptual knowledge); the actual historical series of acts by which he has decided to reveal himself is utterly unpredictable (positive or actual experience) and thus forms the subject matter of the philosophy of revelation.

However, God's freedom also explains Schelling's inability to finish *The Ages of the World*: difficult as it is to know the past, at least what is past can in principle be grasped. The second two sections Schelling had planned, "The Present" and "The Future," are realized through God's freedom, which is, on the terms of Schelling's understanding of freedom, unfathomable. As Lawrence puts it: "The ecstasy of time contradicts the conclusion of the system."[28]

IV. *Gottsein und Dasein*: The Ontology of What is Not

Reality is thus *more* than rational, not opposite to the rational. In *Of Human Freedom*'s claim that "idealism is the soul of philosophy, realism its body; only the two together constitute a living whole" (7:356), Schelling first names the goal he is aiming at, although he had more than hinted at it in 1806, in the unjustly neglected *Presentation of the True Relationship of the Philosophy of Nature to the Revised Fichtean Doctrine* [Darlegung des wahren Verhältnisses der Naturphilosophie zu der verbesserten Fichteschen Lehre]:

> Only at that point where the ideal has become for us itself entirely the actual, too, where the world of thought has become the world of nature, just in this point lies the last, the highest satisfaction and rec-

onciliation of knowledge, as the fulfillment of moral demands is attained only in that they no longer appear to us as thoughts, e.g., as commands, but have become the nature of our soul and have become actual in it. . . . This presentation of God's life, not outside of or above nature but in nature, as a truly real and present life, is certainly the final synthesis of the ideal with the real, of knowing with being, and therefore also the final synthesis of science itself. (7:32, 33–34)

Here at last in the *Ages of the World* is that presentation of God's life. Schelling is ingenious at showing the distance between his view and Christian doctrine when he points out a central contradiction: on the Christian view, God is the purest love; yet at the same time, it is all-important for God to exist.

By itself, however, love does not come to be. To be is se-ity [*Seinheit*], own-ness, seclusion. Love, however, is the nought of own-ness; it does not seek what is its own, and therefore also by itself cannot have being. Hence a being of all beings is by itself without support and supported by nothing; it is in itself the antithesis of personality. (8:210)

Thus either we can retain the orthodox concept of God as perfection and self-sufficiency, or we can begin to understand why he created a world (an understanding which would never become complete in any single human lifetime, but which may be expressed mythologically). Schelling is not going to rest content with the explanation in which both Plato and Hegel take refuge, that of God not being jealous. He has ready to hand, developed through the long years of work on the philosophy of nature, a much more elegant (and, I might add, less frankly anthropomorphic) explanation of the two opposed principles in God, referred to in the freedom essay as God and the ground of God's existence. These were the constituent elements of what Schelling called the first genuine concept of divine personality (7:412).

The presence of this eternal antithesis, what Schelling calls its *Dasein*, has been expressed since the earliest times in a clash of essential oppositions: light and dark, male and female, spiritual and corporeal (8:212). The attempt to separate the antitheses or ask which half of the opposition had priority in time was hardly thinkable; he regards it as the dubious distinction of modern philosophy to have come closest to accomplishing it. Philosophers have striven mightily to set up the most abstract formulation of this antithesis, being and thought, only to be mocked by that which their systems cannot contain:

> Being always stood opposite thought in this sense as something unconquerable, so that philosophy, which would explain everything, found nothing more difficult than to give an explanation of just this being. It had to accept as explanation precisely this incomprehensibility, this active opposition toward all thought, this dynamic darkness, this positive inclination to obscurity. But it would have preferred to do away altogether with the inconvenient, to dissolve the unintelligible entirely into reason or (like Leibniz) into representation [*Vorstellung*]. (8:212)

This inconvenient impenetrability of being is at its most evident in what has long been taken to be the highest being, God. What, then, are the characteristics of this eternal antithesis in God? We ought to be prepared for the stress on the significance of nonbeing to being, since Schelling had emphasized even in the philosophy of nature that it is a mistake to imagine primordial nature as ever having been in harmony with itself, for then it is unintelligible how this harmony could ever end. Life presupposes contradiction, in nature as in everything else

(8:219). Tillich calls Schelling's efforts to rethink nonbeing in *The Ages of the World* his most significant contribution to the history of philosophy: "He determined positively and concretely in the irrational will the amphibolic character of what is not: it is the principle of freedom of God and man, it is the nought from which the world is created, and it is that which should not be, which constitutes the power of sin and error."[29]

Schelling makes nonbeing primary for two reasons: in nature it explains the inexhaustibility, the ever-turning wheel of natural changes to assume an insoluble original contradiction; the second reason nonbeing must be a primary characteristic of all levels of reality is that it makes freedom possible. The image Schelling presents of beginning illustrates the raw and unassimilable wrench of all beginnings: "just in order *that* one begin, that one be the first, a decision must ensue, which, to be sure, cannot happen consciously, by deliberation, but only in the pressure between the necessity and the impossibility of being, by a violence blindly breaking the unity" (8:220). Why pressure? Why violence? Schelling almost seems to be constructing a metaphysical parallel to that old saw of physics which claims that nature abhors a vacuum. For all choice, only that "can be posited for a beginning which distinctively inclines most to the nature of what *is* not" (8:221). This is our introduction to the significance of negation: it alone makes motion (on all levels) possible. It also sets the terms for Schelling's final rejection of idealism as radically incompatible with genuine freedom.

The perfect (and perfectly static) god of idealism cannot move, because it is a unity, and a transition from perfect unity to contradiction is inconceivable. Idealism, "the general system of our times," is insufficient precisely because it understands God only as an empty infinite; it "really consists in the denial or nonrecognition of that primordial negating power" (8:212). Schelling devotes much of the *Ages of the World* to the dialectical unfolding of the three potencies which compose God: the eternal No, the eternal Yes, and the unity of Yes and No, culminating in a diagram of their relationship which is also called *hen kai pan* (8:312). What is of enduring interest in this "ontology of what is not,"[30] as Tillich called it, is the unique importance of the negative potency. It is the active ingredient in God's nature, Schelling carefully explains: "which, as the potency opposed to the essence or that which truly is, cannot be called that which is, although on that account it by no means is not or is nothing" (8:221).

In other words, that which is not is not nothing. The development of God's life can only be grasped as the interaction of being and nonbeing if it is truly to be grasped as *becoming*. The difficulty arises that God's being must therefore first be thought as nonbeing. That which is opposed to God's being, out of which his life takes form, is nonbeing, nothingness (*das Nichts*). In some sense, it takes precedence even over God. Here Schelling is following his line of reasoning at the price of edging close to the limits of language. The problem has become that of how to speak of that with no characteristics or attributes, not even so much as proper grammatical status. He is clear that nonbeing is not a potency but rather what is in itself nonpotent (*das an sich Potenzlose*); it is equally obviously not passion, desire, or nature.

> But just on that account it also cannot be something which is real by necessity; and since as yet we do not know anything which is real by freedom, it cannot in any way be anything real. And yet it cannot be something unreal. Consequently it is in itself neither what is nor what is not, but only the eternal freedom to be. (8:234)

Schelling reflects that when the question "What then could be considered as above all being?" has been posed, and the answer "Nothing" given, the meaning of this "Nothing" has been misconstrued. The negation which precedes all being is also the source of all being: it is the nothing which is at the same time everything. Schelling quotes approvingly an epigram of Angelus Silesius:

Die zarte Gottheit ist das Nichts und Uebernichts,
Wer Nichts in allem sieht, Mensch glaube, dieser
siehts. (8:234)

In Fritz Marti's translation: "The tender godhead is the naught and overnaught / Coulds't see but naught in all, oh man, you'd see God's aught."[31] That which *is* nothing has unlimited freedom to *become* anything. Nonbeing as the eternal freedom to be is also characterized as "the will which wills nothing" (8:235), a will in need of nothing external to it and ruled by nothing. Since this is the highest, most complete condition, it is also that state at which all things aim: "everything rests only insofar as it has found its real nature, its stay and stability [*Bestand*], in the will which wills nothing" (8:235). Thus movement seeks immobility, time strives for eternity; these statements seem unobjectionable enough, if a trifle too poetically expressed. Yet, as discussed in the previous section, when the same principle is applied to the human condition it produces startling results: "Every creature, and especially man, really only strives to return to the position of willing nothing" (8:235).

Schopenhauer can also be read as arguing that the entire pageant of the expression of the will in its inexhaustible variety leads only to the desire that all willing cease, and that this desire is both a metaphysical imperative and a psychological state of certain individuals. Schelling's argument here differs largely in the stress he lays upon the will which does not will as a beginning as well as an end; he wants to press on to a metaphysics of the will and the negation at the heart of the real, impossible though he knows this to be. Yet Schopenhauer's and Schelling's arguments do share the two elements of the metaphysical claim: "the naturelessness which the eternal nature desires", and its psychological counterpart: "it is nothing, like pure delight which is not self-conscious, like calm joy which is completely self-fulfilled and thinks of nothing" (8:236).

Yet this should not be surprising if the individual is recalled to be a microcosm of the macrocosm which is the universe. The significance of the negative potency is as the ineluctably necessary origin of all being; negation is truly "the mother and nurse" (8:243) of all. In the physical realm, nature is what shows the necessary character of this development out of nothing most clearly: "That power of beginning, when posited in the utterable and external, is then the primitive germ of visible nature, that from which nature is developed in the succession of ages. Nature is an abyss of what is past" (8:243).

An abyss or *Abgrund*, inexplicable and in contrast with that which has a ground (*Grund*), nature demonstrates the groundlessness and arbitrariness of necessity right before our eyes. Revealingly, Schelling also compares nature to Penia at Zeus's banquet, driven by poverty and dire need but subsequently producing divine abundance after marriage to the inexhaustible riches of the positive potency (8:244).

This sets the stage for the many retellings of the story of the life of God. Out of the inexplicable dark origin, the blind, dark contradiction, comes the movement of negation, itself constituted by opposing powers and thus in constant dread (*Angst*), inexorably seeking the affirmative potency and ultimately the equilibrium-restoring third potency. This is the story of God's primordial past (8:254), and what makes it possible for Schelling to claim that "we know of no other than a living God; that connection of his highest spiritual life with a natural one is the original secret of his individuality" (8:259).

Schelling is fond of reminding the reader that what he calls "the complete construction of the idea of God" (8:269) cannot be confined to a definition or limited like a geometric figure: it has all the complexity of the living, and thus can never be completely grasped. Returning to the comparisons of health and illness he employed in *Of Human Freedom*, Schelling elaborates: like the health of the sound body, which is an equilibrium of forces that may be destroyed at any time by the false life of disease, there would be no life in God if not for the equilibrium of potencies. Life is a balancing act.

Now we assert the possibility that just this, which now is not, could withdraw from this state of potentiality and again try to rise to that which is. Through this there arises a heightened concept of what is not, which we are often enough forced to acknowledge in nature and in life . . . (8:267)

The remainder of *The Ages of the World* develops what Bolman calls Schelling's existential dialectic.[32] The elegance and economy of Schelling's way of bringing together the relation of the infinite to the finite, temporality, and the reality of evil should not go unnoticed. The ontology of what is not, the primary importance of negation, makes it possible for Schelling to be unequivocal about the negative in God: "his desire to reveal himself, and to posit himself as the superable eternal No, was one and the same decision" (8:310). More poetically expressed: "In the nocturnal vision in which the Lord passed before his prophet, there first came a powerful storm which rent the mountains and cleft the rocks, after this an earthquake, finally a fire. The Lord himself was not in any of them. But there followed a still, small murmur in which he was" (8:311).

The negating must precede the manifestation of the positive. So, too, in the human being, "the contradiction that is life's mainspring and core" (8:321) is that deep within lies that "bitterness which is, indeed must be, the inner [character] of all life . . . the deep discontent lying in all life, without which there is no reality, this toxin of life which has to be conquered, yet without which life would slumber" (8:319). Hogrebe and Bowie would perhaps present this as the nagging sense we all have from time to time of having simply imposed meaning on a world of brute fact; though we for the most part try to ignore or deny the arbitrariness of our choices, we cannot wholly escape that awareness, which causes despair.[33]

One might perhaps wonder if Schelling is providing a working definition of *Angst*, or at least trying to systematize and domesticate it by assigning it a role in the formation of character. In one sense this is correct, as can be seen in his discussion of madness in the *Ages of the World*. Whereas the Sunday's child of the earlier works saw what others too dim of intellect could not, now Schelling's vision has darkened considerably:

> There is no greatness without a continual solicitation to madness which, while it must be overcome, must never be completely lacking. One might profit by classifying men in this respect. The one kind are those in whom there is no madness at all . . . and are so-called men of intellect [*Verstandesmenschen*] whose works and deeds are nothing but cold works and deeds of the intellect. . . . But where there is no madness, there is, to be sure, also no real, active, living intellect. For wherein is intellect to prove itself but in the conquest, mastery, and ordering of madness? (8:338)

The continually repeated refrain of a primordial disorder overcome by a higher power is then the truest, if inexpressible, spectacle of nature, thus also of human nature.[34] Schelling concludes that this is the best description he can give, "although a feeble one, of that primordial state of the all and one from which those who have lately talked so much about pantheism may see what the latter really is" (8:229). He points out that these would-be critics focus in any case only on the 'all' of primordial nature, and not the 'one'; but even their understanding of nature is woefully deficient: "if they were capable of penetrating the outside of things, then they would see that the true basic substance [*Grundstoff*] of all life and being [*Dasein*] is just what is terrible" (8:339).

V. The Controversy of 1811–12 and Beyond

Although the *Weltalter*, in any of its versions, was not published in Schelling's lifetime, the reference to "those who have lately talked so much about pantheism" almost certainly was written in mid-1812, shortly after the Schelling-Jacobi controversy of that year. The falling-out with Jacobi, whose views Schelling had quoted admiringly in his youth, is one measure of the distance he had traveled since the boundless hopefulness and excitement which characterized his earliest writings.

I have alluded above to Lovejoy's view that the ambiguities and difficulties of interpretation in Schelling's philosophical works after 1800 are due in large part to the conflict between incompatible concepts of God: Schelling retains the transcendent, eternally complete Absolute of Neoplatonism even while introducing the idea of an evolving, developing world spirit.[35] Lovejoy further suggests that it was the very public and bitter dispute which erupted between Schelling and Jacobi after the publication of Jacobi's *On the Divine Things and Their Revelation (Von den göttlichen Dingen und ihrer Offenbarung)*[36] that caused Schelling to discard his former views and completely embrace evolutionary theism, which remained his standpoint throughout the later philosophy.

It is certainly true that the heat of the polemic generated some memorable and dramatic claims in Schelling's reply to Jacobi, which appeared in early 1812, bearing the impressive title *F. W. J. Schelling's Memorial on the Treatise on the Divine Things etc. of Friedrich Heinrich Jacobi and the Accusation against Me Made Therein of an Intentionally Deceptive and Lying Atheism.*[37] Still it ought to be borne in mind that the *Memorial* was a polemical broadside, composed for the purpose of attacking and embarrassing Jacobi, and not intended to give a balanced and accurate account of Schelling's own views on God or anything else, as, for example, the friendly, even cordial exchange with Eschenmayer of the previous year had been.[38] Therefore basing conclusions about the direction and significance of the later philosophy on this one work is dangerous at best; perhaps the temptation to do so can be attributed to the fact that it was the last of Schelling's works he chose to publish himself.[39]

Lewis S. Ford has argued that the entire controversy actually rests upon a mistake, that Jacobi's *On the Divine Things*, begun in 1797 as a review of the sixth volume of Matthais Claudius's collected writings for the *Hamburger Correspondenten*, grew and grew to unmanageable proportions until it was finally published as a book in 1811. It contains a resplendently disorganized variety of reflections on religion and the possibility of religious knowledge, as well as dismissive comments directed at "the two daughters of the critical philosophy," but it was not intended as an attack on the new direction in Schelling's thought since 1809.[40] Ford points out that even those comments which might be construed as specifically referring to Schelling have an oddly "generic quality ... they are basically the old ones he had raised against Spinoza"[41] during the *Pantheismusstreit* of 1785.

Schelling's reply in the *Schrift gegen Jacobi* further muddies the waters because it reacts to *Von den göttlichen Dingen* as if were an attack upon evolutionary theism. This is peculiar at best since Schelling himself mocks Jacobi's partial and faulty knowledge of his views, even asking whether the oration "On the Relation of the Creative Arts to Nature" (1807), which Jacobi heard Schelling deliver at the Munich Academy of Sciences, of which Jacobi was then president, was the main source of Jacobi's so-called knowledge (8:29).

Schelling was probably tilting at windmills to some degree; certainly Jacobi could not have been as startled and deeply distressed by the controversy as he later claimed to have been if he had anticipated causing such ill will.[42] It is difficult to reconstruct what Jacobi's attitude toward Schelling was at the time. Certainly Jacobi had felt a certain kinship with both Schelling and Fichte initially, as can be seen from a letter of 1797 to Jens Baggesen:

> Fichte and Schelling are now referring ever more frequently, extensively and emphatically to my writings, and in all the works of the latter one can see how he

> has given them [e.g., Jacobi's writings] flesh and blood.... For my part I must try and see if perhaps these men have succeeded in understanding me better than I do myself, and if I might not—through them—learn something better from myself than I knew I was teaching, which would in no way be impossible.[43]

Yet by 1806 matters stood rather differently: although two friendly letters from Jacobi to Schelling were written in June of 1806, one of which thanks Schelling for his help in preparing the opening day address for the Academy of Sciences,[44] by September things are no longer so friendly, at least from Jacobi's point of view:

> My insight into the rotten and perverse in the most recent philosophy is becoming deeper and more complete with each passing day.... Schelling visits me from time to time; he is very forthcoming to me, and I believe that he sincerely wishes to win my friendship. My genius however warns in no uncertain terms to remain distant and not get involved. Fichte says of the sensual man "it is not his insight but his love that determines his opinion." In Schelling the love of nature dominates exclusively; in me the love of the supersensible [*Übernaturlichen*] takes precedence...[45]

Still, even if Schelling had suspected Jacobi's lack of enthusiasm for his views for some time, it remains for us to inquire what the ideas were that Schelling felt he had to come to the passionate defense of.

First and foremost, Schelling is struggling to define the place and limits of metaphysics. He goes about this by first attacking what he sees as Jacobi's simpleminded or willful misunderstandings of his philosophy of nature as pantheistic; he then turns his attention to the questions of the limits of reason and the possibility of metaphysics, and in so doing he sets the agenda for the philosophy of mythology and revelation.

Schelling immediately seizes upon Jacobi's claim that "this second daughter of the critical philosophy (!) claims ... that above nature there is nothing, and nature alone exists, or put in other words, 'nature is one and all, nothing exists above it'" (8:24). He complains that Jacobi's tone and manner of presentation imply that these exact words frequently occur in his works. This is very misleading, for "these words are not to be found in a single one of my writings" (8:25). He refers to the view of nature he espoused as early as 1802: "We understand nature as absolute identity, insofar as it is seen not as existing, but as the ground of its own being" (8:25). This is an early formulation of the distinction between ground and existence with which Schelling establishes a duality in identity that will allow him to account for the movement in nature and history. Change and transformation is the law of nature and of all life: thus, in the most memorable phrase of the entire polemic, any theology which excludes change produces only "a God who is alien to nature and a nature that is devoid of God" [*ein unnatürlicher Gott und eine gottlose Natur*] (8:70). This claim is echoed in the *Ages of the World*: "We know of no other than a living God" (8:142).

In this first part of the *Memorial*, Schelling is mainly concerned with inaccuracies and what he chooses to see as malicious misinterpretation, but these are relatively minor matters in comparison with the provocative and prophetic claims Schelling makes about metaphysics. He presents Jacobi in historical context in order to tell a cautionary tale that allows us to understand something of how Schelling saw himself. He begins the story by remarking that following all the twistings and turnings of this philosophical personality brings us back to the three principles first announced in the *Spinoza-Büchlein*, which culminate in the declaration that "every manner [of philosophizing that is based on the method] of demonstration ends in fatalism" (8:39).[46] That Jacobi has not changed his basic viewpoint since 1785 is easily seen, continues Schelling, in the claim on page 152 of *On the*

Divine Things: "It is in the interest of science that God not exist" (8:41). This, much more than the accusation of atheism or the various misreadings, is what really seems to enrage Schelling: Jacobi is denying that reason has any access to the highest reality. Schelling, who remains convinced that "philosophy is only really philosophy as long as the belief persists that it is possible for something to be scientifically established about the existence or nonexistence of God" (8:42), observes that it was this question that was at the heart of the pantheism controversy. When Lessing refused Jacobi's invitation to abandon reason for the *salto mortale* of faith, he was comporting himself as a "true philosopher" (8:45); Schelling adds snidely, "Lessing was not the man to readily surrender his mind, for he knew the value of what he had; others may find the sacrifice easier" (8:45–46).

The invocation of Lessing is not accidental; Schelling makes oblique reference to Lessing's thesis in *Education of the Human Race* that "all scientific efforts have as their highest and last goal" (8:55) the demonstration of the truths of revelation as truths of reason. Inasmuch as the highest truth is God, a central focus of Schelling's attack is Jacobi's concept of God; he claims, in arguments reminiscent of the *Ages of the World*, that it is incapable of explaining creation, since a God completely perfect in itself could only be lessened in perfection by the act of creation. (I have referred above, in section III, to Schelling's use of the contrast between the *Deus implicitus* and *Deus explicitus* to explain the nature of the temporal process in which God is expressed.)

Decades later, when Schelling had completed his own transition from the negative philosophy of his youth to the positive philosophy he hoped to capture in the philosophy of mythology, he comes to a calmer and more measured assessment of Jacobi, who is the last figure treated in his lectures *On the History of Modern Philosophy*.[47] How does a story that begins with Bacon and Descartes end with Jacobi? Schelling points out that it is precisely the circumstance that "no other philosopher had conceded so *much* to pure rationalism . . . as Jacobi" that makes him "the most instructive personality in the whole history of modern philosophy" (10:168). That is, Jacobi is exemplary as a kind of limiting case: even though he assigned enormous powers to reason, he also felt strongly that ultimate reality lay beyond reason's grasp. Schelling even gave Jacobi credit for having anticipated his own critique of the Enlightenment:

> He recognized the true character of all modern systems, namely that they, instead of offering us what we really desire to know, and, if we want to be honest, alone consider it is *worth* the effort to know, offer only a tiresome substitute, a knowledge in which thought never gets beyond itself, whereas we really desire to get *beyond* thinking. . . . Thus the early Jacobi. (10:169)

This is a marvelous piece of strategy, as Schelling sees it: concede everything to reason, only to sorrowfully point out that reason cannot capture what is most vital to human beings—personality, freedom, God. Jacobi had diagnosed the singular failing of rationalistic philosophy; but the cure he advocated, the reliance on faith (*Glaube*), or "this comfortable immediate knowledge, by means of which one is lifted over all difficulties with One Word," was "the worst present Jacobi gave to philosophy" (10:172), leading to enormous abuses by his followers. This was of course the *Schwärmerei* Kant had feared, with its concomitant division between the true belivers and everyone else.

Where, then, did Jacobi go wrong, after so unerringly putting his finger on *the* philosophical problem of modern philosophy? In rejecting reason for faith, the natural for the supernatural, he was (perhaps unwittingly) rejecting the basis of the very truths he wished to celebrate. Here we can begin to apprehend the end of the story of modern philosophy as Schelling now sees it. All his earlier work on the philosophy of nature and the structure of knowledge was the necessary preparation for understanding the true significance of the very things Jacobi was so insistent on the importance of. Jacobi, in a sense, stands in for all those who wanted to skip the hard work of philosophizing and rush unimpeded into the arms of the highest reality. The lesson of Jacobi's philosophical efforts is just one illustration of the more general truth that "every philosophy which does not keep its basis in the negative, and which wishes to reach the positive, the divine in an immediate manner, *without* the negative, finally dies of unavoidable spiritual exhaustion" (10:176).

In this inability to deal with beginnings, Jacobi is again an instructive example, in that his "panic-stricken terror of nature" (10:176) and utter incomprehension of even "the thought of matter as living" (10:177) doomed his speculations about the supernatural to a vitiated onesidedness, connected with nothing real or living:

> When Jacobi saw nature taken up fully as an essential element into philosophy, the only weapon left to him was to accuse this system of Pantheism in the commonest and crudest sense, and to pursue it in every possible way. But philosophy *cannot* just concern itself with the highest things, it must, if it is to be the science which grasps everything, *really* connect the highest with the lowest. Whoever throws nature away in advance, as that which is absolutely devoid of spirit, thereby deprives himself even of the material in which and from which he could develop the spiritual. (10:177)

This statement reflects both Schelling's lifelong commitment to system, in the claim that the science which grasps everything must "*really* connect the highest with the lowest," as well as his growing realization that reason alone cannot reveal this connection. This makes him our contemporary in more ways than one. Certainly the passage in *Of Human Freedom* points to this, which claims that beneath all appearance of law and order "lawlessness lurks ... as if it could once again break through, and nowhere does it appear as if order and form were at the origin but rather, that an original chaos was brought to order" (7:359). Ernst Bloch has suggested that Schelling presents us with an early example of what he calls

> Oedipal metaphysics [in which] an original *darkness* or *incognito* is reflected, if not a fantastically contrived *crime*. In this respect, every last investigation of origins is related to the Oedipal form, which treats the incognito basically not just as an unknown of the logical variety, but also as something uncanny, unknown even to itself.[48]

The philosophy of mythology, then, can be read as a reconstruction of the crime, of the unfathomable, of that which answers the question of why there is something rather than nothing. It is anything but a departure or new direction for Schelling, given his earlier concerns; rather it is the only way possible for him to address the questions about origins the earlier work had led to.

VI. Conclusion

In a sense, Schelling never again thought so highly of reason as he did at the very beginning of his career, when he, like so many others, sought to be more Kantian than Kant by making the search for the limits of reason a central part of his philosophical endeavors. His rejection of the claims to objectivity and truth made by Enlightenment science in favor of a more dynamic and developmental model of nature could not fail to raise that question posed to all defenders of evolutionary theories: where does man fit in? If nature is really the unconscious poetry of the spirit, then the opacity and resistance to complete understanding of matter itself must have its parallel in the human being, as indeed proved to be the case: the unconscious was acknowledged in the *System of Transcendental Idealism*. The "solution" Schelling claimed to find in the philosophy of art did not last: the fragile unity of unconscious and conscious production represented by the work of the artist proved to be too slender a foundation for all the philosophical weight Schelling wanted to place on it, although the suggestion that the highest development of reason is aesthetic reason has by no means gone unnoticed.

Schelling's various excursions into the philosophy of identity ended unsatisfyingly, but in his very failure to achieve systematic closure he began to understand the implications of the connections between a static concept of being and the dream of system. It became clearer to him in *Of Human Freedom* that he had to abandon concept for metaphor, to give up an unchanging highest being for the pantheism of a living God. The primordial being is will; with this realization dawns the recognition of the limitations of reason with a vengeance. Reason will never be adequate, even in principle, to understand a being whose essence is will. Thus although Schelling is quite right to insist that man is self-created in the sense that he chooses his own character, and therefore that both the good and the evil man act freely, he has come no closer to understanding what it is in man that turns him to evil, and his frustration at this last and deepest failure is evident.

The middle Schelling can be understood as having moved decisively beyond the whole enterprise of trying to understand the nonrational in rational terms. The philosophy of mythology returns to the emphasis on the individual, the particular, and the symbolic so characteristic of aesthetic reason in the hope that the more flexible framework of myth will be able to catch and retain the richness of reality. That this was only partially successful may be seen from the philosophical point of view not just in Schelling's increasing use of references to *Angst* and *Angst des Lebens* but in his inability to put the philosophy of mythology into a final form.

The later Schelling's philosophy of revelation remains known largely through its spectacularly unsuccessful presentation in the 1841 Berlin Lectures. The story of these lectures, including the events which motivated the king of Prussia to issue the invitation to Schelling to assume Hegel's chair at the University of Berlin, and an anatomy of the zeitgeist which doomed the lectures, is contained in Manfred Frank's edition of the *Philosophie der Offenbarung*.[49] The philosophy of revelation is, as Walter Schulz points out, a solution literally beyond reason to the situation posed by Schelling's own incapacitating awe at the implications of his discovery of the *unvordenklichkeit* of being itself:

> The later Schelling stood between two ages. He could on the one hand no longer maintain unproblematically the rationality of the world, as he had done in the beginning, and on the other hand he did not want to elevate the will as a dark force to an absolute principle, like Schopenhauer and Nietzsche.[50]

Schelling's philosophy of revelation retells the Christian story as a drama of mediation between will and reason, not just in the individual but also in human history. Yet it is a mistake to see in it a disappointed old man's relapse into the comforting pieties of his youth. Schelling felt, rather, that he and others had exposed the pretensions of reason and did not flinch from recognizing the dark side of the will, but were unwilling to cast their allegiance exclusively with either side, leaving Christian metaphysics the only place to stand.

NOTES

Introduction

1. F. W. J. Schelling, *Schellings Werke*, ed. Manfred Schröter. Munich: Beck, 1927. Citation of texts is by volume and page number.

2. Hermann Braun, "Ein Bedürfnis nach Schelling," *Philosophische Rundschau* 37 (1990): 161–96, 298–326.

3. Joseph L. Esposito, *Schelling's Idealism and the Philosophy of Nature*, Lewisburg: Bucknell University Press, 1977; Alan White, *Schelling: An Introduction to the System of Freedom*, New Haven: Yale University Press, 1983; Alan White, *Absolute Knowledge: Hegel and the Problem of Metaphysics*, Athens, Ohio: Ohio University Press, 1983; Werner Marx, *The Philosophy of F. W. J. Schelling*, Bloomington: Indiana University Press, 1984; Andrew Bowie, *Schelling and Modern European Philosophy*, London and New York: Routledge, 1993; Edward Beach, *The Potencie(s) of the Gods*, New York: State University of New York Press, 1994.

4. Esposito, *Schelling's Idealism and Philosophy of Nature*, 9.

5. "The dragonseed of Hegelian pantheism" were the words of King Friedrich Wilhelm IV, quoted in Manfred Frank's introduction to *Schellings Philosophie der Offenbarung 1841/42* (Frankfurt am Main: Suhrkamp, 1977), 11.

6. Ibid., 99.

7. Alan White (see note 2 above) argues that Hegel can be defended against Schelling's criticisms; Andrew Bowie points out how successful many of Schelling's objections have proven to be, even if we know them today by rather different names; both are influenced by Manfred Frank's *Der unendliche Mangel an Sein* (Frankfurt: Suhrkamp, 1975, 1989).

8. Lovejoy, *The Great Chain of Being*, (Cambridge: Harvard University Press, 1936), 232.

9. Frederick Beiser, *The Fate of Reason* (Cambridge: Harvard University Press, 1987); see especially chapters 2 and 3.

Chapter 1. The Enlightenment Under Attack

1. Vol. 3, tr. E. S. Haldane and Frances Simson (New York: Humanities Press, 1974), 504–505.

2. K. L. Reinhold, *Versuch einer neuen Theorie des menschlichen Vorstellungsvermögens* (Prague & Jena: C. Widtmann and I. M. Mauke, 1789), 2.

3. The "Letters" attracted attention far beyond Jena; Kant wrote to Reinhold in December 1787: "I have, excellent praiseworthy sir, read the beautiful letters with which you have honored my philosophy, and which are incomparable for their combination of thoroughness and grace[;] they have also not failed in our area to produce the desired effect." AK, 10, Kant an Reinhold, 28.12.1787, no. 176, p. 513.

4. In an appendix to "Uber den Gebrauch teleologischen Prinzipien in der Philosophie" (1788), which first appeared in the *Teutschen Merkur*, where Reinhold's "talent, insight and praiseworthy style of thought" are singled out for favorable attention in the "Letters." AK 8: 183.

5. Robert Reiniger, *Kant, seine Anhänger und seine Gegner* (Munich: Verlag Ernst Reinhard), 1923.

6. Max Wundt, *Die Philosophie an der Universität Jena in ihrem geschichtlichen Verlauf dargestellt* (Jena: Verlag von Gustav Fischer, 1932), 140.

7. "Ueber die bisherigen Schicksale der Kantischen Philosophie", reprinted as the preface to the *Versuch*, 62.

8. Ibid, 67.

9. Ibid, 67.

10. An examination of Reinhold's role in the development of German Idealism, with special reference to his influence on Fichte, can be found in Daniel Breazeale, "Between Kant and

Fichte: Karl Leonhard Reinhold's 'Elementary Philosophy,' " *Review of Metaphysics* 35 (1982): 785–821.

11. *Briefe*, 2: 63–64; see also 1:87–88, 1:208.

12. Xavier Tilliette, *Schelling: Une Philosophie en devenir* (Paris: Librarie Philosophique J. Vrin, 1970), 1:66.

13. Ernst Cassirer, *Das Erkenntnisproblem* (Berlin: Verlag Bruno Cassirer, 1920), 3:17.

14. Ibid., 3:1.

15. Baum, *Vernunft und Erkenntnis: Die Philosophie F. H. Jacobis* (Bonn: Bouvier, 1969), 1.

16. N. Altwicker, ed., *Texte zur Geschichte des Spinozismus* (Darmstadt: Wissenschaftliche Buchgesellschaft, 1971), 37.

17. Hermann Timm, *Gott und die Freiheit: Die Spinozarenaissance*, Studien zur Religionsphilosophie der Goethezeit (Frankfurt: Vittorio Klostermann, 1974), 1:6.

18. Jacobi, "Etwas das Lessing gesagt hat: Ein Commentar zu den Reisen des Päpste," reprinted in *Jacobis Werke*, 2:325–88.

19. Alexander Altmann, *Moses Mendelssohn: A Biographical Study* (London: Routledge & Kegan Paul, 1973), 593–603.

20. Heinrich Scholz, ed., *Die Hauptschriften zum Pantheismusstreit zwischen Jacobi und Mendelssohn*, Neudrucke seltener philosophische Werke, ed. von der Kantgesellschaft (Berlin: Reuther & Reichard, 1916), 6:293; all references will be to this edition rather than the version in Jacobi's *Werke*, since it is not as widely available.

21. Hermann Timm speaks of three *Auslegungstypen*, but admits: "Lessing is best understood as protagonist of the moral-religious consciousness of emancipation of the German Enlightenment movement, the first New Protestant. His name stands for an undogmatic Christianity, which has freed itself from biblical-confessional dogmatism to [become] a universal religion of humanity . . . as was announced for the first time from the theatrical pulpit of "Nathan." *Gott und die Freiheit*, 17–18.

22. Scholz, *Hauptschriften zum Pantheismusstreit*, 68–69.

23. See Altmann, *Moses Mendelssohn*, esp. 593–670, for an extensive discussion of the circumstances of Mendelssohn's death.

24. Scholz, *Hauptschriften zum Pantheismusstreit*, 78.

25. Altmann, "Lessing und Jacobi: Das Gesprach uber den Spinozismus," *Lessing Yearbook 3* (Max Hueber Verlag, 1971), 50.

26. Henry E. Allison, *Lessing and the Enlightenment* (Ann Arbor: University of Michigan Press, 1970), 72–75.

27. Ibid., 125.

28. Kurt Hildebrandt, *Leibniz und das Reich der Gnade* (The Hague: Nijhoff, 1953), 9–10.

29. Scholz, *Hauptschriften zum Pantheismusstreit*, 88.

30. *God: Some Conversations*, trans. Frederick Burkhardt (New York: Veritas Press, 1940), 78.

31. Altwicker, *Texte zum Spinozismus*, 30.

32. Mauthner, *Jacobis Spinoza-Buchlein, nebst Replik und Duplik* (Munich: Georg Muller Verlag, 1912), xii.

33. W. Dilthey, *Leben Schleiermachers, zweite Auflage* (Berlin and Leipzig: Walter de Gruyter, 1922), 183: "Like most of his contemporaries before 1802, when the edition of Paulus appeared, he knew Spinoza only in Jacobi's version."

34. Scholz, *Hauptschriften zum Pantheismusstreit*, 15, 295ff.

35. Ibid., 39.

36. Ibid., 78.

37. Ibid., 79, 124.

38. Ibid., 80.

39. Ibid., 82.

40. "Historically, the contrast of the typological worldviews of pantheism and personalism are at the basis of Jacobi's philosophy. . . . It is especially noteworthy that, with the exception of Kant, at first everyone young and promising . . .

came down on the side of Spinoza's opposition." Timm, *Gott und die Freiheit*, 139.

41. Scholz, *Hauptschriften zum Pantheismusstreit*, 173–80.

42. A common designation for all three, especially among followers of Kant. See, for example, Robert Reininger's *Kant, Seine Anhänger und Seine Gegner* (Munich: Verlag Ernst Reinhardt, 1932), which devotes a chapter to the *Glaubensphilosophen* Hamann, Herder, Jacob, and Fries.

43. The *Socratische Denkwürdigkeiten* has been translated into English as *Hamann's Socratic Memorabilia: A Translation and Commentary*, ed. and trans. James C. O'Flaherty (Baltimore: Johns Hopkins University Press, 1967).

44. *Socratic Memorabilia*, 7.

45. Oswei Temkin discusses Herder's understanding of the concepts of genesis and epigenesis as they anticipate Schelling's views on the historical character of the natural world in "Ontogeny and History around 1800," reprinted in *The Double Face of Janus* (Baltimore: Johns Hopkins University Press, 1977), 373–89.

46. Scholz, *Hauptschriften zum Pantheismusstreit*, 90.

47. Di Giovanni, "From Jacobi's Philosophical Novel to Fichte's Idealism," *Journal of the History of Philosophy* 27 (1989): 75–100.

48. Frederick Beiser, *The Fate of Reason: German Philosophy from Kant to Fichte* (Cambridge: Harvard University Press, 1987), 158.

49. Nohl, *Die Deutsche Bewegung: Vorlesungen und Aufsatze zur Geistesgeschichte von 1770–1830* (Göttingen: Vandenhoeck und Ruprecht, 1970), 96.

50. See Hermann Timm, "Amor Dei Intellectualis," *Neue Hefte für Philosophie* 12 (1977): 65–68, on how Jacobi's *Kontrasttypologie* indirectly led to Fichte's claim, presented in its most popular form in *The Vocation of Man* (1800), that there are "only two completely consistent systems—although for Fichte these systems are his own and Spinoza's dogmatism." Or as Lewis S. Ford describes the effect of Jacobi's doctrine: "It be-

came quite fashionable to regard Spinoza as the most consistent proponent of one kind of philosophy, the wrong kind": "The Controversy between Schelling and Jacobi," *Journal of the History of Philosophy* 3 (1965): 80.

51. Scholz, *Hauptschriften zum Pantheismusstreit*, 81, 91.

52. See the discussion of the influence of Jacobi on Schelling in this respect in Ingtraud Görland, *Die Entwicklung der Frühphilosophie Schellings in der Auseinandersetzung mit Fichte* (Frankfurt: Vittorio Klostermann, 1973), esp. 55–58.

53. Letter of April 26, 1796, translated in Daniel Breazeale, ed. and trans., *Fichte's Early Philosophical Writings* (Ithaca, Cornell University Press, 1988), 413.

54. Scholz, *Hauptschriften zum Pantheismusstreit*, 171.

Chapter 2. The Knowledge of Reality

1. Scholz, *Hauptschriften zum Pantheismusstreit*, 88.

2. Ibid.

3. Ibid., 89.

4. *Briefe*, vol. 1 (Bonn: Bouvier und Co, Verlag, 1962), 301.

5. Scholz, *Hauptschriften zum Pantheismusstreit*, 146.

6. Ibid., 156–57.

7. Valerio Verra, "Jacobis Kritik am Deutschen Idealismus," *Hegel-Studien* 5 (1969): 212; Hermann Timm, "Die Bedeutung der Spinoza-Briefe Jacobis" in *Friedrich Heinrich Jacobi, Philosoph und Literat der Goethezeit*, ed. Klaus Hammacher (Frankfurt: Vittorio Klostermann, 1971), 69.

8. See the detailed discussions in Baum, *Vernunft und Erkenntnis*, 32–42, 51–69; Klaus Hammacher, *Die Philosophie Friedrich Heinrich Jacobis* (Munich: Wilhelm Fink, 1969), 131–66; Moltke S. Gram, "Things-in-Themselves: The Historical Lessons," *Journal of the History of Philosophy* 18 (1980): 407–31. For the history of the discussion of the problem, see Gerold Prauss, *Kant und das Problem der Dinge an sich* (Bonn: Bouvier, 1974); on Jacobi, esp. 192–96.

9. A thorough discussion of Fichte's early development can be found in the editor's introduction to *Fichte: Early Philosophical Writings*, trans. and ed. Daniel Breazeale (Ithaca: Cornell University Press, 1988), 1–46.

10. See the editorial report on the Briefentwurf an Eisenstuk (Fichte *Gesamtausgabe*, series 3, vol. 1, no. 124a).

11. Fichte, *Gesamtausgabe*, no. 133a (Briefentwurf an F. V. Reinhard, 20.2. 1793).

12. A partial English translation can be found in *Between Kant and Hegel: Texts in the Development of Post-Kantian Idealism*, trans. and annotated by George Di Giovanni and H. S. Harris (Albany: State University of New York Press, 1985).

13. Fichte, *Gesamtausgabe*, 2, no. 171 (Brief an Heinrich Stephani, mid-December 1793).

14. Fichte, *Gesamtausgabe*, 2, no. 189 (Brief an K. L. Reinhold, 1.3. 1794).

15. Eduard Fichte, *Johann Gottlieb Fichte. Lichtstrahlen aus seinen Werken und Briefen nebst einem Lebenabriss. Mit Beiträgen von Immanuel Hermann Fichte* (Leipzig, 1863). Cited in Fichte *Gesamtausgabe*, 2:3, 11.

16. Baggesens Dagboger, Det Kongelige Bibliotek, Kopenhagen, Ms. Ny Kgl. Saml. 8., 504. Cited in Fichte *Gesamtausgabe*, 2:3, 13.

17. The version of the story recorded in his autobiography by Heinrich Steffens, a former student, is typical: "in a close, intimate circle, Fichte used to tell us about the origin of his philosophy and how he was suddenly surprised and seized by the fundamental idea of his philosophy . . ." *Was ich erlebte*, 4 (Breslau: J. Max, 1841), 161.

18. Breazeale, *Fichte: Early Philosophical Writings*, 12–14.

19. Walter Wright in "Fichte and Philosophical Method," discusses the impact of this conviction of the incommunicability of philosophical truth by means of discursive argument on the form of Fichte's philosophical writing (*Philosophical F rum* 19 (2–3): 65–73).

20. "Erste Fichte-Rezeption mit besonderer Berucksichtigung der intellectuellen Anschauung," in *Der Transendentale Gedanke*, ed. K. Hammacher (Hamburg: Meiner, 1981) 532-35.

21. Ibid., 536, 542.

22. Ibid.

23. Fichte, *Gesamtausgabe*, 2:3, 19.

24. Reinhold, *Über das Fundament des Philosophischen Wissens* (Hamburg: Meiner, 1978), 70.

25. Reinhold, "Beytrage zur Berichtigung bisheriger Missverstandnisse der Philosophen" (Jena: Johann Michael Mauke, 1790).

26. Stolzenberg, *Fichtes Begriff der intellektuellen Anschauung*, Deutscher Idealismus, vol. 10, (Stuttgart: Klett-Cotta, 1986), see esp. 40–49.

27. Ibid., 55.

28. Fichte, *Gesamtausgabe*, 2:3, 28.

29. Ibid., 28–35.

30. Ibid., 23.

31. Ibid., 176.

32. Fichte, *Ausgewählte Werke*, 1:469; see also 1:420.

33. *The Ethics*, trans. R. H. M. Elwes (New York: Dover Publications, 1955), see esp. part I, def. 3.

34. See, e.g., Annemarie Pieper's claim in her editorial report on the "Philosophical Letters" that Fichte's formulation was composed "in enger Ahnlehnung on Schelling's Ausspruch im sechsten Brief." *Historische-Kritische Ausgabe*, 1:3 (Stuttgart: Frommann-Holzboog, 1982), 42.

35. Scholz, *Die Hauptschriften zum Pantheismusstreit*, 186.

36. Ibid., 189.

37. In his letter of 8 November to Niethammer, Schelling writes: "Thank you for the generous offer to make me a coworker at the new philosophical journal. I will do what is in my

powers. It is with special satisfaction that I take on the continuing review-essay on the most recent philosophical literature.... I will gradually provide a brief survey of the most recent history of philosophy starting with *Kant* and continuing up to the present." *Briefe* 1:95. In his letter of 16 December 1796, Schelling reports that he has already finished his first installment "as well as I could considering my many other obligations.... I don't know if you and Fichte did not expect something better." *Briefe* 1:96.

38. The "Treatises" have recently been translated into English for the first time by Thomas Pfau: *Idealism and the Endgame of Theory: Three Essays by F. W. J. Schelling* (Albany: State University of New York Press, 1994), who includes an introduction containing valuable historical background.

39. G. W. F. Hegel, *Lectures on the History of Philosophy*, vol. 3, ed. Robert F. Brown, trans. R. F. Brown and J. M. Stewart (Berkeley: University of California Press, 1990), 251.

40. Ibid., 253.

41. *Glauben und Wissen oder die Reflexionsphilosophie der Subjektivität, in der Vollständigkeit ihrer Formen, als Kantische, Jakobische, und Fichtische Philosophie*, in G. W. F. Hegel, *Gesammelte Werke*, ed. H. Büchner and O. Pöggeler (Hamburg, 1968) 4:385–86.

42. Ibid., 261.

43. *Vorlesungen über die Geschichte der Philosophie*, ed. H. Glockner (Stuttgart Frommann, 1928), 3:654.

44. Snow, "Self and Absolute in the Early Schelling," Diss., Emory University, 1984.

45. Translated into English with the title *On University Studies*; trans. E. S. Morgan (Athens: Ohio University Press, 1966).

46. Shaffer, "Romantic Philosophy and the Organization of the Disciplines: The Founding of the Humboldt University of Berlin," in *Romanticism and the Sciences*, ed. Andrew Cunningham and Nicholas Jardine (Cambridge: Cambridge University Press, 1990), 38–54.

47. Ibid.

Chapter 3. The Philosophy of Nature

1. However, Timothy Lenoir, in *The Strategy of Life* (Chicago: University of Chicago Press, 1989), has recently argued that German biologists of the nineteenth century tended to belong to one of two distinct schools, and that the adherents of Schelling-inspired forms of *Naturphilosophie* ought not to be confused with the teleomechanists or vital materialists who took their theoretical direction from Kant and J. F. Blumenbach.

2. Liebig, "Ueber das Studium der Naturwissenschaften und über den Zustand der Chemie in Preussen, 1840," *Reden und Abhandlungen* (Leipzig and Heidelberg: C. F. Winter'sche Verlagshandlung, 1874), 24.

3. Ibid., p. 9.

4. Lenoir, "Generational Factors in the Origin of *Romantische Naturphilosophie*," *Journal of the History of Biology* 11 (1978): 57.

5. See note 1.

6. Gower, "Speculation in Physics: The History and Practice of *Naturphilosophie*," *Studies in the History and Philosophy of Science* 3 (1973): 320.

7. Esposito, *Schelling's Idealism and Philosophy of Nature*, 10.

8. Nelly Tsouyopoulos, *Andreas Röschlaub und die Romantische Medizin: Die philosophische Grundlagen der modernen Medizin* (Stuttgart: Gustav Fischer Verlag, 1982); H. J. Sandkühler, *Natur und geschichtlichen Prozess: Studien zur Naturphilosophie F. W. J. Schellings* (Frankfurt: Suhrkamp, 1984); R. Heckmann, H. Krings, and R. W. Meyer, eds., *Natur und Subjektivität: Zur Auseinandersetzung mit der Naturphilosophie der jungen Schelling* (Stuttgart-Bad Cannstatt: Frommann-Holzboog, 1985); Marie-Luise Heuser-Kessler, *Die Produktivität der Natur: Schellings Naturphilosophie und das neue Paradigma der Selbstorganisation in den Naturwissenschaften* (Berlin: Duncker & Humblot, 1986); Bernd-Olaf Küppers, *Natur als Organismus: Schellings frühe Naturphilosophie und ihre Bedeutung für die moderne Biologie*

(Frankfurt: Klostermann, 1992); Klaus-Jürgen Grün, *Das Erwachen der Materie* (Zurich: Georg Olms Verlag, 1993).

9. One of the most daunting aspects of studying Schelling's *Naturphilosophie* concerns the close connection of many of his views to the scientific milieu of his time; so important are these in many cases all but forgotten historical figures that the editors of the Schelling *Historische-Kritische Ausgabe* have devoted an entire supplementary volume to them.

10. Ernst Cassirer, *Idee und Gestalt* (Berling: G. Cassirer, 1924), 130–31.

11. An English translation of the *Ideas for a Philosophy of Nature* has been provided by Errol E. Harris and Peter Heath (New York: Cambridge University Press, 1988); unfortunately, it does not contain page references to Schelling's *Sämtliche Werke*.

12. *Aesthetica in nuce* (1762), in *Sämtliche Werke*, ed. J. Nadler (Vienna: Thomas-Morus-Presse, 1949–57), 2:198–99.

13. See especially *The Vocation of Man*, Book 2, and the Second Introduction to the *Wissenschaftslehre*.

14. Harris and Heath, *Ideas*, 182–90.

15. *Metaphysical Foundations of Natural Science*, trans. James Ellington (Indianapolis: Hackett, 1985), 41.

16. Ibid., 42.

17. Ibid., 57.

18. Harris and Heath, *Ideas*, p. 165 (xi).

19. "The truth is that the idea of things in themselves had come down to Kant through the tradition and had lost all meaning in the course of inheritance." Note added in the second edition: 2: 33 n.

20. Lawrence, "Schelling as Post-Hegelian and as Aristotelian," *International Philosophical Quarterly* 26 (1986), see especially 323–25. Hideki Mine has explored the impact of Aristotle on Schelling's later philosophy in *Ungrund und Mitwissenschaft: Das Problem der Freiheit in der Spätphilosophie Schellings* (Frankfurt: Peter Lang, 1983), see esp. 57–90.

21. Kant, *Critique of Judgment*, trans. W. S. Pluhar (Indianapolis: Hackett, 1987), 254.

22. Ibid., 282.

23. *Metaphysical Foundations of Natural Science*, 57. Kant adds that this inability of the attractive force to be sensed directed "is doubtless the reason why, in spite of the clearest proofs that attraction must belong to the fundamental forces of nature equally as much as repulsion does, one nevertheless opposes the former force so much, and wants to grant no other forces at all besides those of impact and pressure (both by means of impenetrability)":58–59.

24. Royce, *The Spirit of Modern Philosophy* (Boston: Houghton Mifflin, 1893), 187.

25. Ibid., 188–89.

Chapter 4.   Metaphors for Nature

1. Schelling, "Freiheit und Geschichte in Schellings Philosophie," in F. W. J. Schelling, *Über das Wesen der menschlichen Freiheit* (Frankfurt am Main: Suhrkamp [Suhrkamp Taschenbuch 138], 1975), 13.

2. Some of this material was reprinted by K. F. A. Schelling in the *Sämtliche Werke*, 7:127–288; the proposal for the *Jahrbücher der Medizin* has been reprinted in the *Briefe*, 1:312–14.

3. Ibid., 324.

4. See, e.g., Nelly Tsouyopoulos, "Doctors *contra* clysters and feudalism: The consequences of a Romantic revolution," in A. Cunningham and N. Jardine, eds., *Romanticism and the Sciences* (Cambridge: Cambridge University Press, 1990), 101–29, on the consequences for nineteenth-century medicine of the transition from conceptualizing the body as a lifeless machine which might be destroyed by its own waste products to the Schellingian model of a self-regulating organism responding to stimuli.

5. Rowland Gray-Smith, "God in the Philosophy of Schelling" (Diss., University of Pennsylvania, 1933), 34.

6. Dietrich von Engelhardt, "Schellings philosophische Grundlegung der Medizin," in Sandkühler, *Natur und geschichtlicher Prozess*, 306; von Engelhardt discusses a number of aspects of Schelling's relationship to the medical and scientific community of his time but stresses that this is a complex and still relatively unresearched area.

7. Spelman, "Woman as Body: Ancient and Contemporary Views," *Feminist Studies* 8 (1982): 109–10.

8. Indeed, Schelling's relationship with his first wife, Caroline Böhmer-Schlegel, seems to have been a model of intellectual cooperation and of mutual benefit, intimate to the then unusual point of coauthorship, and even giving rise to pranks played on editors about which of them had written certain reviews, according to Erich Frank, *Rezensionen über schöne Literatur von Schelling und Caroline* (Heidelberg: Carl Winters Universitätsbuchhandlung, 1912), 4–7. Arsenji Gulyga has recently argued, with respect to the disputed authorship of the novel *Nachtwachen*, that Schelling and Caroline may have collaborated: "Schelling als Verfasser der Nachtwachen des Bonaventura," *Deutsche Zeitschrift für Philosophie* 32 (1984): 1027–36.

9. Kleingeld, "The Problematic Status of Gender-Neutral Language in the History of Philosophy: The Case of Kant," *Philosophical Forum* 25 (1993): 134.

10. A thorough examination of Kant's views and their philosophical antecedents can be found in Robin May Schott's *Cognition and Eros: A Critique of the Kantian Paradigm* (Boston: Beacon, 1988). Kleingeld (see note 9) also provides a summary of recent work on Kant's views on women.

11. "Of the Distinction of the Beautiful and the Sublime in the Interrelations of the Sexes," in Mary Mahowald, ed., *Philosophy of Woman*, 2d ed. (Indianapolis: Hackett, 1983), 269.

12. Mendus, "Kant: 'An Honest but Narrow-Minded Bourgeois'?" in *Women in Western Political Philosophy*, ed. Ellen Kennedy and Susan Mendus (New York: St. Martin's, 1987), 21–43.

13. Ibid., 195.

14. *Metaphysical Foundations of Natural Science*, trans. James Ellington (Indianapolis: Hackett, 1985), 48.

15. "That the possibility of fundamental forces should be made conceivable is a completely impossible demand; for they are called fundamental forces precisely because they cannot be derived from any other force . . ." Ibid., 62.

16. *Werke* 8:197.

17. *Critique of Practical Reason*, trans. Lewis White Beck (New York: Bobbs-Merrill, 1956), 58.

18. In no other philosopher except possibly Schopenhauer does the theory seem to have been such a transparent reflection of the man and his personality, as can be seen in this comment by Julius Ebbinghaus: "Fichte was not satisfied merely to present the insight he had achieved and allow it to have its own effect. Instead, he was motivated just as much by a concern for people's relation to this insight and the need for the entire world to submit to the necessity of his thoughts as he was by the question of truth itself. Fichte's sole blind spot regarding himself was that he never realized that underlying all of his speeches (and, at bottom, all the works he left behind are nothing but speeches) was a will to dominate the thoughts of men—a will which on occasion, dispensed neither with threats nor with scorn directed at those who were unwilling to submit." Quoted in Daniel Breazeale, *Fichte's Early Writings*, 37 n. 82.

19. *Politics* 1.13.1260a.13.

20. *Politics* 1.5.1254b.14.

21. There are those who argue that Aristotle, too, assigns women a distinct nature, despite the fact that he explicitly answers this question in the negative elsewhere (*Metaphysics* 10.9.1058a.29–31); my point here is only that independently of the question of whether or not Aristotle conflated social and natural realities with respect to the nature of women, Fichte (and Hegel after him) certainly did.

22. What it means to say that woman is still a part of nature for Fichte is discussed at length in Karen Kenkel's "Fichte's Theory of Sexual Difference," in *Impure Reason: Dialectic of the Enlightenment in Germany* (Detroit: Wayne State University Press, 1992); 279–97.

23. *Philosophy of Right*, 263.

24. *Philosophy of Nature*, 413.

25. Ravven, "Has Hegel Anything to Say to Feminists?" *Owl of Minerva* 19 (1988): 159.

26. *Philosophy of Right,* section 166, 114.

27. Ibid., sections 165, 166, p. 114.

28. Mills, "Hegel's *Antigone,*" *Owl of Minerva* 17 (1986): 151.

29. *Philosophy of History,* trans. J. Sibre (New York: Dorer, 1956), section 59.

30. *Phenomenology of Spirit,* trans. A. V. Miller, paragraph 475.

31. In A. Stopcyzk, *Was Philosophen uber Fraven denken* (Munich: Matthes & Seitz Verlag, 1980) 128.

32. Ravven, "Has Hegel Anything to Say?" 161.

33. On Hegel's philosophy of nature, see *Hegels Philosophie der Natur: Beziehungen zwischen empirischen und spekulativer Naturerkenntnis,* ed. Rolf-Peter Horstmann and Michael John Petry (Stuttgart: Klett-Cotta, 1986).

34. Beach, *The Potencie(s) of the Gods* (Albany: State University of New York Press, 1994), 85.

35. "The laws of nature of the material world, are laws of reason, revelations of a rational will; but when we thus consider all material nature, as the constant work of eternal reason, our contemplation cannot remain at this point, but leads us by thought to view the laws of the universal nature. In other words, soul and nature are one, seen from two different sides; thus we cease to wonder at their harmony." H. C. Oersted, *The Soul in Nature* (London: Bohn, 1852); 384. See also H. A. M. Snelders, "Oersted's Discovery of Electromagnetism," in A. Cunningham and N. Jardine, eds., *Romanticism and the Sciences* (Cambridge: University Press, 1990), 228–40.

36. Wetzels, *Johann Wilhelm Ritter: Physik im Wirkungsfeld der deutschen Romantik* (Berlin and New York: 1973), 32–33.

37. David Farrell Krell rereads *Of Human Freedom* in light of what he sees as a crucial emphasis on the motif of castration, in "The Crisis of Reason in the Nineteenth Century: Schelling's

Treatise on Human Freedom," in *The Collegium Phaenomenologicum*, ed. John Sallis (Dordrecht: Kluwer, 1988), 13–32.

Chapter 5. The Emergence of the Unconscious

1. *The System of Transcendental Idealism* (1800) has been translated by Peter Heath, with an introduction by Michael Vater (Charlottesville: University Press of Virginia, 1978, 1981).

2. The "Vorlesungen zur Geschichte der neueren Philosophie" of 1827 have recently appeared in English translation under the title *On the History of Modern Philosophy*, trans. and with an introduction by Andrew Bowie (Cambridge: Cambridge University Press, 1994); Bowie dates the text as either 1833–34 or 1836–37: ix.

3. Marx, *The Philosophy of F. W. J. Schelling: History, System and Freedom*, trans. Thomas Nenon (Bloomington: Indiana University Press, 1984), 52.

4. This claim has also been made by Michael Vater in his introduction to Heath's translation of the *System;* see especially "The Dominance of the Unconscious," xxvii–xxxii.

5. White, *Schelling: An Introduction to the System of Human Freedom* (New Haven: Yale University Press, 1983), 55.

6. According to Lancelot Law Whyte in *The Unconscious before Freud* (New York: Basic Books, 1960), 125: "Schelling gave the earliest formulation . . . of the following argument, which for minds affected by the Cartesian dualism is of crucial importance: that one organizing principle must pervade both the physical world and consciousness, but that outside our own awareness this principle is not itself conscious." Peter Gay presents a compelling account of the development of Freud's theory of mind and the unconscious which argues that the laws of neurology were an important influence on the formulation of the "laws" of psychology: *Freud: A Life for our Time* (New York: W. W. Norton, 1988); see esp. 117–32.

7. *The Phenomenology of Spirit*, trans. A. V. Miller (Oxford: Oxford University Press, 1977), 408.

8. Ballard, "The Kantian Solution to the Problem of Man within Nature," *Tulane Studies in Philosophy* 3 (1954): 8.

9. Ibid., 9.

10. *Critique of Judgment,* trans. Werner S. Pluhar (Indianapolis: Hackett, 1987), 15.

11. Di Giovanni, review of Errol E. Harris, *An Interpretation of the Logic of Hegel* (Lanham, Md.: University Press of America, 1983), in the *Owl of Minerva* 16(2) (1985): 224.

12. *Critique of Judgment,* 356–57.

13. Ibid., 357 n. 64.

14. That Schelling's *Naturphilosophie* is better understood as a response to Kant than as an emendation or supplement to Fichte has also been stressed by Erich Adickes, *Kant als Naturforscher* (Berlin: Walter de Gruyter, 1925), and more recently by George di Giovanni, "Kant's Metaphysics of Nature and Schelling's *Ideas for a Philosophy of Nature,*" *Journal of the History of Philosophy* 17 (1979): 197–215.

15. "Einleitung," in F. W. J. Schelling, *System des transcendentalen Idealismus* (Hamburg: Felix Meiner Verlag, 1962), xxiv.

16. See chapter 3, section IV.

17. This insight led directly to the discovery of what Schelling claimed to be his unique method. The self makes itself an object, yet also desires to know itself as a subject, to model its knowledge on self-knowledge; thus it is driven to create ever more sophisticated objectifications of itself. This method of demonstrating the progression by means of which the self comes to itself as dialectical is what Schelling claims to have discovered while still working under the "carapace of Fichtean thought": "If anyone among you wishes now or in the future to become acquainted at first hand with the gradual development of recent philosophy, then I cannot do otherwise than recommend to him the study of this system of transcendental idealism; therein he would recognize beneath the carapace of Fichtean thought, the new system, which must sooner or later break through this carapace[;] he would find in this work already the *method* in use, which was only later used on a greater scale; in that he already finds this method, which later became the soul of the system independently of Fichte, he would be convinced, that it was exactly this which was peculiar

to me, yes, was so natural to me that I almost cannot *boast* of it as a discovery, yet precisely for that reason can much less allow *it* to be stolen from me, or allow that someone else boasts of having discovered it" (10:96).

18. White points out that the Heath translation is based on the Felix Meiner edition, which has mistakenly printed *ich frage mich weiter* [I ask myself further]. The K. F. A. Schelling edition reads *ich frage nicht weiter* [I do not ask further]. *Schelling: An Introduction to the System of Freedom*, 58.

19. *Schelling: An Introduction to the System of Freedom*, 5.

20. The references to "tranquility" and the pacification of endless striving in the contemplation of art certainly evoke Schopenhauer's discussions of "peace and calm, true well-being" and artistic contemplations as suddenly lifting "us out of the endless stream of willing." *The World as Will and Representation*, vol 1, trans. E. F. J. Payne (New York: Dover, 1969), 196.

21. Marx, *Philosophy of Schelling*, 57.

Chapter 6.   Of Human Freedom

1. Schelling: *The Ages of the World*, trans. Frederick de Wolfe Bolman (New York: Columbia University Press, 1942), 67.

2. Hegel, *Works*, Freundeausgabe 25:682; quoted in Heidegger, *Schelling's Treatise on the Essence of Human Freedom*, trans. Joan Stambaugh (Athens: Ohio University Press, 1985), 13.

3. White, *Schelling*, 5.

4. Axel Orzechowski ("Der gegenwärtige Schelling: Positionen der heutigen Schelling-Forschung. Ein Bericht," *Zeitschrift für philosophische Forschung* 46 [1993]: 301–6) has provided a brief summary of the wide-ranging variety of perspectives on *Of Human Freedom* discussed at the October 1992 meeting of the Internationale Schelling-Gesellschaft (the theme of the meeting was "Schelling's Path to the Freedom Essay— Legend and Reality"), beginning with Walter Erhardt's claim

that "Schelling always intended to develop a system of freedom," 301.

5. Published in Tübingen in 1812; the full title was: "F. W. J. Schellings Memorial on Herr Friedrich Heinrich Jacobis Writing on the Divine Things and the Attribution Therein to Him of an Intentional and Lying Atheism" [*F. W. J. Schellings Denkmal der Schrift von den Gottlichen Dingen etc des Herrn Friedrich Heinrich Jacobi und der ihm in derselben gemachten Beschuldigung eines absichtlich tauschenden, lugeredenden Atheismus*], 8: 19–36.

6. Vater, Introduction to the *System of Transcendental Idealism* (1800), trans. Peter Heath (Charlottesville: University Press of Virginia, 1978), xxx.

7. Heidegger, *Schelling's Treatise*, 6.

8. One of the most difficult German expressions to translate, it might somewhat clumsily be rendered as "the unpreconceivability of Being," implying that there is always that in reality which will remain beyond thought. See Joseph P. Lawrence, *Schellings Philosophie des ewigen Anfangs* (Würzburg: Konighausen & Neumann, 1989), 10.

9. Wieland, *Schellings Lehre von der Zeit* (Heidelberg: Carl Winter Universitätsverlag, 1956), 23.

10. Brown, *The Later Philosophy of Schelling* (Lewisburg: Bucknell University Press, 1977). A briefer discussion may be found in Edward Beach's *The Potencies of the God(s): Schelling's Philosophy of Mythology* (Albany: State University of New York Press, 1994); see esp. 69–91.

11. White, *Schelling*, 107.

12. The original title was "Correspondence with Eschenmayer concerning the Treatise 'Philosophical Investigations of the Essence of Human Freedom, etc.' " [Briefwechsel mit Eschenmayer bezüglich der Abhandlung 'Philosophische Untersuchungen über das Wesen der menschlichen Freiheit usw.']. It appeared in the *Allgemeinen Zeitschrift von Deutschen für Deutsche* and consisted of a letter from Eschenmayer (8:145–60) and Schelling's reply (8:161–89).

13. Heidegger, *Schelling's Treatise*, 97.

14. Desmond, *Beyond Hegel and Dialectic: Speculation, Cult, and Comedy* (Albany: State University of New York Press, 1992), 307, 309.

15. Ibid., 310.

16. *Ideas for a Philosophy of Nature*, trans. Errol Harris and Peter Heath (Cambridge: Cambridge University Press, 1988), 87.

17. Schelling's reference is a paraphrase of the fourth proposition on the list of the six inevitable consequences of rationalism Jacobi argues for in the *Spinoza-Büchlein*; see chapter 1.

18. Tilliette, "Schelling an der Furt der Identitätsphilosophie," *Der Transzendentale Gedanke*, ed. Klaus Hammacher (Hamburg: Meiner, 1981), 402.

19. Heidegger, *Schelling's Treatise*, 98.

20. Odo Marquard, *Schwierigkeiten mit der Geschichtsphilosophie* (Frankfurt am Main: Suhrkamp, 1973); see esp. 83–107.

21. Marx, *The Philosophy of F. W. J. Schelling*, trans. Thomas Nenon (Bloomington: Indiana University Press, 1984), 65.

22. Nelly Tsouyopoulos has a detailed discussion of the influence of Schelling's ideas on contemporary medical theory in "Schellings Krankheitsbegriff und die Begriffsbildung der modernen Medizin," in R. Heckmann, H. Krings, and R. W. Meyer, eds., *Natur und Subjektivität: Zur Auseinandersetzung mit der Naturphilosophie des jungen Schelling* (Stuttgart-Bad Cannstatt: Frommann-Holzboog, 1985), 265–90, concluding that Schelling's appropriation of the "irritability" theory of John Brown and emphasis on the ideas of self-regulation and equilibrium both effectively discredited the tendency to assign disease to a *causa occulta* and served as a forerunner to the contemporary emphasis on maintaining the body's own defenses against the ravages of stress.

23. Marx, *Is There a Measure on Earth?* trans. Reginald Lilly and Thomas Nenon (Chicago: University of Chicago Press, 1987); see esp. 16–25, 60–70.

24. See, for example, the third book of the *Nichomachean Ethics:* "But perhaps a man is not the kind of man to take care. Still they are themselves by their slack lives responsible for becoming men of that kind, and men are themselves responsible for being unjust or self-indulgent, in that they cheat or spend their time in drinking bouts and the like; for it is activities exercised on particular objects that make the corresponding character . . ." 1114a.3–7.

25. Bowie, *Schelling and Modern European Philosophy* (London: Routledge, 1993), 91. Robert F. Brown makes a similar comparison in "Resources in Schelling for New Directions in Theology," *Idealistic Studies* 20 (1990): 9.

26. White, *Schelling*, 133.

27. Psalms 18:26–27; 2 Samuel 22:26–27.

Chapter 7. Beyond Idealism? *The Ages of the World*

1. Fackenheim, "Schelling's Conception of Positive Philosophy," *Review of Metaphysics* 7 (1953/54): 566.

2. See especially Fuhrmans's claim that "Schelling's entire philosophical output from 1809 on is, in the final analysis, a unity," amounting to, as Schelling himself defined it, " 'nothing other than the progressive proof, growing stronger with every step, of the actually existing God' " (13:31), *Schellings Philosophie der Weltalter* (Düsseldorf: Verlag L. Schwann, 1954), 308.

3. Brown, "Resources in Schelling for New Directions in Theology," *Idealistic Studies* 20 (1990): 3.

4. Lanfranconi, *Krisis: Eine Lektüre der "Weltalter"-Texte F. W. J. Schellings* (Stuttgart: Frommann-Holzboog, 1992), 9.

5. Frederick de Wolfe Bolman, *Schelling: The Ages of the World* (New York: Columbia University Press, 1942). Reprinted by AMS Press, 1967.

6. Schröter, *Die Weltalter: Fragmente, in den Urfassungen von 1811 und 1813* (Munich: C. H. Beck'sche Verlagsbuchhandlung, 1946).

7. See the appendix to *Krisis: Eine Lektüre der "Weltalter"—Texte*, "Die drei frühen 'Weltalter'-Texte. Kommentierte Gliederung," 294–346.

8. Brown, *Later Philosophy of Schelling*, 195.

9. Schulz, *Die Vollendung des deutschen Idealismus in der Spätphilosophie Schellings* (Stuttgart: G. Neske, 1955), 1975.

10. Sandkühler, *Friedrich Wilhelm Joseph Schelling* (Stuttgart: Metzler, 1970).

11. O'Meara, "F. W. J. Schelling: Bibliographical Essay," *Review of Metaphysics* 31 (1977): 283–309.

12. Braun, "Ein Bedürfnis nach Schelling," *Philosophische Rundschau* 37 (1990): 161–96, 298–326.

13. *The Ages of the World*, 5.

14. Hogrebe, *Prädikation und Genesis* (Frankfurt: Suhrkamp, 1989), 9.

15. Trans. A. V. Miller (Oxford: Clarendon Press, 1977), section 16.

16. Harris, "The Cows in the Dark Night," *Dialogue* 26 (1984): 629.

17. Fuhrmans's essay "Schelling und Hegel. Ihre Entfremdung," which appears at the end of vol. 1 of *Briefe und Dokumente*, provides an exhaustive discussion of the circumstances of their break: 451–533. That Hegel's claim to be criticizing Schelling's followers rather than Schelling himself has an ironic counterpart in the tendency of many commentators to conflate Schelling's attacks on Hegelians with his criticisms of Hegel himself has recently been noted by Walter E. Erhardt, in "Schellings letzte Kritik an Hegel zu dessen Lebzeiten," *Hegel-Jahrbuch* 1992: 11–16.

18. Erlangen, 1803.

19. Manfred Frank, ed., *Schelling: Philosophie der Offenbarung 1841/42* (Frankfurt: Suhrkamp, 1977), 131. This passage is from "Paulus-Nachschrift," an unauthorized version of Schelling's Berlin Lectures published without his knowledge or consent, and thus also obviously without having been edited by him.

20. Tilliette, *Une Philosophie en Devenir* (Pan's: J. Vrin, 1970), 2:13; see also Lanfranconi, *Krisis*, 50–58.

21. Lovejoy, *The Great Chain of Being* (Cambridge: Harvard University Press, 1936), 317.

22. There are some notes for the second book, "The Present," in Schröter's edition.

23. Lovejoy, *Great Chain of Being*, 320, 325.

24. Bowie, *Schelling and Modern European Philosophy*, 92.

25. Ibid., 99.

26. Brown, *Later Philosophy of Schelling*, 220–21.

27. Ibid., 220 n. 73.

28. Lawrence, *Schellings Philosophie des ewigen Anfangs*, 195.

29. Tillich, *Die religionsgeschichtliche Konstruktion in Schellings positiver Philosophie, ihre Voraussetzungen und Prinzipien* (Breslau, 1910), 17–19.

30. See note 7.

31. In *Ages of the World*, p. 122.

32. P. 198 n. 45.

33. These and related issues are discussed in Bowie's chapter 5, "Freedom, Ontology and Language"; he points out that "meaning must, in this view, be part of what is always already potentially present in 'matter' in Schelling's sense" (100).

34. In the Stuttgart Lectures, Schelling puts the same point even more dramatically in his claim that "the being of intelligence is madness" (7:469).

35. See note 5.

36. Leipzig: Gerhard Fleischer dem Jüngeren, 1811.

37. *F. W. J. Schellings Denkmal der Schrift von den göttlichen Dingen etc. des Herrn Friedrich Heinrich Jacobi und der ihm in denselben gemachten Beschuldigung eines absichtlich täuschenden, Lüge redendent Atheismus* (Tübingen: J. G. Cotta, 1812); reprinted in *Sämtliche Werke*, 8:19–136.

38. The correspondence with Eschenmayer was discussed in chapter 6; although many of the same topics are discussed, as Eschenmayer does not shy away from questioning central doctrines, Schelling's response is uniformly pleasant and reasonable. Indeed, he even states his regret in the introduction that he and Eschenmayer as separated geographically, for he would have liked to construct a dialogue of their exchange (8:161).

39. With the exception of the preface to the works of Victor Cousin (1842).

40. Ford, "The Controversy between Schelling and Jacobi," *Journal of the History of Philosophy* 3 (1965): 80–81.

41. Ibid, 82.

42. Ford quotes Per Daniel Amadeus Atterbom, *Menschen und Städte, Begegnungen und Beobahtungen eines schwedischen Dichters in Deutschland, Italien, und Österreich 1817–19*, who visited Jacobi in Munich on January 19, 1818, as saying that Jacobi told him that "reading Schelling's *Schrift* against him nearly killed him, forcing him to resign the Presidency of the Munich Academy of the Sciences": 81 n. 33.

43. Letter of 21.10.1797, *Aus Jens Baggesens's Briefwechsel mit Karl Leonhard Reinhold und Friedrich Heinrich Jacobi*, part 2 (Leipzig, 1831), 234–5; cited in *Schelling: Historische-Kritische Ausgabe* Werke, 4:43.

44. See the letters of 13.6.1806 and 30.6.1806 in *Briefe*, 1:380–81.

45. Letter of 16.9.1806 to Jakob Fries, quoted in *Briefe*, 1:380 n. 50.

46. See chapter 1, section II, for the list of the six original propositions.

47. Recently translated and with an introduction by Andrew Bowie (Cambridge: Cambridge University Press, 1994).

48. Bloch, *The Utopian Function of Art and Literature: Selected Essays*, trans. Jack Zipes and Frank Mecklenburg (Cambridge: MIT Press, 1988), 260.

49. Frankfurt: Suhrkamp, 1977.

50. Schulz, *Die Vollendung des deutschen Idealismus*, 23.

SELECTED BIBLIOGRAPHY

English Translations of Schelling

Schelling, Friedrich Wilhelm Joseph. *The Unconditional in Human Knowledge: Four Early Essays.* Trans. and ed. Fritz Marti. Lewisburg: Bucknell University Press, 1980.

———. *Ideas for a Philosophy of Nature.* Trans. Errol Harris and Peter Heath. New York: Cambridge University Press, 1988.

———. *Idealism and the Endgame of Theory: Three Essays by F. W. J. Schelling.* Trans. and ed. Thomas Pfau. Albany: State University of New York Press, 1994.

———. *System of Transcendental Idealism* (1800). Trans. Peter Heath. Charlottesville: University Press of Virginia, 1978, 1981.

———. *Bruno, or on the Divine and Natural Principle of Things.* Ed. and trans. Michael Vater. Albany: State University of New York Press, 1984.

———. *The Philosophy of Art.* Trans. Douglas Stott. Minneapolis: University of Minnesota Press, 1989.

———. *On University Studies,* trans. E. S. Morgan. Athens, Ohio: Ohio University Press, 1966.

———. "Schelling's Aphorisms of 1805." Trans. Fritz Marti, *Idealistic Studies* 14 (1984): 237–56.

———. *Of Human Freedom.* Trans. James Gutmann. La Salle, Ill.: Open Court, 1954.

———. "Concerning the Relation of the Plastic Arts to Nature." Trans. Michael Bullock. Appendix to Herbert Read, *The True Voice of Feeling.* New York: Pantheon Books, 1953.

———. *Schelling: The Ages of the World.* Trans. Frederick de Wolfe Bolman. New York: Columbia University Press, 1942.

———. *On the History of Modern Philosophy*. Trans. Andrew Bowie. Cambridge University Press, 1994.

———. *Schelling's Treatise on "The Deities of Samothrace."* Trans. Robert F. Brown. Missoula, Mont.: Scholars Press for the American Academy of Religion, 1976.

———. "On the Source of the Eternal Truths." Trans. Edward Beach. *The Owl of Minerva* 19 (1990): 55–67.

Primary Sources

Fichte, Johann Gottlieb. *Ausgewählte Werke*, ed. Fritz Medicus. Hamburg: Meiner, 1962. Cited as Fichte.

———. *Gesamtausgabe der Bayerischen Akademie der Wissenschaften*, ed. Reinhard Lauth and Hans Jacob. Stuttgart-Bad Cannstatt: F. Frommann, 1962–. Cited as Gesamtausgabe.

Hamann, Johann Georg. *Sämtliche Werke*, ed. Josef Nadler. Vienna: Thomas-Morus-Presse, 1949–57.

Hegel, Georg Wilhelm Friedrich. *Gesammelte Werke*, ed. H. Büchner and O. Pöggeler. Hamburg: Meiner, 1968.

———. *Vorlesungen über die Geschichte der Philosophie*, ed. H. Glockner. Stuttgart: Frommann, 1928.

Jacobi, Friedrich Heinrich. *Werke*, ed. F. H. Jacobi and F. Köppen. Leipzig: Fleischer, 1812–15. Cited as Jacobi.

Kant, Immanuel. *Akademie* edition: *Kants gesammelte Schriften*. Königlich Preussische Akademie der Wissenschaften. Berlin: Walter de Gruyter & Co. and Predecessors, 1902–. Cited as AK.

Reinhold, Karl Leonhard. *Beytrage zur Berichtigung bisheriger Missverstandnisse der Philosophen*. Jena: Johann Michael Mauke, 1790–1794.

———. *Uber das Fundament des philosophischen Wissens; über die Möglichkeit der Philosophie als strenge Wissenschaft*, with an introduction by Wolfgang Schrader. Hamburg: Meiner: 1978.

———. *Versuch einer neuen Theorie des menschlichen Vorstellungsvermögens*. Prague & Jena: C. Widtmann and I. M. Mauke, 1789.

Schelling, Friedrich Wilhelm Joseph. *Briefe und Dokumente*, ed. H. Fuhrmans, Bonn: Bouvier, 1962. Cited as *Briefe*.

———. *Historische-Kritische Ausgabe*, ed. Hans Michael Baumgartner et. al. Stuttgart: Frommann-Holzboog, 1976–

———. *Schellings Werke*, ed. Manfred Schröter. Munich: Beck, 1927. Citation of texts is by volume and page number.

———. *Die Weltalter: Fragmente, in den Urfassungen von 1811 und 1813*. Munich: C. H. Beck'sche Verlagsbuchhandlung, 1946. Cited as WA.

Secondary Sources

Adickes, Erich. *Kant als Naturforscher*. Berlin: Walter de Gruyter, 1925.

Allison, Henry E. *Lessing and the Enlightenment*. Ann Arbor: University of Michigan Press, 1970.

Altmann, Alexander. *Moses Mendelssohn: A Biographical Study*. London: Routledge & Kegan Paul, 1973.

Altwicker, Norbert, ed. *Texte zur Geschichte des Spinozismus*. Darmstadt: Wissenschaftliche Buchgesellschaft, 1971.

Bäck, Leo. "Spinozas erste Einwirkungen auf Deutschland." Diss., Berlin, 1895.

Ballard, Edwin G. "The Kantian Solution to the Problem of Man within Nature." *Tulane Studies in Philosophy*, 3. The Hague: Martinus Nijhoff, 1964: 7–40.

Barion, Jakob. *Die Intellektuelle Anschauung bei J. G. Fichte und Schelling*. Abhandlungen zur Philosophie und Psychologie der Religion, Heft 22. Würzburg: C. J. Becker Universitäts-Druckerei, 1929.

Bar On, Bat-Ami, ed. *Modern Engendering: Critical Feminist Readings in Modern Western Philosophy*. Albany: State University of New York Press, 1994.

Baum, Gunther. *Vernunft und Erkenntnis: Die Philosophie F. H. Jacobis*. Bonn: Bouvier, 1969.

Baumgardt, David. "Spinoza und der deutsche Idealismus." *Kant-Studien* 32 (1927): 182–192.

Baumgartner, Hans Michael. *Schelling: Einführung in seine Philosophie.* Freiburg: Karl Alber, 1975.

Beach, Edward. *The Potencie(s) of the Gods.* Albany: State University of New York Press, 1994.

Behler, Ernst. "Die Geschichte des Bewusstseins: Zur Vorgeschichte eines Hegelschen Themas." *Hegel-Studien* 7 (1972): 169–216.

Beiser, Frederick. *The Fate of Reason.* Cambridge: Harvard University Press, 1987.

Bloch, Ernst. *The Utopian Function of Art and Literature: Selected Essays.* Trans. Jack Zipes and Frank Mecklenburg. Cambridge: MIT Press, 1988.

Bowie, Andrew. *Schelling and Modern European Philosophy: An Introduction.* London: Routledge, 1993.

Bracken, Joseph. "Freedom and Causality in the Philosophy of Schelling." *New Scholasticism* 50 (1976): 164–82.

———. "Schelling's Positive Philosophy." *Journal of the History of Philosophy* 15 (1977): 324–30.

Braun, Hermann. "Ein Bedürfnis nach Schelling." *Philosophische Rundschau* 37 (1990): 161–96; 298–326.

Braun, Otto. *Hinauf zum Idealismus! Schelling-Studien.* Leipzig: Fritz Eckhardt Verlag, 1908.

Breazeale, Daniel. "Fichte's Aenesidemus Review and the Transformation of German Idealism." *Review of Metaphysics* 34 (1981): 545–68.

———. "Between Kant and Fichte: Karl Leonhard Reinhold's 'Elementary Philosophy.'" *Review of Metaphysics* 35 (1982): 785–821.

———. "How to Make an Idealist: Fichte's 'Refutation of Dogmatism' and the Problem of the Starting Point of the Wissenschaftslehre." *Philosophical Forum* 19 (1987–88): 97–123.

———. "Fichte on Skepticism." *Journal of the History of Philosophy* 29 (1991): 427–53.

——. ed and trans. *Fichte's Early Philosophical Writings.* Ithaca: Cornell University Press, 1988.

Bröcker, Walter. "Rückblick auf die Existenzphilosophie." *Philosophische Perspektiven* 4 (1972): 191–97.

Brown, Robert F. *The Later Philosophy of Schelling.* Lewisburg: Bucknell University Press, 1977.

——. "The Transcendental Fall in Kant and Schelling." *Idealistic Studies* 14 (1984): 49–66.

——."Resources in Schelling for New Directions in Theology." *Idealistic Studies* 20 (1990): 1–17.

Brüggen, M. "Jacobi und Schelling." *Philosophisches Jahrbuch des Görres-Gesellschaft*, 1967/68: 419–29.

Bubner, Rüdiger, ed. "Das älteste Systemprogramm. Studien zur Frühgeschichte des deutschen idealismus." *Hegel-Studien*, Beiheft 9. Bonn: Bouvier Verlag Herbert Grundmann, 1973.

Buchheim, Thomas. "Das 'objektive Denken' in Schellings Naturphilosophie." *Kant-Studien* 81 (1990): 320–38.

Buchner, Hartmut, ed. *Anhang zur Kritisches Journal der Philosophie hrsg. F. W. J. Schelling und G. W. F. Hegel.* Hildesheim: Georg Olms Verlagsbuchandlung, 1967.

Burtt, E. A. *The Metaphysical Foundations of Natural Science.* New York: Harcourt, Brace, 1925.

Cassirer, Ernst. *Das Erkenntnisproblem in der Philosophie und Wissenschaft der neueren Zeit.* Berlin: Verlag Bruno Cassirer, 1920.

——. *Idee und Gestalt.* Berlin: G. Cassirer, 1924.

Collingwood, R. G. *The Idea of Nature.* Oxford: Clarendon Press, 1945.

Copleston, F. C. "Pantheism in Spinoza and the German Idealists." *Philosophy* 21 (1946): 42–56.

——. *A History of Philosophy*, vols. 6–7. New York: Image Books, 1965.

Cunningham, Andrew, and Nicholas Jardine, eds. *Romanticism and the Sciences*. Cambridge: Cambridge University Press, 1990.

Desmond, William. *Beyond Hegel and Dialectic: Speculation, Cult, and Comedy*. Albany: State University of New York Press, 1992.

Dietzsch, Steffen. *Friedrich Wilhem Joseph Schelling*. Cologne: Pahl-Rugenstein Verlag, 1978.

di Giovanni, George, and H. S. Harris, ed. and trans. *Between Kant and Hegel: Texts in the Development of Post-Kantian Idealism*. Albany: State University of New York Press, 1985.

di Giovanni, George. "Kant's Metaphysics of Nature and Schelling's *Ideas for a Philosophy of Nature*." *Journal of the History of Philosophy* 17 (1979): 197–215.

———. "Grazing in the Sunlight: On H. S. Harris's 'The Cows in the Dark Night.'" *Dialogue* 26 (1987): 653–64.

———. "From Jacobi's Philosophical Novel to Fichte's Idealism. *Journal of the History Of Philosophy* 27 (1989): 75–100.

Dilthey, Wilhelm. *Gesammelte Schriften*, vol. 4, ed. Herman Nohl; vol. 15, ed. Ulrich Herrman. Göttingen: Vandenhoeck & Ruprecht, 1970.

———. *Leben Schleiermachers*, 2nd ed. Berlin and Leipzig: Walter de Gruyter, 1922.

Durner, Manfred. "Aktuellen Perspektiven der Philosophie Schellings." *Philosophisches Jahrbuch der Görresgesellschaft* 88 (1981): 363–71.

———. "Schellings Begegnung mit den Naturwissenschaften in Leipzig." *Archiv für Geschichte der Philosophie* 72 (1990): 220–36.

Düsing, Klaus. *Die Teleologie in Kants Weltbegriff*. Bonn: Bouvier, 1968.

———. "Spekulation und Reflexion: Zur Zusammenarbeitm Schellings und Hegels in Jena." *Hegel-Studien* 5 (1969): 95–128.

Bibliography 247

———. "Ein Brief von Schelling an Steffens über Naturphilosophie." *Hegel-Studien* 9 (1974): 39–42.

Easton, Susan M. "Hegel and Feminism." In *Hegel and Modern Philosophy*, ed. David Lamb. London: Croom Helm, 1987.

Engelhardt, Dietrich von. "Grundzüge der Naturwissenschaftlichen Naturforschung um 1800 und Hegels spekulative Naturerkenntnis." *Philosophia Naturalis* 13 (1972): 290–315.

Eschenmayer, Karl August. *Die Philosophie in ihren Uebergang zur Nichtphilosophie.* Erlangen: Walterschen, 1803.

Esposito, Joseph. *Schelling's Idealism and Philosophy of Nature.* Lewisburg: Bucknell University Press, 1977.

Fackenheim, Emil. "Schelling's Conception of Positive Philosophy." *Review of Metaphysics* 7 (1953/54): 563–82.

———. "Schelling's Philosophy of the Literary Arts." *Philosophical Quarterly* 4 (1954): 310–26.

Fichte, J. G. *The Vocation of Man*, trans. Peter Preuss. Indianapolis: Hackett, 1987.

Ford, Lewis S. "The Controversy between Schelling and Jacobi." *Journal of the History of Philosophy* 3 (1965): 75–89.

Förster, Wolfgang. "Schelling in der westdeutschen Gegenwartsphilosophie." *Deutsche Zeitschrift für Philosophie* 16 (1968): 859–71.

———. "Die Philosophie Schellings in ihren entgegensetzten Rezeptionslinien." *Deutsche Zeitschrift für Philosophie* 23 (1975): 289–305.

Frank, Erich. *Rezensionen über schöne Literatur von Schelling und Caroline.* Heidelberg: Carl Winters Universitätsbuchhandlung, 1912.

Frank, Manfred. *Der unendliche Mangel an Sein: Schellings Hegelkritik und die Anfänge der Marxschen Dialektik.* Frankfurt: Suhrkamp, 1975, 1989.

Frank, Manfred, ed. *Schellings Philosophie der Offenbarung 1841/42* Frankfurt am Main: Suhrkamp, 1977.

———. *Eine Einführung in Schelling Philosophie.* Frankfurt: Suhrkamp, 1985.

Frank, Manfred, and E. Kurz, eds. *Materialien zu Schellings philosophischen Anfängen.* Frankfurt: Suhrkamp, 1975.

Freier, Hans. *Von deutscher Philosophie, Art und Kunst: Ein Votum für Friedrich Heinrich Jacobi gégen F. W. J. Schelling.* Heidelberg: Mohr und Zimmer, 1812.

———. *Die Rückkehr der Götter.* Stuttgart: Metzler, 1976.

Fuhrmans, Horst. *Schellings Letzte Philosophie.* Berlin: Junker und Dünnhaupt, 1940.

———. "Schellings Briefe. Eine Übersicht," *Zeitschrift für philosophische Forschung* 8 (1954): 414–37.

———. *Schellings Philosophie der Weltalter.* Düsseldorf: Schwann, 1954.

———. "Dokumente zur Schelling-Forschung," *Kant-Studien* 47 (1955/56): 182–191, 273–87, 378–96.

Gay, Peter. *Freud: A Life for Our Time.* New York: W. W. Norton, 1988.

Görland, Ingtraud. *Die Entwicklung der Frühphilosophie Schellings in der Auseinandersetzung mit Fichte.* Frankfurt: Vittorio Klostermann, 1973.

Gower, Barry. "Speculation in Physics: The History and Practice of Naturphilosophie." *Studies in the History and Philosophy of Science* 3 (1973): 301–56.

Gram, Moltke S. "Things-in-Themselves: The Historical Lessons," *Journal of the History of Philosophy* 18 (1980): 407–31.

Gray-Smith, Rowland. "God in the Philosophy of Schelling." Diss., University of Pennsylvania, 1933.

Grün, Klaus-Jürgen. *Das Erwachen der Materie.* Zurich: Georg Olms Verlag, 1993.

Gulyga, Arsenji. "Schelling als Verfasser der *Nachtwachen des Bonaventura.*" *Deutsche Zeitschrift für Philosophie* 32 (1984): 1027–36.

Habermas, Jürgen. *Das Absolute und die Geschichte: von der Zweispältigkeit in Schellings Denken.* Bonn: H. Bouvier, 1954.

———. "Dialektischer Idealismus im übergang zum Materialismus: Geschichtsphilosophische Folgerungen aus Schellings Idee einer Contraction Gottes." In *Theorie und Praxis*. Frankfurt: Suhrkamp, 1971.

Hammacher, K. *Die Philosophie Friedrich Heinrich Jacobis*. Munich: Wilhelm Fink, 1969.

———, ed. *Friedrich Heinrich Jacobi*. Frankfurt: Vittorio Klostermann, 1971.

———, ed. *Der Transcendentale Gedanke: Die Gegenwärtige Darstellung der Philosophie Fichtes*. Hamburg: Felix Meiner, 1981.

Hammacher K., and A. Mues, eds. *Erneuerung der Transzendentalphilosophie im Anschluss an Kant und Fichte*. Reinhard Lauth zum 60. Geburtstag. Stuttgart-Bad Cannstatt: Frommann-Holzboog, 1979.

Hamann, Johann Georg. *Hamann's Socratic Memorabilia: A Translation and Commentary*, ed. and trans. James C. O'Flaherty. Baltimore: Johns Hopkins University Press, 1967.

Hansen, Lee Ann. "From Enlightenment to *Naturphilosophie:* Marcus Herz, Johann Christian Reil, and the Problem of Border Crossings." *Journal of the History of Biology* 26 (1993): 39–64.

Harris, H. S. *Hegel's Development: Toward the Sunlight (1770–1807)*. Oxford: Clarendon Press, 1972.

———. "The Cows in the Dark Night." *Dialogue* 26 (1987): 627–44.

Hartkopf, Werner. *Die Dialektik in Schellings Transzendental und Identitätsphilosophie*. Meisenheim am Glan: Anton Hain, 1975.

———. "Die Anfänge der Dialektik bei Schelling und Hegel," *Zeitschrift für philosophische Forschung* 30 (1976): 545–66.

———. "Schellings Naturphilosophie," *Philosophia Naturalis* 17 (1979): 349–372.

Hasler, Ludwig, ed. *Schelling: Seine Bedeutung für eine Philosophie der Natur und der Geschichte: Referate und Kolloquien der Internationalen Schelling-Tagung Zurich 1979*. Stuttgart-Bad Cannstatt: Frommann-Holzboog, 1981.

Hayes, Victor. "Schelling: Persistent Legends, Improving Image." *Southwestern Journal of Philosophy* 3 (1972): 63–73.

Haym, R. *Die Romantische Schule. Ein Beitrag zur Geschichte des deutschen Geistes*. Darmstadt: Wissenschaftliche Buchgesellschaft, 1912.

Heckmann, R., H. Krings, and R. W. Meyer, eds. *Natur und Subjektivität: Zur Auseinandersetzung mit der Naturphilosophie der jungen Schelling*. Stuttgart-Bad Cannstatt: Frommann-Holzboog, 1985.

Heidegger, Martin. *Schellings Abhandlung über das Wesen der menschlichen Freiheit*, ed. Hildegard Fieck. Tübingen: Max Niemeyer, 1971.

Hegel, G. W. F. *Lectures on the History of Philosophy*, vol. 3, ed. Robert F. Brown, trans. R. F. Brown and J. M. Stewart. Berkeley: University of California Press, 1990.

———. *Phenomenology of Spirit*, trans. A. V. Miller. Oxford: Clarendon Press, 1977.

———. *The Philosophy of History*, trans. J. Sibree. New York: Dover, 1956.

Henrich, Dieter. "Fichtes ursprüngliche Einsicht." In *Subjektivität und Metaphysik. Festschrift für Wolfgang Kramer*. Frankfurt: Vittorio Klostermann, 1966.

———. "Aufklärung der Herkunft des Manuskriptes 'Das älteste Systemprogramm des deutschen Idealismus.' " *Zeitschrift für philosophische Forschung* 30 (1976): 510–28.

———. *Ist systematische Philosophie möglich? Stuttgarter Hegel-Kongress 1975*. Bonn: Bouvier Verlag Herbert Grundmann, 1977.

Herder, Johann Gottfried. *God: Some Conversations*, trans. Frederick Burckhardt. New York: Veritas Press, 1940.

Heuser-Kessler, Marie-Luise. *Die Produktivität der Natur: Schellings Naturphilosophie und das neue Paradigma der Selbstorganisation in den Naturwissenschaften*. Berlin: Duncker & Humblot, 1986.

Hildebrandt, Kurt. *Leibniz und das Reich der Gnade.* The Hague: Nijhoff, 1953.

Holz, Harald. *Spekulation und Faktizität.* Bonn: Bouvier, 1970.

———. "Die Beziehungen zwischen Schellings Naturphilosophie und dem Identitätsphilosophie in den Jahren 1801/02." *Philosophisches Journal des Görresgesellschaft* 8 (1971): 270–94.

———. "Das Problem des Vollkommenen Menschen bei Kant und Schelling." *Kant-Studien* 64 (1973): 336–62.

———. *Die Idee der Philosophie bei Schelling.* Freiburg, Munich: Verlag Karl Alber, 1977.

Horstmann, Rolf-Peter, and Michael John Petry, eds. *Hegels Philosophie der Natur: Beziehungen zwischen empirischer und spekulativer Naturerkenntnis.* Stuttgart: Klett-Cotta, 1986.

Jähnig, Dieter. *Schelling: Die Kunst in die Philosophie.* 2 vols. Pfüllingen: Verlag Gunther Neske, 1969.

Jaspers, Karl. *Schelling. Grösse und Verhängnis.* Munich: R. Piper, 1955.

Kant, Immanuel. *Critique of Judgement*, trans. Werner S. Pluhar. Indianapolis: Hackett, 1987.

———. *Critique of Practical Reason*, trans. Lewis White Beck. New York: Bobbs-Merrill, 1956.

———. *Metaphysical Foundations of Natural Science*, trans. James Ellington. Indianapolis: Hackett, 1985.

Kasper, Walter. *Das Absolute in die Geschichte.* Mainz: Matthais-Grünewald-Verlag, 1965.

Kenkel, Karen. "Fichte's Theory of Sexual Difference." In *Impure Reason: Dialectic of the Enlightenment in Germany*, ed. Daniel Wilson and Robert C. Holub. Detroit: Wayne State University Press, 1992: 279–97.

Kleingeld, Pauline. "The Problematic Status of Gender-Neutral Language in the History of Philosophy: The Case of Kant." *Philosophical Forum* 25 (1993): 134–50.

Kluback, William. "The Political Dimensions of Schelling's Lecture: 'On the Source of the Eternal Truths.'" *Idealistic Studies* 12 (1982): 169–79.

———. "A Few Remarks on Schelling's Philosophy of Love and Evil." *Idealistic Studies* 13 (1983): 132–39.

Knittermeyer, H. *Schelling und die Romantische Schule.* Munich: Ernst Reinhart, 1929.

———. "Hundert Jahre nach Schellings Tod." *Philosophische Rundschau* 4 (1956): 1–57.

Krell, David Farrell. "The Crisis of Reason in the Nineteenth Century: Schelling's Treatise on Human Freedom." In *The Collegium Phaenomenologicum,* ed. John Sallis, 13–32. Dordrecht: Kluwer, 1988.

Kroner, Richard. *Von Kant bis Hegel.* 2 vols. Tübingen: J. C. B. Mohr, 1924.

———. "The Year 1800 in the Development of German Idealism." *Review of Metaphysics* 1 (1948): 1–31.

Küppers, Bernd-Olaf. *Natur als Organismus: Schellings frühe Naturphilosophie und ihre Bedeutung für die moderne Biologie.* Frankfurt: Klostermann, 1992.

Lanfranconi, Aldo. *Krisis: Eine Lektüre der "Weltalter"-Texte F. W. J. Schellings.* Stuttgart: Fromann-Holzboog, 1992.

Lauth, Reinhard. *Die Entstehung von Schellings Identitätsphilosophie in der Auseinandersetzung mit Fichtes Wissenschaftslehre 1795 bis 1801.* Freiburg/Munich: Verlag Karl Alber, 1975.

———. "Une Philosphie en Devenir." *Revue Metaphysique et de Morale* 80 (1975): 240–53.

———. ed. *Philosophie aus einem Prinzip: Karl Leonhard Reinhold.* Conscientia: Studien zur Bewusstseinsphilosophie, vol. 6. Bonn: Bouvier Verlag Herbert Grundmann, 1975.

Lawrence, Joseph P. "Schelling as Post-Hegelian and as Aristotelian." *International Philosophical Quarterly* 26 (1986): 315–30.

———. "Art and Philosophy in Schelling." *Owl of Minerva* 20 (1988): 5–19.

———. *Schellings Philosophie des ewigen Anfangs.* Würzburg: Köningshausen & Neumann, 1989.

Bibliography

Leibbrand, Werner. *Die Spekulative Medizin der Romantik.* Hamburg: Claasen Verlag, 1956.

Lenoir, Timothy. "Generational Factors in the Origin of Romantische Naturphilosophie." *Journal of the History of Biology* 11 (1978): 57-100.

———. *The Strategy of Life: Teleology and Mechanics in Nineteenth Century German Biology.* Chicago: University of Chicago Press, 1989.

Lieber, Hans Joachim. "Kant's Philosophie des Organischen und die Biologie seiner Zeit." *Philosophia Naturalis* 1 (1950-52): 553-70.

Liebig, Justus von. *Reden und Abhandlungen.* Leipzig nad Heidelberg: C. F. Winter'sche Verlangshandlung, 1874.

Lovejoy, A. O. *The Great Chain of Being.* Cambridge: Harvard University Press, 1936.

Löw, Reinhard. *Philosophie des Lebendigen: Der Begriff des Organischen bei Kant, sein Grund und seine Aktualität.* Frankfurt: Suhrkamp, 1980.

Lukacs, Georg. "Schellings Irrationalismus." *Deutsche Zeitschrift für Philosophie* 1 (1953): 53-102.

———. *Die Zerstörung der Vernunft,* vol. 1. Darmstadt und Neuwied: Hermann Luchterhand, [1962] 1973.

McCarthy, Vincent. "Schelling and Kierkegaard on Freedom and Fall." In *The Concept of Anxiety,* ed. Robert L. Perkins. Macon: Mercer University Press, 1985: 89-109.

———. *Quest for a Philosophical Jesus: Christianity and Philosophy in Rousseau, Kant, Hegel, and Schelling.* Mercer University Press, 1987.

McFarland, J. D. *Kant's Concept of Teleology.* Edinburgh: Edinburgh University Press, 1970.

Mahowald, Mary B., ed. *Philosophy of Woman,* 2nd ed. Indianapolis: Hackett, 1983.

Marquard, Odo. *Schwierigkeiten mit der Geschichtsphilosophie.* Frankfurt: Suhrkamp, 1973.

——. *Transzendentaler Idealismus. Romantische Naturphilosophie. Psychoanalyse.* Cologne: Dinter, 1987.

Marti, Fritz. "Theological Epistemology in Augustine, Kant, and Schelling." *Modern Schoolman* 55 (1977): 21–35.

——. *Religion and Philosophy: Collected Papers.* Washington, D. C.: University Press of America, 1979.

——. "Schelling, Theologian for the Coming Century." *New Scholasticism* 56 (1982): 217–27.

Marx, Werner. *The Philosophy of F. W. J. Schelling: History, System and Freedom.* Trans. Thomas Nenon. Bloomington, Indiana University Press, 1984.

——. *Is There a Measure on Earth?* Trans. Reginald Lilly and Thomas Nenon. Chicago: University of Chicago Press, 1987.

Mauthner, Fritz. *Jacobis Spinoza Büchlein, nebst Replik und Duplik.* Munich: Georg Muller Verlag, 1912.

Medicus, Fritz. *Fichtes Leben.* Leipzig: Verlag von Felix Meiner, 1922.

Mende, Erich. "Die Entwicklungsgeschichte der Faktoren Irritabilität und Sensibilität in deren Einfluss auf Schellings 'Prinzip' als Ursache des Lebens." *Philosophia Naturalis* 17 (1979): 327–48.

Mendus, Susan. "Kant: 'An Honest but Narrow-Minded Bourgeois'?" In *Women in Western Political Philosophy,* ed. Ellen Kennedy and Susan Mendus. New York: St. Martin's Press, 1987: 21–43.

Meyer-Schubert, Astrid. *Mutterschosssehnsucht und Geburtsverweigerung: Zu Schellings früher Philosophie und dem frühromantischen Salondenken.* Vienna: Passagen Verlag, 1992.

Mills, Patricia Jagentowicz. "Hegel's *Antigone.*" *Owl of Minerva* 17 (1986): 131–52.

Mine, Hideki. *Ungrund und Mitwissenschaft: Das Problem der Freiheit in der Spätphilosophie Schellings.* Frankfurt: Peter Lang, 1983.

Nauen, Franz. *Revolution, Idealism, and Human Freedom: Schelling, Hölderlin, and Hegel, and the Crisis of Early German Idealism.* The Hague: Nijhoff, 1971.

Neubauer, J. "Dr. John Brown and Early German Romanticism." *Journal of the History of Ideas* 28 (1967): 367–82.

Nohl, Hermann. *Die Deutsche Bewegung: Vorlesungen and Aufsatze zur Geistesgeschichte von 1770–1830.* Göttingen: Vandenhoeck und Ruprecht, 1970.

O'Meara, Thomas F. "F. W. J. Schelling: Bibliographical Essay." *Review of Metaphysics* 31 (1977): 283–309.

———. *Romantic Idealism and Roman Catholicism: Schelling and the Theologians.* Notre Dame: Univeristy of Notre Dame Press, 1982.

Oersted, H. C. *The Soul in Nature.* London: Bohn, 1852.

Oesterreich, Peter. "Schellings Weltalter und die ausstehende Vollendung des deutschen Idealismus." *Zeitschrift für Philosophische Forschung* 39 (1985): 70–85.

Orzechowski, Axel. "Der gegenwärtige Schelling: Positionen der heutigen Schelling-Forschung. Ein Bericht." *Zeitschrift für philosophische Forschung* 46 (1993): 301–6.

Pieper, Anne-Marie. "Ethik 'a la Spinoza': Historischsystematisch Überlegungen zu einem Vorhaben des jungen Schell-ing." *Zeitschrift für Philosophische Forschung* 31 (1977): 545–64.

Prauss, Gerold. *Kant und das Problem der Dinge an sich.* Bonn: Bouvier, 1974.

Ravven, Heidi. "Has Hegel Anything to Say to Feminists?" *Owl of Minerva* 19 (1988): 149–68.

Reardon, Bernard. *Religion in the Age of Romanticism: Studies in Early Nineteenth Century Thought.* Cambridge: Cambridge University Press, 1985.

Reininger, Robert. *Kant, seine Anhänger und seine Gegner.* Munich: Verlag Ernst Reinhardt, 1923.

Rintelen, Fritz-Joachim von. "Philosophical Idealism in Germany: The Way from Kant to Hegel and the Present." *Philosophy and Phenomenological Research* 38 (1977): 1–32.

Rockmore, Tom. "Kant's and Fichte's Theory of Man." *Kant-Studien* 68 (1978): 305–20.

Royce, Josiah. *The Spirit of Modern Philosophy.* Boston: Houghton Mifflin, 1893.

———. *Lectures on Modern Idealism*. New Haven: Yale University Press, 1919.

Sandkühler, H. J. "Schelling ou le Compromis entre L'Idealisme et le Materialisme." *Archives de Philosophie* 38 (1975): 379–94.

———. *Natur und geschichtlichen Prozess: Studien zur Naturphilosophie F. W. J. Schellings*. Frankfurt: Suhrkamp, 1984.

———. *Friedrich Wilhelm Joseph Schelling*. Stuttgart: Metzler, 1970.

Schlanger, Judith. *Schelling et la réalité finie: Essai sur la Philosophie de la Natur et de l'Identite*. Paris: Presses Universitaires de France, 1966.

Schleiden, Matthais. *Schellings und Hegels Verhältnis zur Naturwissenschaft*, ed. Olaf Breidbach. Weinheim: Acta Humaniora, 1988.

Scholz, Heinrich, ed. *Die Hauptschriften zum Pantheismusstreit zwischen Jacobi und Mendelssohn*. Neudrücke seltener philosophischer Werke, ed. von der Kantgesellschaft, vol. 6. Berlin: Reuther & Reichard, 1916.

Schott, Robin May. *Cognition and Eros: A Critique of the Kantian Paradigm*. Boston: Beacon, 1988.

Schröter, Manfred. "Bericht über den Muncher Schelling-Nachlass." *Zeitschrift für philosophische Forschung* 8 (1954): 437–45.

———. "Bemerkungen zu Fuhrmans Schelling-Briefausgabe." *Zeitschrift für philosophische Forschung* 18 (1964): 164–8.

———. *Kritische Studien über Schelling und zur Kulturphilosophie*. Munich: R. Oldenbourg, 1971.

Schulz, Walter. "Das Verhzältnis des späten Schelling zu Hegel." *Zeitschrift für philosophische Forschung* 8 (1954): 336–52.

———. "Anmerkungen zu Schelling." *Zeitschrift für philosophische Forschung* 29 (1975): 321–36.

———. *Die Vollendung des deutschen Idealismus in der Spätphilosophie Schellings*. Pfullingen: G. Neske, [1955] 1975.

Seidel, G. J. "Creativity in the Aesthetics of Schelling." *Idealistic Studies* 4 (1974): 170–80.

———. *Activity and Ground: Fichte, Schelling and Hegel.* Hildesheim and New York: Georg Olms Verlag, 1976.

Smid, Stefan. "Schelling's Idea of Ultimate Reality and Meaning," *Ultimate Reality and Meaning* 9 (1986): 56–69.

Snow, Dale E. and James Snow. "The Limits of Idealism: Schopenhauer and the Early Schelling on the Nature of Reality," *Ultimate Reality and Meaning* 14 (1991): 84–98.

Snow, Dale E. "The Role of the Unconscious in Schelling's *System of Transcendental Idealism,*" Idealistic Studies 19 (1989): 231–250.

———. "F. H. Jacobi and the Development of German Idealism," *Journal of the History of Philosophy* 25 (1987): 397–415.

———. "Self and Absolute in the Early Schelling," Diss., Emory University, 1984.

Spelman, Elizabeth. "Woman as Body: Ancient and Contemporary Views." *Feminist Studies* 8 (1982): 108–39.

Spinoza, Benedict. *The Ethics,* trans. R. H. M. Elwes. New York: Dover Publications, 1955.

Steffens, Heinrich. *Was ich erlebte,* 10 vols. Breslau: J. Max, 1841.

Steinkamp, Fiona. "Schelling's Account of Primal Nature in *The Ages of the World.*" *Idealistic Studies* 24 (1994): 173–90.

Stolzenberg, Jürgen. *Fichtes Begriff der intellektuellen Anschauung: Die Entwicklung in den Wissenschaftslehren von 1793/94 bis 1801/02.* Deutscher Idealismus, vol. 10. Stuttgart: Klett-Cotta, 1986.

Stopcyzk, Annegrel. *Was Philosophen über fraven denken.* Munich: Matthes & Seitz, 1980.

Studia Philosophica. Jahrbuch der Schweizerischen Philosophischen Gesellschaft, vol. 14. Verhandlung der Schelling-Tagung in Bad Ragaz, 1954. Basel: Verlag für Recht und Gesellschaft, 1954.

Temkin, Owsei. *The Double Face of Janus and Other Essays in the History of Medicine.* Baltimore: Johns Hopkins University Press, 1977.

Theunissen, Michael. "Schellings Anthropologischer Ansatz." *Archiv für Geschichte der Philosophie* 47 (1965): 174–89.

Tillich, Paul. "Schelling und die Anfänge des existentialistischen Protestes." *Zeitschrift für philosophische Forschung* 9 (1955): 197–208.

———. *Mysticism and Guilt-Consciousness in Schelling's Philosophical Development.* Trans. Victor Nuovo. Lewisburg: Bucknell University Press, 1974.

———. *Die religionsgeschichtliche Konstruktion in Schellings positiver Philosophie, ihre Voraussetzungen und Prinzipien.* Breslau, 1910.

Tilliette, Xavier. *Schelling: Une Philosphie en Devenir.* 2 vols. Paris: Librarie Philosophique J. Vrin, 1970.

———. "La Nouvelle Image de l'idealisme allemand." *Revue Philosophique de Louvain* 71 (1973): 46–67.

———. "Schelling und das Problem der Metaphysik." *Perspektiven der Philosophie* 2 (1976): 123–43.

Timm, Hermann. *Gott und die Freiheit: Die Spinozarenaissance. Studien zur Religionsphilosophie der Goethezeit,* vol. 1. Frankfurt am Main: Vittorio Klostermann, 1974.

———. "Amor Dei Intellectualis: Die teleologische Systemidee des romantischen Spinozismus." *Neue Hefte für Philosphie* 12 (1977): 64–91.

Vater, Michael. "Heidegger and Schelling: The Finitude of Being," *Idealistic Studies* 5 (1975): 20–58.

———. "Hymns to the Night: On H. S. Harris's 'The Cows in the Dark Night.'" *Dialogue* 26 (1987): 645–52.

Verra, Valerio. "Jacobis Kritik am Deutschen Idealismus." Hegel-Studien 5 (1969): 201–23.

Vörlander, Karl. *Immanuel Kant: Der Mann und das Werk.* 2d ed. Hamburg: Felix Meiner, 1977.

Watson, J. *Schelling's Transcendental Idealism.* Chicago: S. C. Griggs, 1882.

Wetzels, Walter. *Johann Wilhelm Ritter: Physik im Wirkungsfeld der deutschen Romantik.* Berlin and New York: De Gruyter, 1973.

White, Alan. *Absolute Knowledge: Hegel and the Problem of Metaphysics.* Athens, Ohio: Ohio University Press, 1983.

———. *Schelling: An Introduction to the System of Freedom.* New Haven: Yale University Press, 1983.

Whyte, Lancelot Law. *The Unconscious before Freud.* New York: Basic Books, 1960.

Wieland, Wilhelm. *Schellings Lehre von der Zeit.* Heidelberg: Carl Winter Universitätsverlag, 1956.

Williams, L. Pearce. "Kant, *Naturphilosophie,* and Scientific Methods." In *Foundations of Scientific Method: The Nineteenth Century,* ed. R. N. Giere and R. S. Westfall. Bloomington: Indiana University Press, 1973.

Wilson, John E. *Schellings Mythologie: Zur Auslegung der Philosophie der Mythologie und der Offenbarung. Spekulation und Erfahrung,* vol. 31. Stuttgart-Bad Cannstatt: Frommann-Holzboog, 1993.

Wolfinger, Franz. *Denken und Transzendenz—zum Problem ihrer Vermittlung. Der unterschiedliche Weg der Philosophien F. H. Jacobis und F. W. J. Schellings.* Frankfurt am Main: Bern-Circenster, 1981.

Wright, Walter E. "Fichte and Philosophical Method." *Philosophical Forum* 19 (1988): 65–73.

———. "Self and Absolute in the Philosophy of Fichte." Diss., Vanderbilt University, 1971.

Wundt, Max. *Die Philosophie and der Universität Jena in ihrem geschichtlichen Verlauf dargestellt.* Jena: Verlag von Gustav Fischer, 1932.

Zac, Silvain. "Jacobi Critique de Spinoza." *Proceedings of the First Italian International Congress on Spinoza,* ed. Emilia Giancotti. Naples: Bibliopolis, 1985: 173–83.

Zeltner, Hermann. "Gleichgewicht als Seinsprinzip. Schellings Philosophie des Gleichgewichts." *Studium Generale* 14 (1961): 495–908.

Zimmerli, Walther. "Die intellektuelle Anschauung beim frühen Schelling." *Proceedings of the XVth World Congress of Philosophy* 5 (1975): 839–43.

INDEX

Absolute, 6, 51–53, 55–57, 60–62, 65, 73–74, 85–86, 90, 93, 123, 137, 185–186, 189, 206; concept of the absolute self, 41–45, 102, 127–130, 138. See also Intellectual intuition
Aenesidemus. See Schulze, G. E.
Aesthetic intuition, 134, 137, 139–140
Allison, Henry, 19, 20
Altmann, Alexander, 16, 19
Angst, 9, 203, 204, 214
Antithesis, as philosophical principle, 199–200; as scientific principle, 87–88, 129
Antigone, 107–108, 110
Archaos, 168
Aristotle, 39, 83, 105–106, 171–173, 227n. 20; Nichomachean Ethics, 237n. 24; view of women, 230n. 21
Art, 120–123, 134–135, 137–140; and history, 122
Atterbom, Per Daniel Amadeus, 240n. 42
Augustine, 158

Baader, Franz, 167
Bacon, Francis, 210
Baggesen, Jens, 39, 40, 207
Ballard, Edward G., 123

Bardili, Christoph Gottfried, 187
Baum, Gunther, 16
Bayle, Pierre, 20, 21
Beach, Edward, 111–112
Becoming, 81, 178–179, 185, 187, 201–205
Being, 9, 22, 36, 83, 145, 148–149, 151–152, 156, 166, 171, 185, 192, 199–205, 205, 215; of God, 85–86, 159–165, 199–200; of the self, 41–45, 70, 93–94, 139, 169. See also Absolute; Will
Berlin, Humboldt University of, 65
Berlin Lectures, 3, 182, 214, 238n. 19
Big Bang, 177
Biology, 19th century German, 226n. 1
Birth, 148, 161–162, 164, 176
Bloch, Ernst, 1, 213
Blumenbach, J. F., 226n. 1
Böhme, Jakob, 146–147, 196
Bolman, Frederick de Wolfe, 141, 185, 203
Bowie, Andrew, 2, 177, 192, 203, 217n. 7, 239n. 33
Braun, Hermann, 1, 184
Breazeale, Daniel, 40, 218n. 10, 223n. 9, 230n. 18
Brown, Robert F., 147, 182–183, 196–197, 237n. 25

262 Index

Cassirer, Ernst, 1, 15
Castration, 116–117
Cato, 173–174, 193
Character, 171–174; Schelling's theory of, 54, 66, 155, 169, 171–174, 193, 205, 214
Christ, 173–174
Christian, Christianity, 26, 182, 195, 198, 219n. 21; metaphysics, 215; theory of creation, 150
Claudius, Matthais, 207
Consciousness, 7, 61–62, 76–77, 86–87, 94–95, 134–135, 142, 167, 232n. 6; aesthetic, 120–121; need for a first principle of, 38–40; transcendental, 114–115
Cotta, J. G., 183
Creation, 150, 176, 187, 191, 195, 210
Criticism, as philosophical system, 5, 31, 52, 54, 56, 71

Dasein, 85, 199, 205. See also Jacobi, concept of *Daseyn*.
Davidson, Donald, 2
Derrida, Jacques, 1
Descartes, 20, 116, 151, 159, 210; concept of *cogito*, 39, 194
Desire, 116–118, 148, 161–162, 164; and freedom, 154
Desmond, William, 150
Dialectic, existential, 204; of production, 111–112; of sublation, 111–112; original discovery of the method of, 233n. 17
di Giovanni, George, 28, 124, 187–188
Dilthey, Wilhelm, *Leben Schleiermachers*, 219n. 33
Disease, 148, 166–167, 174, 178–179, 203
Dogmatism, as philosophical system, 5, 31, 52–54, 56–57, 71, 73, 75, 78, 83–84, 135

Easton, Susan, 106–107
Ebbinghaus, Julius, 230n. 18
Education, 64–66
Electricity, 76
Electromagnetism, 113
Engelhardt, Dietrich von, 229n. 6
Enlightenment, 11, 17, 18, 23, 24, 31, 117, 149; concept of science, 6, 213; German, 219n. 21; view of reason, 5, 28–29, 151; Schelling's critique of, 4–6, 58, 66, 143, 146, 155, 158, 211
Erhardt, Walter, 234n. 20, 238n. 17
Eschenmayer, Karl August, 148, 206, 235n. 12, 240n. 38; *Die Philosophie in ihrem Uebergang zur Nichtphilosophie*, 188
Esposito, Joseph, 3, 68
Eternity, 156, 169–172, 195–197
Evil, 7, 146–147, 149–150, 152, 158, 175–180, 191–192; Christian view

of, 150; as principle in Schelling's system, 3, 60, 157–162, 165–174, 214. *See also* Metaphysics of evil.
Existence, 85, 159, 163–165, 175, 191

Fackenheim, Emil, 181
Faith, 5, 22–30. *See also* Jacobi, *Glaube*
Fall, the, 8, 185–192
Fatalism, 22, 23, 25, 153–154, 209
Female, 99, 104–106, 109–110, 115–117, 161–162. *See also* Other, otherness; Woman
Feminism, 6, 7
Feuerbach, Ludwig, 1, 3
Fichte, J. G., 2, 6, 11, 29, 30, 46, 54, 98, 115–116, 121, 125, 142, 161, 162, 169–170, 194, 207, 208, 223n. 9, 223n. 19, 225n. 37, 230n. 18, 232n. 14; "Attempt at a New Presentation of the Science of Knowledge," 53; concept of the self, 36–45, 49, 102–103, 223n. 17; criticism of Reinhold, 37–38, 40, 44–45; "First Introduction to the Science of Knowledge," (1797) 42, 53; intellectual intuition, 40–45, 103, 224n. 34; "Personal Meditations on Elementary Philosophy," 40, 43–44; philosophy of nature, 93–96, 102–106; "Review of *Aenesidemus*," 38–42, 50; Schelling's criticisms of, 68–69, 144, 157, 187–189; *Science of Knowledge (1794)*, 41–43, 45, 51, 104, 135; *Science of Right*, 105–106; "Second Introduction to the Science of Knowledge," 41, 53; view of women, 102–106, 230n. 21, 230n. 22; *The Vocation of Man*, 221n. 50
Ford, Lewis S., 207, 221n. 50, 240n. 42
Frank, Erich, *Rezensionen über schöne Literatur von Schelling und Caroline*, 229n. 8
Frank, Manfred, 215, 217n. 5, 217n. 7, 238n. 19
Freedom, 30–31, 108–109, 122–124, 130, 134–135, 149, 168–170, 171–174, 179, 182, 190–197, 200; connection with life, 151–158; Jacobi's emphasis on, 26–27, 30; in Schelling's early thought, 52–56, 69–70, 89; Schelling's "idealism of freedom," 142–146, 153–154, 193
Freud, Sigmund, 7, 115, 121, 129, 162, 232n. 6
Fries, J. F., 62, 63, 221n. 42
Fuhrmans, Horst, 182, 237n. 2, 238n. 17

Gay, Peter, 232n. 6
Genius, 62–66, 137–139, 144, 205

German idealism, 3, 99, 146, 150, 153, 183, 218n. 10
Germany, intellectual history, 152–153
Glaubensphilosophen, 24, 26, 221n. 42
God, 7, 22, 30, 55–56, 62, 144 147–151, 159–165, 175–180, 193–205, 206–213; as principle in Schelling's philosophy, 3, 85–86, 153–154, 182, 185, 188, 214, 237n. 2; pantheism of a living God, 154–157, 163–165, 175, 196–198; possibility of knowledge of, 12, 30, 149; relation to nature, 117, 151–152, 209
Görland, Ingtraud, 222n. 52
Gower, Barry, 67–68
Groundless. See *Ungrund*.
Grund, 193–194, 203, 205; of Being, 159–162, 205
Gulyga, Arsenji, 229n. 8
Gutmann, James, 155, 167

Habermas, Jürgen, 1
Hamburger Correspondenten, 207
Hamann, J. G., 24, 25, 58, 69, 221n. 42; *Socratic Memorabilia*, 24–25
Harris, H. S. 187–188
Hegel, 37, 62–64, 65, 98, 111, 112, 115–116, 139, 142, 145, 162, 163, 187, 198, 215; concept of freedom, 108–109; concept of history, 119–122; criticisms of Schelling, 63–66, 187–188, 238n. 17; *Differenzschrift*, 119; *Faith and Knowledge*, 63; *Lectures on the History of Philosophy*, 11; *Logic*, 149; *Phenomenology*, 64, 107–108, 109, 119–122, 187–188; *Philosophy of Nature*, 107; *Philosophy of Right*, 107–108, 117; reputation of, 1, 2, 4; Schelling's criticisms of, 3, 70, 238n. 17; view of nature, 106–110; view of women, 106–110, 230n. 21
Hegelianism, 1, 217n. 5
Hegelians, 3, 238n. 17
Heidegger, Martin, 1, 142, 145, 149, 150
Hemsterhuis, Frans, 77
Herbart, G. H., 42
Herder, J. G., 20, 24, 58, 221n. 42, 221n. 45; *On the Origin of Language*, 25, genetic method, 25, 81; *God: Some Conversations*, 25; *Vom Erkennen und Empfinden*, 28
Herschel, F. W., 113
Heydenreich, Karl Heinrich, *Letters on Atheism*, 58
Hildebrandt, Kurt, 20
History, 96, 107–109, 111, 122–123, 190–192; the end of, 119–122
Hogrebe, Wolfram, 185, 203
Hölderlin, Friedrich, 42
Hume, David, 27, 72; Schelling's criticism of, 80, 134

Idealism, 55–62, 174–180, 181–185, 197–198, 200–202; aesthetic,

Index

135–140; rejection of;
200–201; Schelling's concept of, 55, 115–116, 120,
132, 140–141, 146,
156–158, 169
Imagination, 59, 60–61, 63–65
Individuality, 85, 89, 107,
154, 179, 203; and evil,
168–169
Induktion, method of, 84
Infinite, 72–73, 138, 189, 200;
transition to the finite,
53–56, 74, 185–186, 204
Intellectual intuition, Fichte's
concept of,. 40–45, 103,
224n. 34; Reinhold's concept of, 43–44; Schelling's
concept of, 42, 48, 49,
50–55, 62–66, 124,
129–130, 133, 135–137, 186
Intuition, role in knowledge,
58–60, 62–63, 69–70, 132.
See also Aesthetic intuition
Irrational, 114, 123, 130,
139–140, 151–152,
161–163, 168

Jacobi, F. H., 4, 11, 12, 26, 33,
35, 37, 41, 45–46, 48, 58,
62–64, 79, 126, 132, 141,
149, 194, 206–213; *Allwills
Briefsammlung*, 28; attack
on rationalism, 15, 22, 25,
26, 30; conflict between
faith and reason, 19, 22–30;
criticism of the Enlightenment, 18, 23–30, 211; critique of reason, 22–23,
53–54; *David Hume on Belief or Realism and Idealism*, 15, 26, 27, 34; *Daseyn*
(existence), 8, 27–28, 57,
64; *Glaube* (faith), 23,
26–27, 34, 49, 62–63, 153,
186, 211; idealism versus
realism, 29–30, 35–36;
interpretation of Spinoza,
21–28, 220n. 33, 221n. 50;
intuition, 15, 27, 29, 34, 36;
irrationalism, 26, 30; *Kantkritik*, 15, 34–36; *On the
Divine Things and Their
Revelation*, 8, 206–207,
209–210, 240n. 42; "On
Transcendental Idealism,"
34; revelation as first principle, 23; role in the pantheism controversy, 5,
14–24, 152–154; *salto
mortale*, 26, 30, 210;
"Something Lessing Said,"
16; *Spinoza-Büchlein*,
14–26, 27, 28, 29, 34, 209,
236n. 17; *Woldemar*, 28, 30.
See also Schelling-Jacobi
Controversy
Jaspers, Karl, 1, 140
Jena, University of, 13
Jenaische Allgemeine Literaturzeitung, 12
Judas, 173–174, 193

Kabbala, 20, 23
Kant, Immanuel, 2, 6, 12, 20,
22, 30, 54, 72, 79, 97, 98,
106, 111, 114–116, 121,
123–125, 132, 134, 139,
142, 152, 155, 161, 181,
186, 211, 213, 218n. 3,
218n. 4, 221n. 42, 225n. 37;
Anthropology, 102; as defender of the Enlightenment, 4, 5, 8; concept of
matter, 76–77, 90, 101–102,

228n. 23; *Critique of Judgment*, 82–84, 102, 124, 162; *Critique of Practical Reason*, 103, 170; *Critique of Pure Reason*, 14, 33, 34, 35, 42, 48–49, 100–101; Kantians, 13, 135, 148; "The Only Possible Proof for a Demonstration of God's existence," 34; *Metaphysical Foundations of Natural Science*, |75–76, 101, 228n. 23; moral philosophy, 95, 99–100, 103, 123, 164, 170; "Observations on the Feeling of the Beautiful and the Sublime," 99; philosophy of nature, 99–102, 226n. 1, 232n. 14; reputation of, 4, 11, 13; and Reinhold, 12–14, 37–38; Schelling's criticisms of, 46–50, 59–61, 169–172; view of women, 99–102, 109, 229n. 10; "What is Orientation in Thinking?" 34

Kenkel, Karen, 230n. 22
Kierkegaard, Soren, 1, 3, 28, 183
Kleingeld, Pauline, 99, 229n. 10
Krell, David Farrell, 231n. 27

Landshut, University of, 97
Lanfranconi, Aldo, 183
Language, 25, 81–82, 148, 185, 201; theosophical, 147–148
Lawrence, Joseph, 83, 145–146, 197, 227n. 20, 235n. 8

Lebensphilosophie, 16
Leibniz, 19–20, 26, 71, 116, 123, 177–178, 199; concept of matter, 77
Leipzig, 96
Lenoir, Timothy, *The Strategy of Life*, 226n. 1
Lessing, G. E., 53, 210; as Spinozist, 16, 21; *The Education of the Human Race*, 18, 19, 210; "Nathan the Wise," 17, 219n. 21; role in the pantheism controversy, 17–21; *Wolfenbüttler Fragmente*, 19;
Liebig, Justus von, 67
Life, 83–86, 88–90, 116, 153–155, 162, 175–180, 186, 193, 199, 209; false, 166, 168, 176, 203; of God, 203
Love, 117, 173, 177–178, 198
Lovejoy, A. O., 4, 189–190, 192, 206

Madness, 205, 239n. 34
Man, 113–115, 154, 158, 164–175, 179–180, 191, 193, 196, 202, 205; relation to nature, 115–118
Marti, Fritz, 202
Marx, Karl, 1, 98, 114, 183
Marx, Werner, 119–120, 139, 162; *Is There a Measure on Earth?*, 167
Matter, 72, 74–77, 83–88, 90–92, 212, 213, 228n. 23, 239n. 33; Newtonian concept of, 75, 101–102, 239n. 33
Mauthner, Fritz, 21

Medicine, 6, 96–97, 167, 228n. 4, 229n. 6, 236n. 22
Melancholy, 175, 184
Mendelssohn, Moses, 21, 24, 26; as defender of the Enlightenment, 5; enlightened patheism, 21–22; *Morning Hours*, 14, 17, 18, 21; role in the pantheism controversy, 14–22; "To Lessing's Friends," 17, 18
Mendus, Susan, 100
Metaphysics, 3–4, 176, 183–195, 200, 208–213; Christian 215; Oedipal, 213; of evil, 146, 150, 152, 157–162, 165, 176–180; and the irrational, 123, 133–135, 140, 159–165; of the will, 2, 137, 145, 166–169, 202, 215
Mills, Patricia, 108
Mine, Hideki, 227n. 20
Montesquieu, 98
Munich Academy of Sciences, 207, 208

Nature, 57–62, 78, 90–91, 97, 100, 128–129, 136–137, 139–140, 199–200, 203, 205, 209–213, 231n. 35; God's relation to, 117, 159–165, 193–194, 209; purposiveness in, 82–85, 90, 95
Naturphilosophie, 67–70, 93, 112–114, 176; 226n. 1, 226n. 8, 227n. 9, 232n. 14. *See also* Nature; Philosophy of nature

Negation, 131, 199–205, 212
Negative philosophy. *See* Philosophy
Neoplatonism, 189–190
Newton, 84, 90, 101, 104, 157
Niethammer, Immanuel, 224n. 37; *Philosophisches Journal*, 55
Nietzsche, Friedrich, 115, 143, 183, 215
Nohl, Herman, 28
Nonbeing, 79, 199–205
Novalis, 42

Oedipus, 107, 213
Oersted, H. C., 113, 231n. 35
O'Flaherty, James, 25
O'Meara, Thomas, 184
Organism, as philosophical principle, 74, 84–89, 96, 124–125, 153–154, 160–161, 228n. 4
Orzechowski, Axel, 234n. 4
Other, otherness, 113–115, 160–161, 194. *See also* Female.

Pantheism, 16–23, 152–153, 205–206, 212, 214, 220n. 40; enlightened, 21–22; Hegelian, 217n. 5; of a living God, 154–157, 196–198; Schelling's concept of, 151–157
Pantheism controversy, 4, 14–24, 151, 207; repercussions of, 24–31, 210
Personality, 144, 148, 155, 172–175; dark origins of, 151; divine, 159, 198–199
Pfau, Thomas, 225n. 38

Philosophy, 64–66, 70–71, 119, 156, 211; European, 116; negative philosophy, 9, 146, 184, 188, 210; philosophy of art, 114, 120, 124, 134, 136–140, 214, 234n. 20; philosophy of identity, 114, 127–128, 157, 187–188, 209, 214; philosophy of mythology, 9, 180–184, 208, 210, 213, 214; philosophy of nature, 6, 20, 55–57, 67–74, 84, 93–97, 110–118, 127–129, 142, 159, 164, 198, 199, 208; philosophy of revelation, 9, 180–184, 197, 208, 214–215; positive philosophy, 9, 112, 180–181, 188, 210; philosophy and science, 14, 67–69, 83, 87–88, 90–91, 128–129, 193

Physicalisch-medicinischen Societät of Erlangen, 97

Pieper, Annemarie, 224n. 34

Plato, 4, 48, 59, 64, 71, 72, 123, 198

Plotinus, 4, 20

Poetry, and philosophy, 65–66, 69, 125

Potencies, 200–203

Practical reason. *See* Reason.

Procreation as metaphor, 112, 115–118

Rationalism, 15, 17, 20–22, 25, 26, 30, 147, 211

Ravven, Heidi, 106–107

Reason, 8–9, 11, 33, 58, 101–102, 122, 140, 143, 151, 192, 214; creative, 53–55, 148, 154–155; in conflict with faith, 8, 19–20, 24–31; practical, 30–31, 54, 56, 103–104; transcendental, 114–115

Reid, Thomas, 26

Reinhold, Karl Leonhard, 37–40, 45, 46, 187; concept of *Vorstellung*, 13, 43–44; criticism of Kant, 13; *Elementarphilosophie*, 13; *Essay Toward A New Theory of the Faculty of Representation*, 12, 13, 43; first principle of consciousness, 38–40; intellectual intuition, 43–44; "Letters on the Kantian Philosophy," 12–13, 218n. 3, 218n. 4, 218n. 10; *On the Foundation of Philosophical Knowledge*, 43; Schelling's criticisms of, 14, 59

Reininger, Robert, *Kant, Seine Anhänger und Seine Gegner*, 221n. 42

Religion, 21, 182, 207

Ritter, J. W., 113

Romanticism, romantics, 36, 67, 117

Rorty, Richard, 2

Röschlaub, Andreas, 97

Rousseau, Jean-Jacques, *Emile*, 100

Royce, Josiah, 91

Ruge, Arnold, 3

Sandkühler, H. J., 184

Sartre, Jean-Paul, 165

Schelling, Caroline Böhmer-Schlegel, 229n. 8
Schelling, Friedrich Wilhelm Joseph, works cited by title: *Ages of the World*, 8, 90–91, 117, 141, 147, 151, 177, 183–205; *Bruno*, 86, 187–188; "Epicurean Confession of Faith of Heinz Widerporsten," 91; *Erlanger Lectures*, 194–195; "Further Presentations of the System of Philosophy," 187; *Ideas for a Philosophy of Nature*, 68–76, 77, 82, 113, 152; *Introduction to the Sketch of a System of the Philosophy of Nature*, 94–96, 112, 126, 128–129, 130–131; *Jahrbücher der Medizin als Wissenchaft*, 96–97; "Lectures on the History of Modern Philosophy," 119, 125, 210, 233n. 17; *Memorial on the Divine Things*, 143, 206–210, 240n. 42; *Of Human Freedom*, 7, 54, 116, 138, 140, 141–180, 181, 189, 190–192, 197–199, 212, 214, 231n. 37, 234n. 4; "Of the I As Principle of Philosophy," 42–43, 45, 47, 48, 50–53, 56, 57, 117; *On Myths*, 110; "On the Possibility of a Form for Philosophy," 47, 157; "On the Relation of the Creative Arts to Nature,", 207; *On the World Soul*, 82–88, 126; *On University Studies*, 64, 81, 138; "Philosophical Letters on Dogmatism and Criticism," 5, 12, 50–53, 56, 72, 124, 224n. 34; *Philosophy and Religion* (1804), 187–192, 195; *Presentation of the True Relationship of the Philosophy of Nature to the Revised Fichtean Doctrine*, 197; *Stuttgart Lectures*, 7, 116–117, 239n. 34; *System of Transcendental Idealism*, 7, 60, 76, 77, 80, 88, 94, 110, 114–115, 119–140, 144, 145, 146, 161, 213; "Treatises Explicatory of the Idealism in the *Science of Knowledge*," 55–62, 68–70, 72, 77, 81–82, 86, 93, 126, 132, 134, 225n. 38
Schelling, K. F. A., 183
Schelling-Jacobi controversy of 1811–12, 143, 205–213
Schlegel, Friedrich, 42
Schleiermacher, Wilhelm, 21, 63, 220n. 33
Schmid, K. F. C., 13
Schopenhauer, Arthur, 115, 152, 183, 202, 230n. 18; metaphysics of the will, 2, 215; philosophy of art, 234n. 20
Schott, Robin May, 229n. 10
Schröter, Manfred, 183
Schultz, Christian Gottfried, 12
Schulz, Walter, 96, 125, 150, 183–184, 215
Schulze, G. E., 40, 43; *Aenesidemus*, 38–39, 41, 50

Schutz, G. G., 13
Schwärmerei, 8, 211
Science, 82–87, 90, 114, 125; metaphysical foundations of, 67–70, 112–113, 128–129. See also Philosophy and Science
Self, as philosophical principle, 5, 6, 41–42, 45–51, 56–62, 70–75, 77–81, 125–130, 131–136, 144, 168, 170–172, 233n. 17. See also Personality
Self-consciousness, 37, 61, 95, 131–133, 140; philosophy as the history of, 77, 93–94, 96, 114, 119–120, 125–128, 139
Self-will, 164–168, 179, 191
Shaffer, Elinor, 65
Silesius, Angelus, 201–202
Sin, 166, 200
Spelman, Elizabeth, 98
Spinoza, 20, 29, 34, 69, 85–86, 116, 121, 126, 142, 153–156, 221n. 40, 221n. 50; the absolute, 51–52; concept of God, 56, 73; as dogmatist, 33; *Ethics*, 21, 51; influence on Schelling, 45–54; *On the Improvement of the Intellect*, 21; renaissance, 14, 45, 220n. 33; Schelling's criticisms of, 72–74, 153–157; Spinozism, 16–19, 24, 26; *Theological-Political Tractatus*, 19
Spinoza-Büchlein. See Jacobi, F. H.
Steffens, Heinrich, 187, 223n. 17
Stolzenberg, Jürgen, 43–44

Temkin, Oswei, 221n. 45
Teutschen Merkur, 12, 13, 218n. 4
Thales, 195
Theosophy, 146–148
Thing in itself, 33–36, 78–79, 102, 132, 135; Jacobi's criticism of, 35–36, 222n. 8; Schelling's criticism of, 79–81, 227n. 19
Tillich, Paul, 1, 4, 200, 201
Tilliette, Xavier, 42–43, 157
Time, 8, 59–60, 131–133, 192–197, 204; independence of, 156, 169, 170–171
Timm, Hermann, 34, 219n. 21, 221n. 40, 221n. 50
Tsouyopoulos, Nelly, 228n. 4, 236n. 22

Unconscious, 94–95, 114–115, 119–140, 144–145, 232n. 6; as principle in Schelling's philosophy, 7, 127–129, 213–214
Ungrund, 145, 161, 176–177, 187, 193–194. See also *Grund*
Unvordenklichkeit, 145–146, 215, 235n. 8

Vater, Michael, 145, 187–188, 232n. 4
Verra, Valerio, 34
Vorstellung. See Reinhold, K. L.

Wetzels, Walter, 113

White, Alan, 121, 135, 142, 147, 177, 217n. 7, 234n. 18
Wieland, Wilhelm, 42, 146–147
Wilhelm IV, King Friedrich, 217n. 5
Will, 57, 111–112, 137, 166, 168, 171, 176, 196–197, 200, 202, as primordial Being, 145, 148, 152, 156–158, 169–170, 214
Wolff, Christian, 26; *Theologia Naturalis*, 20
World soul, 82–86, 152, 189
Woman, 98–99; Fichte's view of, 99–102, 109, 229n. 10; Schelling's view of, 110–118. *See also* Female
Wright, Walter, 223n. 19
Whyte, Lancelot Law, 232n. 6

Printed in the United States
32017LVS00006B/38